215/-n

215/-n

*Atlas of the Great Barrier Reef*

W. G. H. MAXWELL

Associate Professor in Geology,
University of Sydney, Sydney, N.S.W. (Australia)

# ATLAS OF THE
# GREAT BARRIER REEF

ELSEVIER PUBLISHING COMPANY

Amsterdam – London – New York

1968

ELSEVIER PUBLISHING COMPANY
335 Jan van Galenstraat
P.O. Box 211, Amsterdam, The Netherlands

ELSEVIER PUBLISHING COMPANY LTD.
Barking, Essex, England

AMERICAN ELSEVIER PUBLISHING COMPANY, INC.
52 Vanderbilt Avenue
New York, New York 10017

Library of Congress Catalog Card Number: Map 68–6

With 166 illustrations

Printed in The Netherlands

0444407073

# Acknowledgements

The ideas and information presented in the following pages have been developed over the previous nine years during which long periods were spent in the Great Barrier Reef Province and in the laboratories and libraries of the Universities of Queensland, Sydney and Texas. In the course of the research I have come into contact with many people who have contributed, directly or indirectly, to the ultimate production of this volume. Foremost among them were Professor Dorothy Hill, Dr. F. W. Whitehouse and the late Professor W. H. Bryan, who by their teachings and research, first stirred my interest in geological science and later, in reef studies. In 1964, I was encouraged by Professor Edgar Owen to spend one year at the University of Texas where I was associated with an active research school in sedimentology and marine geology, supported by Dr. Robert L. Folk, Dr. Earle McBride, Dr. Allan Scott and by the visiting lecturer, Dr. Lloyd C. Pray, from the Marathon Research Center, Denver, Colo. During this period, opportunities were afforded for fruitful discussions with Dr. E. G. Purdy and Dr. Robley Matthews at Rice University, and Dr. A. Kidwell at the Jersey Production Research Center, Tulsa, Okla. Since 1964, co-operative projects with Mr. W. Sugden of the University College of Townsville and the more recent participation by Dr. J. P. Swinchatt of Colgate University, have led to valuable exchanges of ideas and information. Dr. Peter Woodhead, scientific director of the Great Barrier Reef Committee's Research Station, Heron Island, and Dr. T. Wilson of Australian Gulf Oil Co. have provided information and assistance with the marine survey.

Many of my graduate students have participated in various phases of research on the Great Barrier Reef, providing useful assistance to the main project and making significant contributions in their independent studies of reef sedimentation. R. W. Day, P. J. G. Fleming, J. S. Jell, R. G. McKellar, P. J. Conaghan, W. R. Maiklem, K. O. Reid and B. M. Thomas were active in this work. Research and technical assistance were provided by L. G. Johnson, B. Wood, N. Zillman and R. Beiers, while R. Neehouse, A. Bartlett, J. Gardiner, L. Leathart and L. Juleff performed much of the processing of samples in the laboratories. Laboratory facilities were provided by the universities of Queensland, Sydney and Texas and special assistance with X-ray analysis was offered by the University of Queensland. Marine work was carried out from the Heron Island Research Station and from the vessels "Emperor II" owned by Mr. R. Sheilds, "C-Gem" owned by Mr. C. E. Doherty and "Nancy E" owned by Mr. K. S. Lamberton. Clerical assistance was provided by Miss J. Scott of the University of Queensland and Miss M. Breckenridge of the University of Sydney. The final manuscript was prepared by Miss A. Wette of the University of Sydney.

Financial support which made this undertaking possible came initially from the research funds of the University of Queensland. In 1963 a substantial grant from the Jersey Production Research Company, Tulsa, Okla., greatly expanded the scope of the research, and from 1965 extremely generous support has been received from the American Petroleum Institute, and the Petroleum Research Fund of the American Chemical Society.

To all of these people and to the institutions which have made the work possible through their financial support or through provision of facilities, I express my sincere appreciation.

# Contents

# *Chapter 1* | Introduction

Man's interest in organic reefs is as old and as varied as the terms which he first used for their description. The origin of "reef" itself is lost in antiquity—believed to have been derived from the Old Norse "rif" (meaning rocky ridge) in the 14th century, it was applied initially to any submerged rock and restricted subsequently to organic reefs. "Coral" may be traced back through 14th century French, Latin and Greek to what has been suggested as a Semitic origin (ONIONS, 1966, p. 214). Indo-Malayans introduced the term "adal" (meaning closing), long before its appearance as "atoll" in 17th century literature. As early as the 6th century, Europeans speculated on the nature of reef composition (SEXTUS EMPIRICUS; ISIDORE, Bishop of Seville) identifying coral organisms as plants; later writers (FERRANTE IMPERATO, 1599; PEYSSONNEL, 1753) established them as animal. However, man's early interest in the organism was subordinate to his concern with the reef mass as a whole. It was the geometry and distribution of such masses that occupied his thoughts. To the mariner, they were navigational hazards, to the oceanic islander they were havens for food, to the naturalist they were among the most spectacular, the most awesome of nature's phenomena. They still are all of these. But to-day they also represent one of earth's most provocative challenges to science, a challenge that was taken up more than one hundred years ago.

In the 19th century, great minds dwelt on the problem of their origin, major controversies raged and even today some remain unsettled. With the growth of marine sciences in the 20th century, and particularly the progress of marine biology, attention was diverted from the more contentious issue of origin to the more objective analysis of reef communities in terms of their faunal composition and of the factors controlling such composition. Expeditions in the early part of this century to the Bahaman, Florida, Caribbean, Oceanic and Great Barrier Reef provinces provided the wealth of biological and hydrological information that is still in process of assimilation. During World War II, the strategic importance of reefs in the Pacific Ocean led to urgent studies, largely geomorphological, that stimulated the interest of marine geologists as well as that of biologists and culminated in reef research programmes in the post-war period on a scale unprecedented. In the present decade, the intensive exploration for petroleum has resulted in the discovery of major oil-fields in ancient reef provinces and consequent recognition of the need for better understanding of the reef environment. This, together with offshore mining developments, has led to another great surge in marine geological research, a surge that is still accelerating and one that will carry the traditionally land-locked geologist into the largest, possibly the most exciting, most rewarding realm on earth.

In this book, a small part of the marine realm has been taken and examined, largely from a geologist's viewpoint. From such examination, one fact emerges that is indisputable, viz, the interdependence of many disciplines in the understanding of any aspect, however small, of the Great Barrier Reef Province. Biology, hydrology, meteorology, chemistry, mineralogy, sedimentology, geomorphology, stratigraphy, tectonics, geophysics—all are fields that invite attention in one's attempt to glean an understanding of the structure and evolution of this province. Evidence from many of these fields is vaguely defined, and may well be termed circumstantial. Much of it defies precise assessment, much may be misinterpreted. However, in the total synthesis a pattern does emerge and this is developed and examined in the present work.

The essence of the study has been regional and many of the conclusions reached have been influenced by the ideas of numerous earlier and contemporary workers on modern reefs. Although it is not always possible to recognise the extent of such influences nor to specify their proper source, one must acknowledge the major, fundamental contributions of authors such as DARWIN (1842), DANA (1872), GUPPY (1890), SAVILLE-KENT (1893), GARDINER (1898, 1931), WOOD-JONES (1910), VAUGHAN (1919), YONGE (1930, 1940), KUENEN (1933), STEERS (1938), FAIRBRIDGE (1950), ILLING (1954) and CLOUD (1962). No total claim is made on the origi-

*1*

nality of the views presented in this work, on their finality or their validity. This is a geological appreciation, and like others of its kind, must change ultimately under the impact of new discovery and revised assessment.

The evolution of the Great Barrier Reef Province has been taken as an episode in the geological history of the South-Western Pacific. Biological and hydrological factors have been assessed as accurately as possible in terms of the present situation and projected backward into geological time where tectonic, geomorphological and sedimentary processes, slowly effective on such factors, have left their imprint in the stratigraphic record of the continent and the geophysical character of the continental shelf. The theme of the thesis developed in the subsequent chapters may be summarised as follows. Reefs develop as a result of the growth of colonial, lime-secreting animals and plants that require limiting conditions of temperature and light penetration for their survival, a suitable supply of nutrient and a degree of aeration for their growth and an adequate source of carbonate-rich water for skeletal secretion. As these factors vary from one area to another, so the nature of the reef structure varies, until one factor falls below the minimal level and no reef can survive. The geological history of a region—tectonic, volcanic, sedimentary and eustatic—largely determines its bathymetric character. Crustal downwarping and block faulting produce the deeper basins and troughs; opposing movements and vulcanicity result in the formation of the shallower shelves, platforms and ridges that come within the range of light penetration. Accumulation of sediment and submergence of old strand-line features as sea-level rises, provide similar bathymetric elevations. These processes, then, lead to a bathymetric situation favourable to reef colonisation. However, the reef organisms also require suitable water temperatures, nutrient, aeration and carbonate—factors that are dependent on water circulation. Where warm, equatorial or tropical waters sweep across the bathymetric highs, the second condition of temperature is satisfied. On the other hand, warm water is normally deficient in carbonate and, therefore, another source must be provided if prolific skeletal growth is to occur. From the deeper, oceanic areas colder, carbonate-rich water may be brought into the vicinity of potential reef areas either by divergence of surface currents resulting in upwelling, or by the upward deflection of deeper currents that encounter steep, continental slopes. As the water approaches the surface, it is warmed and excess carbonate is extracted by the reef organisms. Thus we find that shallow areas flanked by steep slopes

and in the path of warm surface currents, support relatively dense reef populations along their margin. However, as a result of this dense, marginal growth, penetration of undepleted water further into the area is restricted and the zone behind the marginal or shelf-edge reefs cannot support as many reefs. In contrast to this situation, is the one found adjacent to a gentle continental slope. Here the gradually rising water is slowly warmed and its carbonate content depressed. Similar loss of carbonate may occur where the zone of divergence and upwelling is remote from suitably shallow areas. In both cases, the shelf-edge reefs are fewer, more dispersed and less restrictive on the entry of oceanic water. As a result there is a more uniform, though less abundant development of reefs throughout the entire area.

The final factor influencing reef development involves aeration and removal of organic waste. The most vigorous growth of essential organisms occurs in the surf-zone, immediately below the surf-zone, and in areas of strong tidal activity. Growth directions of individual reefs are, therefore, influenced by the orientation of wave fronts which depend largely on the prevailing wind system, and by tidal currents. The density and vigour of the reef population will depend on the effectiveness of penetration of undepleted oceanic water, the efficiency of removal of depleted water and the degree of aeration by surf action. Provided these conditions are met, reefs may develop anywhere on the shelf, even at the very mouths of muddy streams.

As the reef masses develop they are subjected to the constant attack of waves and destructive organisms, and as one witnesses the enormous magnitude of this assault one might wonder that any reef survives. However, the destruction, particularly of the marginal fauna, may be likened to the trimming of a hedge— the severity of wave attack on the reef is matched by the vigour of new growth. Furthermore, the marginal fauna is dominated by branching species of coral, not, as one might expect, by the strong, massive brain corals that are better designed to resist wave destruction. It is their ability to recover and to renew growth that ensures their survival. Constant erosion, however, produces large quantities of reef-debris which mantles the reef surfaces and fringes their bases. Because of the enormous size of the Queensland continental shelf and because of the depths from which the reefs rise, the debris is comparatively restricted in its areal distribution. Except for near-shore reefs, shelf depths are too great to permit effective movement of the bottom carbonate sediments by wave and current, and it is normal to find abrupt transition from terrigenous to carbonate facies. Much of the carbonate debris has been derived from older, higher reef surfaces which were exposed after the last fall in sea-level, and material of this origin is generally recognisable by its degree of recrystallisation. On present evidence it would seem that the expansion or contraction of the sedimentary carbonate facies can occur only when eustatic changes upset the normal equilibrium between wave destruction and organic growth, and bring reef detritus into the range of wave and current activity.

Many factors have combined to make the Great Barrier Reef Province unique. Most important in this combination are the favourable geological and bathymetric structure of the South-West Pacific, the effective circulation of the surface currents, the unusually high tidal range which is responsible for strong tidal currents, and the persistence of the prevailing Trade Winds which induce heavy wave activity. These features, their variations and their influences on the development of the province, are examined in the following chapters.

# Chapter 2 | Regional setting of the Great Barrier Reef

The Great Barrier Reef Province is but one of many such provinces in the South-West Pacific region and its history has been influenced probably as strongly by the events and processes which have occurred and are still occurring in this vast marine domain, as by the controls exerted by the adjacent land mass of Queensland. Because the land influence is more readily examined, its importance has been emphasized by many authors, perhaps at the expense of the marine factors. Consideration of the geologic and hydrologic character of the South-West Pacific leads to a clearer understanding of the Great Barrier Reef Province, especially with respect to its history, its areal distribution, its regional facies differentiation, the nature of the sedimentation and the effect which the province is having and has had on the character of the Queensland Continental Shelf.

The term South-West Pacific (Fig. 2), as used in this work, refers to the region that extends from the eastern Australian coast to the eastern edge of the Kermadec Ridge–New Zealand Complex, and that is bordered in the north by the New Guinea–Solomon–Samoan Line, and in the south by the Indian–Antarctic Ridge. In area it approaches 5,000,000 sq. miles (13,450,000 km²)—more than 1.6 times the area of the Australian continent. Physiographically it consists of a series of broad basins and rises, steep ridges and deep trenches (Fig. 2). South of latitude 20°S, the features have a predominantly meridional trend. North of this latitude the trend changes to north-west and west-north-west. Depths reach a maximum of 3,000 fathoms (5,500 m) with an average of 1,500 fathoms (2,730 m).

Six groups of major features are recognizable, viz.
(1) the Eastern Plateau and Ridge System with peripheral trenches;
(2) the Eastern Basins;
(3) the Central Zone of Rises and Troughs;
(4) the Western Basin;
(5) the Northern Basins;
(6) the Western Continental Peripheral Zone.

## THE SOUTH-WEST PACIFIC

### The Eastern Plateau and Ridge System with Peripheral Trenches

(a) The Kermadec and Tonga Trenches flank the eastern margin of the South-West Pacific region, and descend abruptly to depths of 3,500 and 5,000 fathoms (6,370 and 9,100 m). Their width is of the order of 60 miles (96 km) and they extend over a distance of 1,300 miles (approx. 2,100 km).
(b) The Hikurangi and Bounty Troughs are shallower features to the east of New Zealand.
(c) The New Zealand Complex and the Kermadec–Tonga Ridge form the high eastern margin of the South-West Pacific. In addition to the land mass, the complex includes the submarine Campbell Plateau, Chatham Rise and Bounty Rise which, for the greater part, are less than 550 fathoms (1,000 m) below sea level. The complex extends northward as the Kermadec–Tonga Ridge, the total length of both features exceeding 2,500 miles (approx. 4,000 km). The ridge has an average width of 120 miles (193 km) and a maximum depth of 1,500 fathoms (2,730 m). Situated along its length are the Kermadec and Tonga Groups of volcanic islands and reefs. The ridge abuts against the west-trending Samoan Group. Diverging westward from the main ridge is a branch on which the Fijian Islands are situated.

### The Eastern Basins

The Fiji Basin extends westward from the Kermadec–Tonga Ridge for 600 miles (965 km) and rises against the shallower floor of the New Hebrides and New Caledonia Ridges and the Auckland Peninsula. An arm of the basin extends further westward into the Central Zone (group 3), connecting the Norfolk and Auckland Troughs, while a northern arm between the New Caledonia and New Hebrides Ridges connects the Fiji Basin with the Papuan Trough, i.e., with the

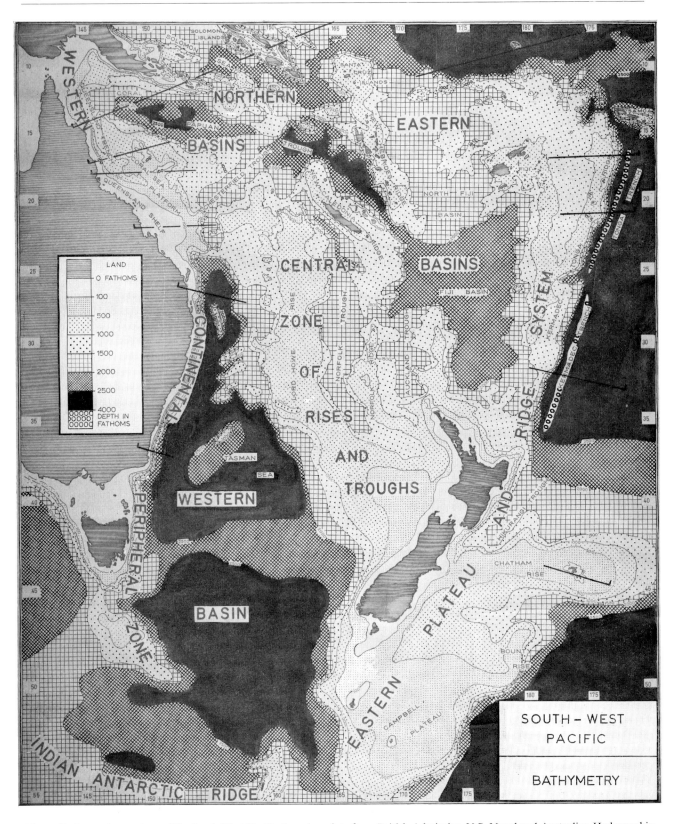

Fig. 1. Bathymetric structure of the South-West Pacific (based on data from British Admiralty, U.S. Naval and Australian Hydographic Charts).

axial part of the Coral Sea in the Northern Basins (group 5). The main part of the Fiji Basin averages 2,000–2,300 fathoms (3,600–4,150 m). The shallower, northern part is less than 2,000 fathoms (3,600 m) in depth.

### The Central Zone of Rises and Troughs

The Central Zone of Rises and Troughs includes the *New Hebrides, New Caledonia* and *Norfolk Ridges*, the *Auckland Peninsula, Lord Howe Rise* and the *Norfolk* and *Auckland Troughs*. This zone trends north-north-west and separates the Eastern and Western Basins, i.e., the Fiji Basin and the Tasman Sea Basin. The New Hebrides, New Caledonia, Norfolk and Auckland Peninsula Ridges are all comparable in magnitude and proportions. The main part of each rises sharply from depths of 1,500 fathoms (2,730 m) and the average depth is between 500 and 1,000 fathoms (910 and 1,820 m). The Lord Howe Rise is a larger feature, approximately 200 miles (320 km) wide and 1,600 miles

(1,575 km) in length, with an average depth between 600 and 800 fathoms (1,090 and 1,460 m). In the north it terminates abruptly against the deep Papuan Trough of the Coral Sea. Separating these positive features of the Central Zone are the Auckland and Norfolk Troughs and the south-western part of the Papuan Trough which joins the Fiji Basin. The Auckland Trough may be regarded as a shallow arm of the Fiji Basin, less than 2,000 fathoms (3,600 m) in depth. The Norfolk Trough occurs along the axial part of the Central Zone and is a well defined feature, 1,200 miles (1,930 km) long and 100–180 miles (160–290 km) wide, with an average axial depth of 1,600–1,900 fathoms (2,920–3,470 m) and a maximum recorded depth of 2,080 fathoms (4,806 m). The deeper part of this trough occurs where the axial trend changes from north to north-west.

### The Western Basin–Tasman Sea

The Western Basin–Tasman Sea is a large triangular

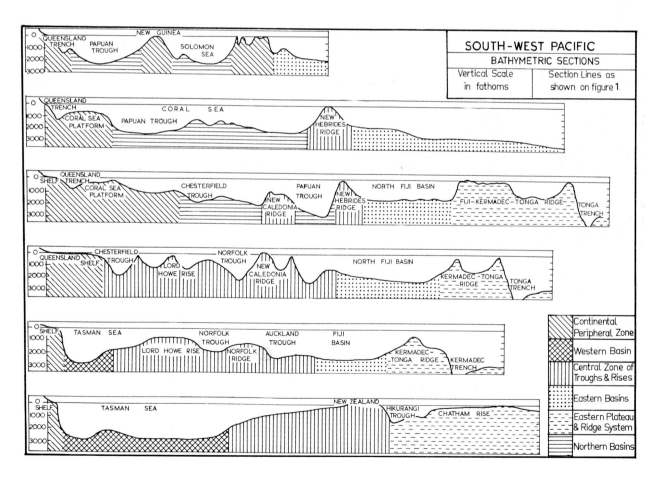

Fig. 2. Bathymetric cross-sections across the South-West Pacific, showing the major topographic units. The locations of the sections are indicated on Fig. 1.

region which expands southward and tapers north-ward as it approaches the southern margin of the Great Barrier Reef Province. The floor of the basin proper is 2,500–2,700 fathoms (4,570–4,940 m) below sea level. In the west it rises steeply to merge with the continental slope of south-eastern Australia, while its eastern border grades more gently into the Lord Howe Rise. Several large sea-mounts occur within the basin.

### The Northern Basins

The Northern Basins include the *Coral* and *Solomon Seas* which occur north of latitude 20°S. The *Papuan Trough* forms the axial depression of the Coral Sea and is one of the significant features of the South-West Pacific. It follows a north-west to westerly trend that is concordant with the grain of New Guinea but discordant with that of the Australian continent and the southern oceanic areas already discussed. It extends from the Fiji Basin to the North Queensland Continental Shelf and is flanked on the north by Papua and the New Hebrides. Its southern limit is defined by the Coral Sea Platform and the northern end of the Central Zone of Rises and Troughs. Four important off-shoots from the axial trough include the *Queensland Trench*, the *Chesterfield Trough*, the unnamed northern connection with the Solomon Sea and the unnamed eastern channel joining the Papuan Trough with the Fiji Basin. The Queensland Trench has exerted a very strong influence on the development of the Great Barrier Reef. The Solomon Sea, between New Guinea and the Solomon Islands, trends concordantly with these two bordering high zones and opens north-eastward through a break in the Solomon–New Hebrides Ridges into the deep abyssal region of the equatorial Pacific.

### The Western Continental Peripheral Zone

The Western Continental Peripheral Zone includes the *Coral Sea Platform* and the *Eastern Australian Continental Shelf*. The Coral Sea Platform is the comparatively shallow, gently sloping borderland that fringes the Central Queensland Shelf and that is separated from the Northern Queensland Shelf by the Queensland Trench. Its depth ranges from 100 to 1,000 fathoms (183–1,830 m), the greater part occurring between 100 and 500 fathoms (183–910 m). Maximum width of the platform is 300 miles (483 km), and maximum length approximately 600 miles (965 km). It is

the site of a major reef province that includes such groups as Lihou, Marion, Tregosa, Saumarez, Malay, Willis and Osprey.

The Continental Shelf of Eastern Australia and New Guinea varies greatly in its width, topographic character, sediment cover and organic structure. Except for the Central Queensland Region and the Torres and Bass Straits, the shelf is narrow—mostly less than 30 miles, and the shelf edge occurs between 60 and 80 fathoms (110–146 m). The shelf widens progressively southward from Cape York to latitude 22°, east of Mackay, where it reaches a maximum width of 200 miles (320 km). South from here it recedes sharply westward and is intersected by the Capricorn Channel before continuing southward as a narrow shelf.

## WATER CIRCULATION

The complexity of the water character of the Pacific Ocean has long been recognised, and as SVERDRUP et al. (1942, p. 669) have emphasized, the slow rate of circulation and the enormous area have not permitted a uniform surface water body to develop over the entire ocean. In the Southern Hemisphere the major oceanic gyral consists of the South Equatorial Current in the north, the West Wind Drift in the south between 40° and 60° latitude, and the Peru Current in the east. The western side is defined, rather obscurely by the East Australian Current and its branches. Within the major gyral there are two cells, a large eastern and a smaller western one, separated approximately along longitude 170°W. It is the western cell which occupies the South-West Pacific Region and controls the hydrologic character of the East Australian Continental Shelf.

Three major wind systems exert a dominant influence on water circulation in the South-West Pacific. In the northern part the Trade Winds are strongest and most persistent from May to November, when they are prevalent between 0° and 25°S latitude (Fig. 3). During the summer, from December to April, the Equatorial Trough moves southward and the Trade Wind Belt is similarly displaced to 10–30°S (WYRTKI, 1960). The high velocity and constancy of these winds result in strong surface drag which is manifested in the Trade Wind Drift. The summer Monsoon blows from the north of the Equatorial Trough for four months. Its direction varies from north-east to north-west, and in February it extends as far south as 15°S latitude (Fig. 3). The main system in the southern region is the West Wind, which prevails between 40° and 60°S latitude. It turns northward from April to October and

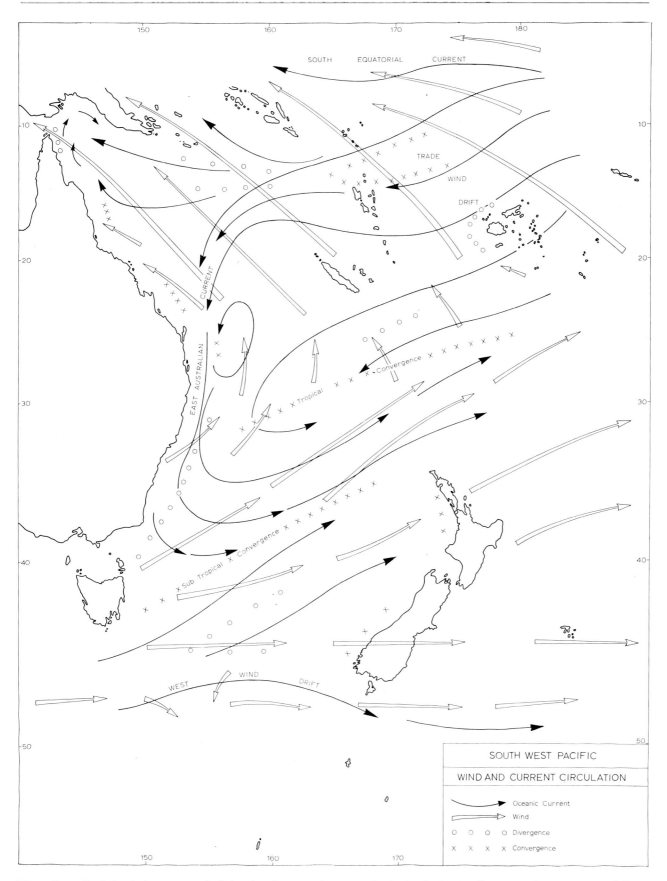

Fig. 3. Generalised circulation pattern of wind and surface oceanic currents in the South-West Pacific. Zones of convergence and divergence are also indicated.

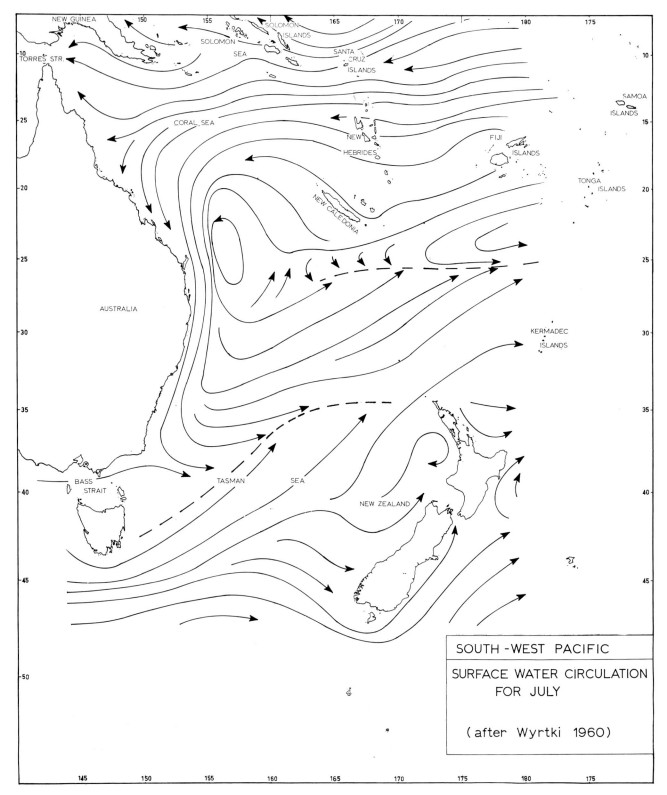

Fig. 4. Circulation pattern of surface currents in the South-West Pacific, for July (winter). Based on data from WYRTKI (1960).

passes into the Trade Wind. Thus, mainly south-west winds develop over the Tasman Sea. The total result of the three systems is to produce an atmospheric cell comparable in magnitude and movement with the western oceanic cell, as shown on Fig. 3. It is evident then that the surface oceanic and atmospheric circu-

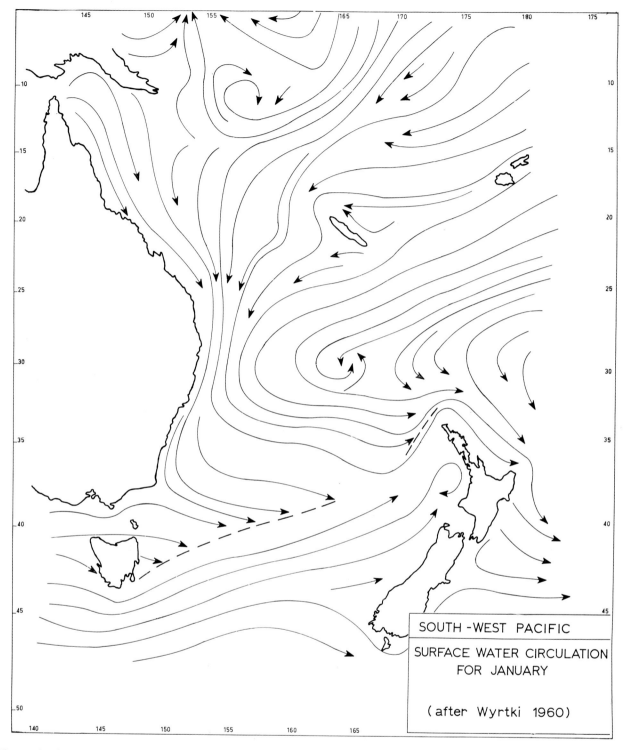

Fig. 5. Circulation pattern of surface currents in the South-West Pacific, for January (summer). Based on data from WYRTKI (1960). Note the southward flow along the North Queensland Shelf and the southward displacement of the main zones of convergence.

lation patterns are in accord, when allowance is made for the slight sinistral deflection of the oceanic currents in response to the Coriolis force.

The northern part of the region is defined by the narrow, fast-moving South Equatorial Current which flows north-westward as it approaches New Guinea. Distinct from this current is the broad, west-flowing Trade Wind Drift which occupies the zone between the South Equatorial Current and the Tropical Convergence, near latitude 30°S. It normally flows with considerable velocity, but fluctuates widely with seasonal changes in the wind pattern. From April to December (Fig. 5) it moves water in a westerly direction across the Coral Sea where it diverges. Part of the northern branch flows into the Solomon Sea while a drift continues westward to the Northern Queensland Shelf where it curves northward. The main southern branch becomes the East Australian Current. In the summer (December–March), a drastic change is wrought in the current pattern (Fig. 4), because of the strong monsoonal effect. Under this influence, equatorial water masses move into the northern region from the north and north-west and flow southward to merge with the East Australian Current.

The East Australian Current is the strong, narrow, southward flow which results from the building up of water in the Coral Sea by the Trade Winds. Because of the Australian land mass and New Guinea, this build-up can only be relieved southward. According to WYRTKI (1960) this is achieved by a southward volume transport of $10-25 \times 10^6$ m³/sec. The current forms to the north of the Chesterfield Reefs, and sweeps over the Queensland Shelf between $20°$ and $25°S$ latitude where it curves southward. Its deflection by the land mass results in stronger, deeper flow between latitudes $25°$ and $30°S$ (off Cape Byron), particularly in the summer. During the winter, a counter current develops in response to the strong southerly winds. There are two important areas of convergence associated with the current viz. one on its western edge to the north of Fraser Island, slightly south of the Great Barrier Reef (latitudes $22-25°S$), and a second (latitudes $23-29°S$) on the eastern margin where the Trade Drift water masses merge. The complexity of water movements in the area between Fraser Island and the Swain Reefs (on the widest section of the continental shelf) has been demonstrated by float measurements carried out by Dr. P. Woodhead (personal communication, 1967). Beyond the second area of convergence the current widens as it curves eastward under the influence of the westerly and south-westerly winds (latitudes $35-45°S$) and reacts with the West Wind Drift and the Trade Wind Drift to form the Subtropical and Tropical Convergences. Strong divergence and upwelling occur where the current swings eastward away from the Southern Shelf.

The northern branch of the Trade Wind Drift which persists westward beyond the divergence near the Solomon Sea, flows across the deep Coral Sea and meets the Queensland Shelf as far south as $15°S$ latitude. The main flow is deflected northward and north-westward along the continental edge and across the shelf between Queensland and New Guinea. In the summer months from December to March, monsoonal drift from the west deflects the flow away from the shelf and causes a small cell or gyral to develop over the western part of the Coral Sea (Fig. 4), with possible divergence in the area offshore from Cape York.

The southern region of the South-West Pacific is characterised by the West Wind Drift which sweeps eastward to the south of Australia. A small but significant branch diverges north-eastward from the main drift and flows along the western side of New Zealand, into the Tasman Sea, where it meets the East Australian Current and produces the Subtropical Convergence. Sinking occurs along this zone as well as along the New Zealand coast.

There are several important areas of Convergence and Divergence in the South-West Pacific. The Subtropical Convergence which occurs between Tasmania and the northern tip of New Zealand, is the boundary between the southward-moving subtropical water masses and the north-eastward-moving subantarctic water masses of the West Wind Drift. The zone of convergence moves southward in the summer, disappears between October and November and reappears to the north during the winter. Because of the higher salinity of the subtropical water, it is believed that more of this subtropical water sinks along the Convergence than subantarctic water.

The second important zone is the Tropical Convergence between the eastward-moving East Australian Current and the Trade Wind Drift. Its position corresponds fairly closely with the southern limit of the South-East Trades where wind directions change from south-west to south-east and thereby cause convergent flow. It is not as strongly developed nor as constant as the Subtropical Convergence, and it disappears in February when the Trade Wind Drift turns south, passing directly into the Subtropical Convergence. It shifts northward in March. Other regions of convergence and sinking occur along the western New Zealand coast. Divergences are developed in the Coral Sea and between Tasmania and New Zealand. Slight divergence may occur off the Queensland Shelf between latitudes $10°$ and $16°S$.

WATER MASSES

In the South-West Pacific, the major water masses include:

(*1*) Pacific Bottom Water which forms around the

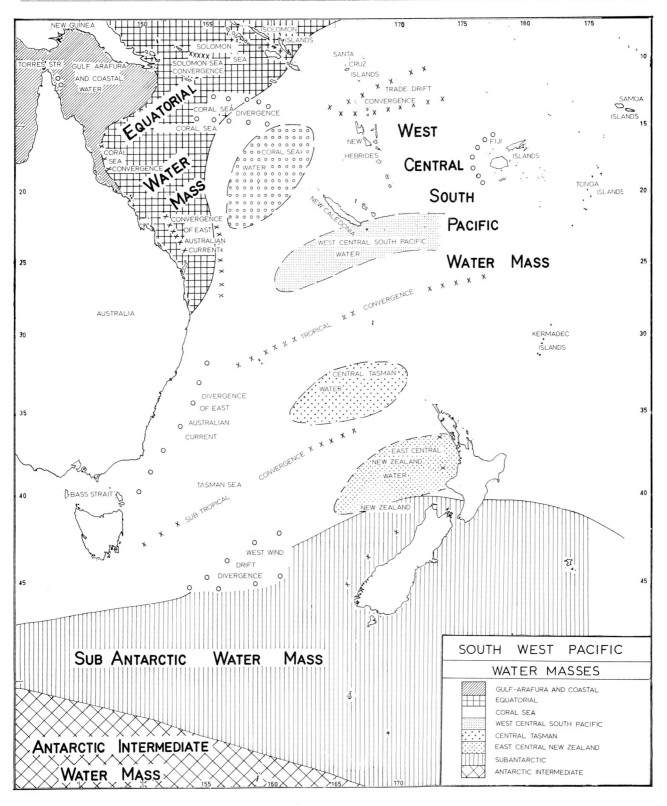

Fig. 6. The main water masses of the South-West Pacific, and the zones of convergence and divergence. Note the southern extension of Equatorial Water and Gulf Arafura Water.

Antarctic continent, sinks and moves northward (average salinity 34.7‰, temperature 0°C).

(*2*) Pacific Deep Water which ranges from 555 to 2,220 fathoms (1,000–4,000 m) and has a net southward flow, above the Pacific Bottom Water (average salinity 34.8‰, temperature 0–2°C).

(*3*) The Antarctic Intermediate Water which descends near the Antarctic Convergence and flows northward as cold (3–7°C), low salinity water (33.8‰).

(*4*) The Subantarctic Water Mass which flows southward and eastward between the Subtropical and Antarctic Convergences, and is warmer than the Antarctic Intermediate Water.

(*5*) The Central Water Mass of the South Pacific which extends to depths of 500 fathoms (900 m) in the west, and is variable in character (average salinity 35.7‰, temperature 16–26°C).

(*6*) The Equatorial Water Mass which forms a band between 10°S and 10°N latitude and extends to depths of 555 fathoms (1,000 m) (average salinity 35.3‰, temperature 27°C).

(*7*) The complex surface water layer of approximately 55 fathoms (100 m) depth which covers most of the Equatorial and Central Water Masses.

The greater part of the South-West Pacific above 550 fathoms (1,000 m) is occupied by the three major water masses shown on Fig. 6 and 7, viz.: Equatorial, Central and Subantarctic. In the northwest, the Equatorial Water Mass extends southward from the Solomon Sea to the coast of New South Wales. It is augmented by Arafura and Gulf water which enters through Torres Strait and mixes along the Queensland Shelf and the western part of the Coral Sea. To the east, the Equatorial Water meets the main Central Water Mass which originates in the region of the Subtropical Convergence and is spread northward and north-westward by the Trade Wind System. Variations in water properties, due largely to the influence of adjacent water masses (Equatorial and Subantarctic), have led to the recognition of four water masses within this extensive central body, viz.:

(*a*) The West Central South Pacific Water proper, which is typically developed in the region of New Caledonia, and has an average salinity of 35.7‰ and a temperature of 26°C.

(*b*) The Central Tasman Water Mass between Lord Howe Island and the Auckland Peninsula, which has

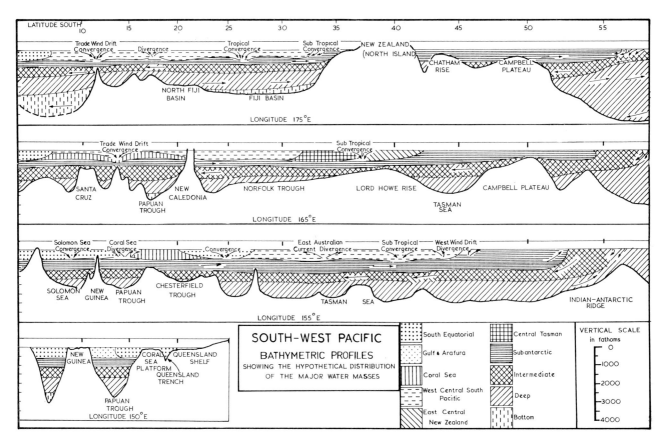

Fig. 7. Meridional profiles of the South-West Pacific illustrating the hypothetical distribution of water types.

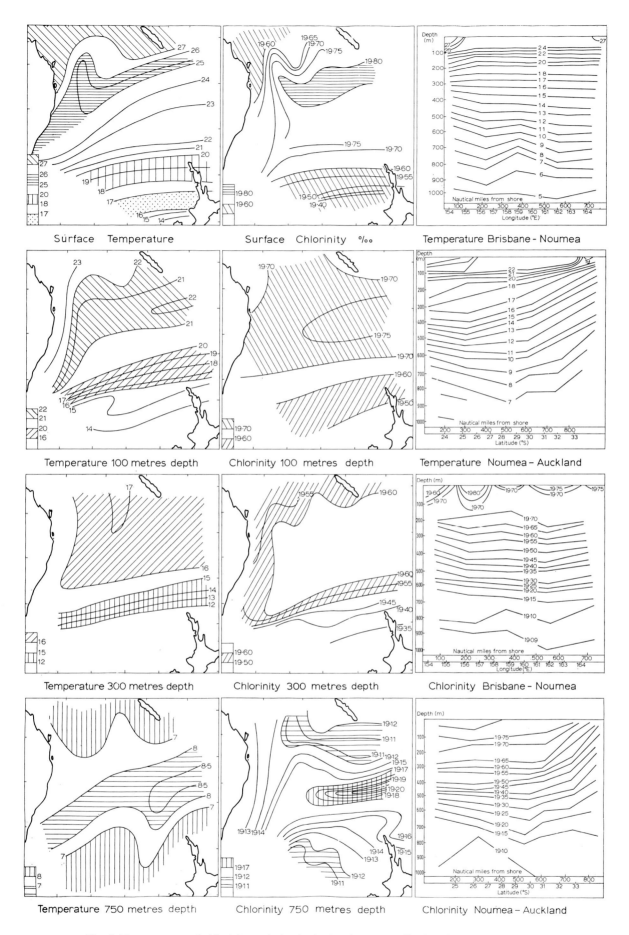

Fig. 8. Temperature and chlorinity variation in the South-West Pacific, based on ROCHFORD (1959).

*15*

an average salinity of 35.6% and a temperature of 19°C.

(*c*) The East Central New Zealand Water Mass which has developed in response to the adjacent Subantarctic Water Mass. It represents a colder, less saline variant of the Central Pacific body and has an average salinity of 35.0% and a temperature of 16.3°C.

(*d*) The Coral Sea Water Mass which is developed in the northwestern region adjacent to the Equatorial Water Mass. It has an average salinity of 35.0% and a temperature of 21.3°C.

The Subantarctic Water Mass originates in the zone between the Subtropical and Antarctic Convergences, by vertical mixing which results in low salinity water. In response to the strong West Wind System, it moves eastward and part is deflected northward along the New Zealand coast where it encounters the Central Water Mass which it modifies to produce the East Central New Zealand Water Mass.

From the data published by ROCHFORD (1959) and SVERDRUP et al. (1942) the properties of the water masses in the South-West Pacific may be tabulated as shown in Table I.

TABLE I

PROPERTIES OF PACIFIC WATER MASSES

| Water mass | Salinity | Chorinity | Temperature |
|---|---|---|---|
| Equatorial | 35.3 | 19.56 | 27.20 |
| Arafura | 34.2 | 18.95 | 29.0 |
| Coral Sea | 35.6 | 19.71 | 21.3 |
| West Central South Pacific | 35.8 | 19.80 | 26.00 |
| Central Tasman | 35.6 | 19.71 | 19.00 |
| East Central New Zealand | 35.0 | 19.38 | 16.30 |
| Subantarctic | 34.5 | 19.09 | 5.60 |

In the survey undertaken by ROCHFORD (1959) the vertical distribution of water properties (Fig. 8) reveals marked breaks between 27.5 and 55 fathoms (50–100 m) and these presumably indicate the base of the complex surface water layer. Below this level, there is a uniform change in water properties to depths of 500 fathoms (900 m), the approximate base of the Central Pacific and Equatorial Water Masses.

In view of the salinity and temperature characteristics of the main water masses, their succession in terms of increasing density would be Arafura, South Equatorial, West Central South Pacific, Coral Sea, East Central New Zealand, Central Tasman and Subant-

arctic. In the summer months when the monsoonal influence is strongest, the surface water on the North Queensland Shelf would belong to the Arafura Mass which is low density, low salinity and high temperature water. During the major part of the year, South Equatorial Water of moderate salinity (35.3%) and high temperature displaces the lighter Arafura water. Further east, colder (21.3°C) more saline water (35.6%) of the Coral Sea Mass extends under the South Equatorial and West Central South Pacific Masses. In the Coral Sea, where the main Trade Wind Drift branches to form the current of the Solomon Sea on the north and the East Australian Current on the south, probable upwelling of the denser, saline Coral Sea Water occurs in the region of divergence. Part of this is carried westward to the steep continental slope of northern Queensland and deflected northward where its influence is reflected in the intensive development of reefs. The other main movements of water are along the Queensland Trench, across the Coral Sea Platform and along the Chesterfield Trough. The gently shelving floor of the Coral Sea Platform allows gradual intermixing with the South Equatorial and West Central South Pacific surface waters, thus reducing the density and salinity of the Coral Sea Water and finally destroying its identity before reaching the central part of the Queensland Shelf. The importance of the Coral Sea Water in reef development is found in its salinity–temperature characteristics, both of which favour high carbonate-ion concentrations that are essential to the skeletal growth of reef organisms. The Queensland Trench, Chesterfield Trough and deep north-western margin of the Coral Sea permit this high carbonate water to reach the northern and southern parts of the Queensland Shelf where reef development is most intensive.

### REEF DISTRIBUTION IN THE SOUTH-WEST PACIFIC

There are nine major reef provinces in the South-West Pacific, viz:

(*1*) the Great Barrier Reef Province;

(*2*) the Eastern New Guinea Province;

(*3*) the Solomon Islands Reefs;

(*4*) the Coral Sea Platform Group;

(*5*) the Chesterfield Group;

(*6*) the New Caledonia Province;

(*7*) the Fiji Province;

(*8*) the Tonga Province;

(*9*) the New Hebrides–Santa Cruz Province.

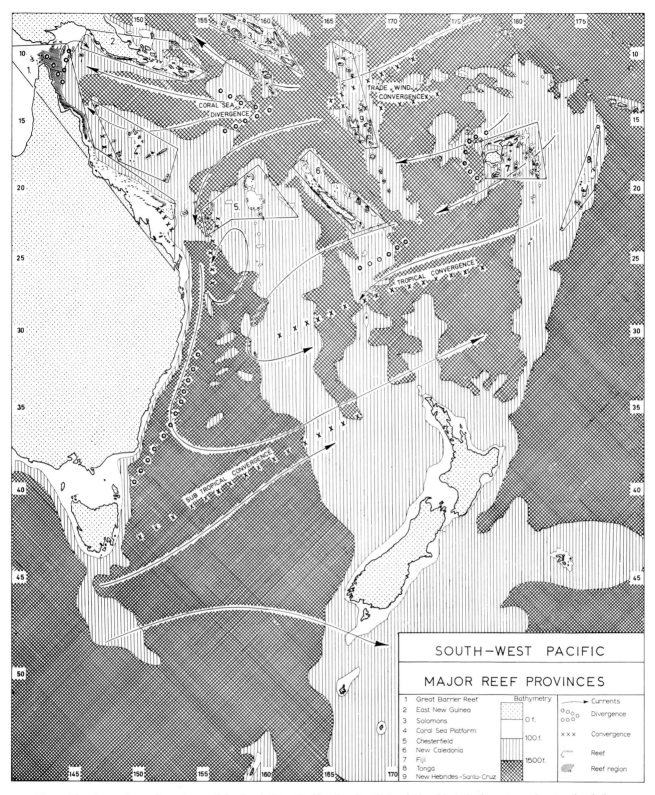

Fig. 9. The nine major reef provinces of the South-West Pacific, showing their relationship to bathymetry and water circulation.

In addition to these areas of major development (Fig. 9), small scattered reefs occur, such as those around Lord Howe Island, Minerva Reefs south of Fiji, Conway and Hunter Reefs in the North Fiji Basin, and the Indispensable Reefs south of the Solomons. However, the greatest concentrations of reef are found in the nine major provinces, some of which have more prolific and more extensive reef growth than

*17*

the others. The sequence in which the major provinces have been listed above may be regarded as one reflecting decreasing density and area of reef development—the most concentrated, most extensive reef growth is found in the Great Barrier Reef Province, the least in the New Hebrides–Santa Cruz Province.

The distribution of the major provinces as well as the differences between them are the result of bathymetric and hydrologic factors that are fairly readily examined. All of the provinces are located on major oceanic rises and ridges or on the continental shelf. All reach their maximum development near the margins of the rises and shelves, adjacent to deep troughs and trenches. Reef development declines sharply as the distance from the deep water increases. Thus, the dense northern and southern regions of the Great Barrier Reef are near the deep western Coral Sea, Queensland Trench and Chesterfield Trough; the East New Guinea and Solomon Island Provinces are bordered by the deep Coral and Solomon Seas; the Coral Sea Platform Reefs and Chesterfield Reefs are marginal developments on oceanic rises and are flanked by the Queensland Trench, Papuan Trough and Chesterfield Trough —southward along the rises they disappear; the New Caledonia Province is set tightly between the Norfolk and Papuan Troughs; the Fiji and Tonga Provinces are flanked by the Fiji Basin and Tonga Trench; the New Hebrides–Santa Cruz Province lies between the Coral Sea and the North Fiji Basin. No major reef province has developed in the central parts of the Lord Howe Rise or the Eastern Plateau and Ridge System, and reefs are sparse and scattered on the central part of the Queensland Shelf—these are areas that are separated from the deeper troughs by greater distances.

Proximity of deep troughs and trenches appears to favour reef growth, but this alone does not account for the varied development of the nine provinces. The hydrology of the water masses also exerts a controlling influence. The first four provinces are covered mainly by South Equatorial Water (35.3% salinity, 27.2°C) and in the very north-west by Arafura Water (34.2% salinity, 29.0°C). The remainder occur in the West Central South Pacific Water which has a higher salinity (35.8%) but lower temperature (26.0°C) than the other water masses. Thus, it might appear that higher temperatures have more beneficial effect on reef growth than higher salinity. This is possibly true for organisms in

which massive lime secretion is not essential—soft corals, sponges, plants and the many other soft inhabitants of reef communities. An important though poorly defined water mass is the Coral Sea Mass of high salinity (35.6%) and relatively low temperature (21.3°C). This water underlies much of the South Equatorial and West Central South Pacific, in the region bordered by the Great Barrier Reef, East New Guinea and Solomons, Coral Sea Platform, Chesterfield Group and New Caledonia. One might speculate that this water, with temperature and salinity range favourable for high carbonate-ion concentrations, flows through the troughs and trenches that flank these areas of strong reef development, and provides the essential lime for skeletal secretion.

The final factor influencing the distribution and character of the reef provinces is oceanic circulation and tidal movement. From the generalized pattern illustrated on Fig. 3, it is obvious that the Trade Wind Drift and the Eastern Australian Current control circulation in the reef areas of the South-West Pacific. In addition to renewing oceanic waters in the provinces, the currents through divergence and convergence, cause upwelling of colder, more saline waters and downsinking of surface water. In the Coral Sea, the main divergence of the Trade Wind Drift occurs and it is probable that Coral Sea Water surfaces and is carried in the direction of the Papuan Trough, the Queensland Trench, the Chesterfield Trough, and the Solomon Sea—the seaways which flank the five major reef provinces. The extensive Coral Sea Platform shields the central region of the Great Barrier Reef from this high salinity, carbonate-enriched water and it is in this central region that reef growth is most subdued. Two other important zones of divergence occur—the first around the western side of the Fiji Province and the second to the south of New Caledonia. Both appear to be responsible for the reef growth in these provinces. The New Caledonia Province is more favourably situated with respect to the southern divergence and this probably accounts for its reef development being more prolific than that of Fiji. The New Hebrides–Santa Cruz Province is influenced by the Trade Wind Convergence, a zone where probable downsinking occurs. Thus, no colder, deeper, more saline water is available to this province and there is a noticeable decline in reef growth relative to that of other provinces.

# Chapter 3 | Geological framework

The framework of the South-West Pacific may be defined broadly in terms of crustal thickness. If one recognises the two main crustal types, viz. continental, with an average thickness of 33 km, and oceanic, with an average thickness of 6 km as well as transitional crustal material, then the South-West Pacific represents a complex intermixture of crustal types and gradations. MENARD (1964, p. 227) suggested that the region could be regarded as one where there had been extreme stretching of the continental margin, with consequent but almost random thinning of the crust. He cited crustal thicknesses of 30, 18, 13.6, 10.5 and 5.7 km in the region. While there appear to be complete gradations from thick continental to thin oceanic crustal type, distinct crustal elements can be recognised and these may be considered the major units in the geological framework of the South-West Pacific. They include:

(*1*) the Australian Continental Mass;
(*2*) the Continental Belt of New Guinea, New Caledonia and New Zealand;
(*3*) the Transitional Region of Melanesia.

## The Australian Continental Mass

The Australian Continental Mass consists of three main elements: (*a*) the Precambrian shield nuclei, which dominate the western two-thirds of the continent, (*b*) the Palaeozoic geosynclines which form the eastern and western margins of the continent as well as bisecting the main shield area, and (*c*) the large cratonic basins which separate the shield nuclei and which form enormous downwarped regions between the main shield area and the eastern (Tasman) geosynclinal belt.

Within the ancient shield nuclei, geosynclinal sequences have been recognised, but by the end of Precambrian

time, these nuclei had been stabilised. Late in the Proterozoic the Adelaidean–Amadeus geosynclinal belt formed and it separated the stable south-western shield from the narrower shield zone that extended from the Mt. Isa area in the north through Broken Hill and south to western Tasmania. The Tasman Geosyncline was well established by the Silurian and, presumably, the large marine basins fringing Western Australia were offshoots from a Westralian Geosyncline, formed at the same time. During the Early Palaeozoic, the extensive area between the shield and Tasman Geosyncline subsided unevenly and various parts of it were sites of terrestrial sedimentation. Major orogenies in the Middle Devonian resulted in the formation of new, active marine basins in both eastern and western Australia along the geosynclinal belts. A second phase of orogenic upheaval after the Permian, terminated the active history of most of these basins, and the greater part of the Australian continent witnessed no further marine sedimentation until the Cretaceous, when seas invaded the large, slowly subsiding cratonic basins and some of the smaller, more active basins that had developed on the old geosynclinal belts. Final stabilisation of Australia had occurred by the end of the Mesozoic, and except for extensive block faulting and vulcanicity, as well as localized terrestrial sedimentation, the continent remained comparatively inactive throughout the Cainozoic. Two of the striking features of eastern Australia's evolution were the extensive, prolonged vulcanicity that occurred during the Siluro-Devonian, Permian, Triassic and Tertiary, and the widespread development of carbonate provinces, in some of which organic (coral) reefs thrived, from Ordovician to Early Permian.

## The Continental Belt of New Guinea, New Caledonia and New Zealand

All three land areas of this belt have had complex histories which included geosynclinal development and Tertiary marine transgression. New Guinea, as suggested by GLAESSNER (1950), is composite in its tectonic framework, having combined elements of the South-East Asiatic, Australian and Melanesian regions to form its present complex mass. These elements contain ancient metamorphic and igneous basements, thick, folded, geosynclinal sequences of Palaeozoic, Mesozoic and Tertiary ages, shelf sediments of Tertiary age and arcs of active and recently active volcanoes. The eastern end of New Guinea is composed of three elements which have their counterparts in both New Caledonia and New Zealand. The first element is the Aure Trough and it contains a thick, strongly folded sequence of Late Tertiary sediments, the northerly trend of which is not concordant with the main north-west trend that is characteristic of the greater part of the island. GLAESSNER (1950) suggested that it represented the foredeep of the Morobe Arc. This is the second element and consists of low grade metamorphic rocks of Cretaceous and younger age, intruded extensively by granitic material, and now forming the main part of the Owen Stanley Mountains. The Finisterre Mountains, which form the third element, consist of Miocene sediments (predominantly limestone) which have been folded. It is evident then that Eastern New Guinea has evolved as a geosynclinal region with associated shelf and basin zones, during the Late Mesozoic and Tertiary. The main Palaeozoic basement developments lie further west.

In New Caledonia, the work of ROUTHIER (1953) has shown the existence of extensive pre-Permian basement metamorphics and a thick sequence of marine sediments ranging from the Permian to the Quaternary. Geosynclinal conditions developed during the Tertiary when the region appears to have been related to Eastern New Guinea.

The complex framework of New Zealand has developed around Precambrian nuclei in the north-western part of the South Island and along Early Palaeozoic and Late Palaeozoic-Early Mesozoic geosynclinal belts. Important orogenies during the Cretaceous were succeeded by smaller ones in the Middle and Late Tertiary. Throughout the Tertiary history of New Guinea, New Caledonia and New Zealand, intensive vulcanicity and extensive carbonate deposition were typical.

## *The Transitional Region of Melanesia*

Included in the Transitional Region of Melanesia are the Northern and Western Basins (Coral Sea, Tasman Sea), the Eastern Basins, the Eastern Plateau and Ridge System (Fiji, Tonga, Chatham Rise and Campbell Plateau) and the Solomon, Santa Cruz and New Hebrides belt between the Northern and Eastern Basins. The region has been so named because of its transitional crustal thicknesses between true continental and oceanic.

Most of the islands are similar geologically, with pre-Miocene basements of igneous and metamorphic rocks and overlying Tertiary sediments (predominantly limestone) and volcanics (predominantly andesite). HOUTZ and PHILLIPS (1963) suggested that the Fijian Group originated as volcanic islands during the Eocene and were subsequently intruded by both basic and acid magmas, prior to the main phases of vulcanicity and marine sedimentation that occurred during the Miocene and Pliocene. This view is in accord with those of GLAESSNER (1950, p. 875) and MENARD (1964, p. 227) both of whom postulated a thinning of the crust in the Melanesian region. GLAESSNER (1950) further suggested that because of this, "all pre-Tertiary rocks were either regionally metamorphosed or replaced by plutonic intrusions".

Less is known of the submarine part of the Melanesian region. MENARD (1964, p. 229) suggested that the thickness of the crust varied with its depth below sea level and thus implied that the deeper basins had the thinnest crusts, some in fact approaching the true oceanic type. The Chatham Rise and Campbell Plateau off New Zealand have yielded Tertiary rocks on dredging. ADAMS (1962) calculated a crustal thickness of 20 km for this region. It may be speculated that the rises of the Central Zone would have comparable thicknesses, but available seismic data in this region is inconclusive.

In summary, the framework of the South-West Pacific consists of the Archaean nuclei and marginal Palaeozoic geosynclinal zone in the west, the younger Mesozoic and Tertiary geosynclinal zone of the New Guinea –New Zealand belt with which are associated older, possibly Precambrian nuclei, and the thin crustal region of Melanesia with its locally thickened zones of Tertiary islands. The whole area is bordered on the north and east by deep, thin oceanic crust.

When the geological grain of the Australian continent is examined in conjunction with the bathymetric character of the South-West Pacific, two patterns emerge (Fig. 10). The most obvious is the north to north-north-west trend of the geosynclinal belts of the continent and of the bathymetric features south of the Coral Sea. Less obvious is the west-south-west to west-north-west trend which is reflected on the continent by the Euroka Ridge and Longreach Spur in the

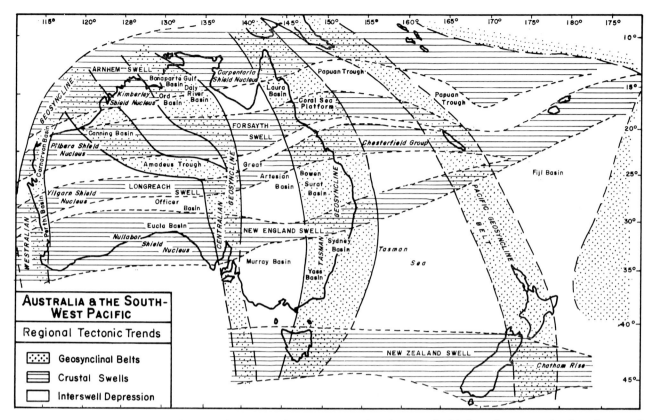

Fig. 10. Regional tectonic trends of the South-West Pacific, showing meridional geosynclinal belts and cross trends of gentler crustal warping.

Great Artesian Basin, the Amadeus Trough in central Australia and elements of the shield region of western Australia, and in the South-West Pacific by the Papuan Trough, the Solomon Sea, the ridge between Tasmania and New Zealand (South Island) and the Chatham Rise.

The main northerly pattern is associated with geosynclinal belts: the Late Proterozoic Centralian Belt which includes the Adelaidean, Amadeus and north-western branches; the Palaeozoic Westralian Belt with its marginal basins; the Palaeozoic Eastern Belt (Tasman Geosyncline); the Mesozoic–Tertiary Pacific Belt with geosynclinal sequences in New Guinea, New Caledonia and New Zealand; and the active, marginal zone of the Kermadec–Tonga–Solomons Groups. Thus there are five main elements in this pattern, the oldest in the centre of the continental mass, the youngest along the South-West Pacific margin.

The westerly pattern is recognised mainly in areas of Precambrian shield rock and in younger intrusives and metamorphics. This very association implies basement uplift in latitudinal zones, and one might regard these zones as crustal swells separated by deeper troughs and basins. Their association with the older rocks might also imply that they too originated early in crustal de-

velopment. Five major zones have been recognised (Fig. 10) and named, from south to north, the New Zealand, New England, Longreach, Forsayth and Arnhem Swells. All appear to increase westward.

The areas of intersection of the two patterns are frequently the site of significant geological developments. In most cases on the continent, extensive exposure of granitic and metamorphic rocks occur where swells are transected by geosynclines: e.g., the Cape York Complex, the Forsayth–Charters Towers Complex, the Anakie High and the New England Bathylith—formed where the Tasman Geosyncline crosses the Arnhem, Forsayth, Longreach and New England Swells. Where the latitudinal crustal troughs or depressions are intersected by geosynclinal belts, the geosyncline widens and deepens: e.g., Laura Basin, Bowen–Surat Basin, Amadeus Trough. Between the geosynclinal belts, shield rocks are exposed on the swells, whereas large cratonic basins (Great Artesian, Murray) develop over the inter-swell depressions. It may be inferred that the westerly swells and depressions are ancient features which still react epeirogenically as positive and negative belts respectively, and that the character of the geosynclinal belts is affected by these older cross trends. On the assumption that the sialic crust originally

*21*

thinned progressively across the South-West Pacific and that it is influenced by both patterns, it is possible to draw conclusions on the tectonic framework of this region.

Evidence for a Pacific Geosynclinal Belt from New Guinea, through New Caledonia to New Zealand is found in the geosynclinal sequences of these land areas and in the high submarine topography that runs in a semi-meridional belt between them. One might regard the central Coral Sea area (Papuan Trough) as the zone of intersection of a westerly crustal depression and intergeosynclinal belt. The main part of the Tasman Sea and the Fiji Basin are also located in the crustal depressions between geosynclinal belts. The southern island of New Zealand, with its Precambrian shield areas and Palaeozoic geosynclinal sequences occurs on the New Zealand Swell which extends through Tasmania to the Chatham Rise. The effect of the westerly pattern on the sialic crust would probably be manifested in thickening along the swells, but the overall gradient eastwards would be caused by the geosynclinal belts, and one would expect greater crustal thickness along the Pacific Belt and along the marginal zone. The main areas of subsidence and uplift should occur at the intersection of geosynclinal belts with interswell depressions and swells respectively. One might speculate that the Coral Sea Platform and New Caledonia have been active elements, whereas the Papuan Trough, Tasman Sea and Fiji Basin have been quiescent.

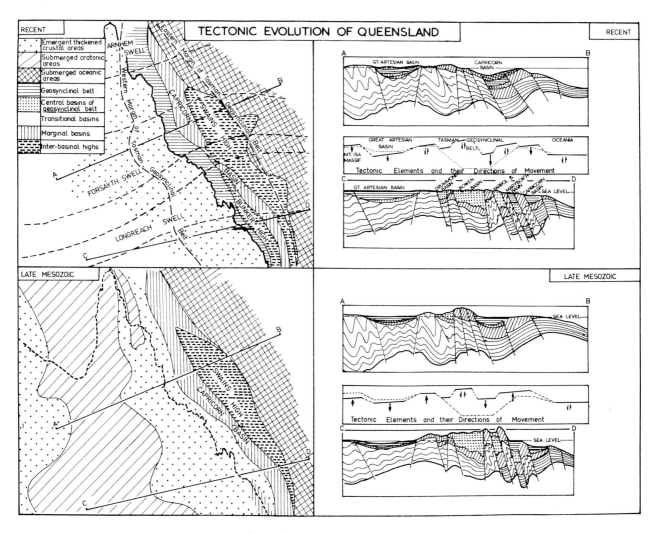

Fig. 11, first part. Legend see p. 23.

EASTERN QUEENSLAND

*Tectonic framework and evolution*

The influence exerted by the mainland on the evolution of the Great Barrier Reef Province is one which is not readily assessed. Some indication of its magnitude is gained through consideration of the geological character of the region and through examination of its present sediment-source potential. The major geological feature in eastern Queensland is the Tasman Geosyncline which, during its several phases of development from Ordovician to Early Triassic time, was the site of heavy marine sedimentation, intensive vulcanicity and orogenic upheaval. By Early Mesozoic time, the belt had achieved relative stability, and widespread freshwater deposition then occurred during this era. Crustal

movements continued but they were non-orogenic in character and smaller in scale than the earlier deformations. Similar terrestrial sedimentation, on a more restricted scale, persisted through the Cainozoic. Again, faulting and block movement were important and widespread volcanic extrusion occurred.

The main tectonic framework of eastern Queensland evolved during the Palaeozoic (Fig. 11) and it consists essentially of the various units of the Tasman Geosyncline. Younger features of Mesozoic and Cainozoic age are significant, but their histories appear to have been controlled largely by the framework developed in the preceding era.

Two groups of tectonic elements may be recognised: the belts of old metamorphic and igneous rocks which acted as positive elements throughout most of the Palaeozoic and subsequent eras, and the intervening

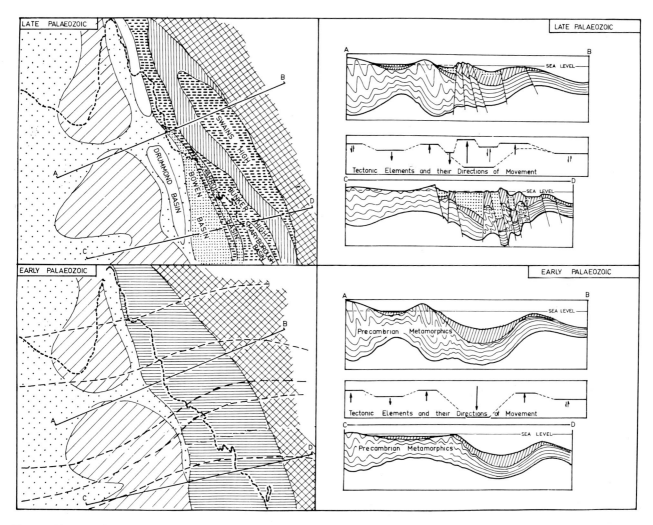

Fig. 11. The tectonic evolution of Queensland. Maps and cross-sections illustrating the main tectonic elements of Queensland and the adjacent oceanic region during the Palaeozoic, Mesozoic and Cainozoic. The degree and direction of movement of the various elements are indicated by arrows on the cross-sections.

basins of sedimentary rocks. The main positive elements form three sub-parellel, sub-meridional belts and include the North Coast–Anakie High (HILL, 1951), the Eungella–Gogango–Auburn High (HILL, 1951; HILL and DENMEAD, 1960) and the dichotomous South Coastal High (HILL, 1951). Four groups of basins are separated by the highs and, from west to east, they are the Hodgkinson–Star–Drummond Basins, the Bowen–Surat Basins, the Yarrol Basin and the Maryborough Basin. The smaller Esk Rift occurs in the South Coastal dichotomy. Stratigraphic evidence suggests that seven major tectonic episodes occurred during the evolution of eastern Australia.

The first tectonic episode involved the downbuckling of the main geosynclinal belt in Early Palaeozoic time and the intensive sedimentation and vulcanicity which produced thicknesses of the order of 20,000 ft. of argillite, greywacke, radiolarian chert and interbedded andesite. Along the marginal shelf areas extensive carbonate deposition occurred and major coral reefs developed.

The second tectonic episode began after widespread orogenic disruption during the Middle Devonian. As a result of deformation, uplift, intrusion and metamorphism of the geosynclinal sediments, positive tectonic elements emerged and new negative belts began to subside: the western Hodgkinson–Star–Drummond Basins and the eastern Yarrol Basin. Deposition of argillaceous and arenaceous material, largely of volcanic derivation, began at a rapid rate but as tectonism declined, carbonate sedimentation dominated the region and coral reefs developed along the western shelf of the Yarrol Basin. During this later phase, deposition in the western basins which had been mainly terrestrial, was reduced.

Episode three witnessed the rapid downwarp of the Bowen, Esk and Maryborough Basins and the stabilisation of the earlier basins. Again, vulcanicity was intensive and the sequences in all three basins include a high proportion of andesite and acid volcanics, greywacke and shale, followed by the main development of coal measures of Late Permian–Early Triassic age. The fourth episode terminated the geosynclinal phase and introduced the tectonic pattern that was to develop during the Mesozoic and Cainozoic eras. Eastern Queensland was subjected to orogenic forces of varying intensity which resulted in folding, thrusting and uplift of basins and highs, igneous intrusion and finally, rifting and vulcanicity. Sedimentation resumed in the grabens and intramontane basins of this rejuvenated region, together with intensive pyroclastic activity. The most active tectonic zone was the subsiding Mary-

borough Basin which had not achieved the same stability as that of the other basins.

The fifth episode began towards the end of the Jurassic when crustal movements, accompanied by intrusive and extrusive activity, affected the Maryborough Basin. Renewed subsidence of this belt was in contrast with the regional, marginal upwarping that affected the rest of eastern Queensland.

The sixth episode in the Late Cretaceous culminated in the folding of the Maryborough Basin sediments and the formation of small, isolated freshwater basins throughout eastern Queensland, together with extensive basaltic extrusion. A long interval of tectonic stability and peneplanation was climaxed by the lateritisation of large areas of surface material, both on the present mainland and on part of the present continental shelf.

The seventh and final episode extended through the Late Cainozoic to the present. Strong marginal upwarp of the Queensland coastal belt was followed by fracturing and differential movement of the resultant blocks as well as differential erosion that resulted in the topographic pattern that is evident to-day.

The seven tectonic episodes that have been recognised on the mainland must be taken into consideration in any assessment of the development of the continental shelf and adjacent regions. The trends of the main tectonic elements of the Tasman Geosyncline are interrupted quite sharply by the coastline and the sparse geophysical and geological data suggest that these elements continue on to the shelf, and that submergence of large parts of the shelf has resulted not only from post-Pleistocene eustatic changes but from major crustal adjustments associated with the later tectonic episodes recognised on the mainland. These will be considered in a subsequent section.

GEOMORPHOLOGY

Eastern Queensland belongs entirely to one of the three major topographic divisions of Australia, viz. the Eastern Highlands (BRYAN, 1930). In the main, these consist of uplifted, dissected areas which extend southward from Cape York in a widening belt that reaches a maximum width of 400 miles (approx. 645 km) in southern Queensland. The greater part of the belt is less than 2,000 ft. (610 m) high, while a large portion is less than 1,000 ft. (305 m). Four subdivisions are recognised within the Eastern Highlands: the Main Divide, the Coastal Ranges, Coastal Plain and the Intermediate Plateau Remnants (Fig. 12). The Main

Divide separates the Pacific Drainage from the western and southwestern river systems. In character it varies from true mountain range to insignificant plainland, frequently lower than adjacent topography. There appears to be little correspondence between its course and the structural trend of the Palaeozoic rocks. Some authors believe that it developed mainly as a result of Mesozoic and Cainozoic upwarp and that its present position is located to the west of its pre-Miocene position.

The Coastal Ranges include a discontinuous belt of dissected mountains that diverge from the Main Divide in southern Queensland and rejoin it near Cairns. Elevations of more than 5,000 ft. (1,525 m) are reached in the north where the Coastal Range is much higher than the Main Divide. The Coastal Plain varies from a few miles to 120 miles (193 km) in width and consists mainly of sand drift superimposed on clean rock, of recently elevated plains of marine deposition and of widespread alluvial deposits.

Between the Main Divide and Coastal Ranges are the Intermediate Plateau Remnants and low mountain ranges. These include the large tablelands of Cape York Peninsula, Atherton Tableland, Harvey Plateau, Alice Tableland, Carnarvons, Buckland Tableland, the Upper Burdekin region and the northern Hughenden area. The plateau belt is drained by three major river systems: the Burdekin, Fitzroy, and Burnett. Both the Burdekin and Fitzroy have basins of more than 53,000 square miles (142,500 km²). The Burdekin Basin contains high volcanic (basaltic) terrain in the north, granites and Tertiary sediments in the centre and southwest and Palaeozoic metamorphics and sediments in the east and south. Almost no Mesozoic rocks occur. By contrast, Mesozoic rocks occupy the southern third of the Fitzroy Basin, with Permian sediments and

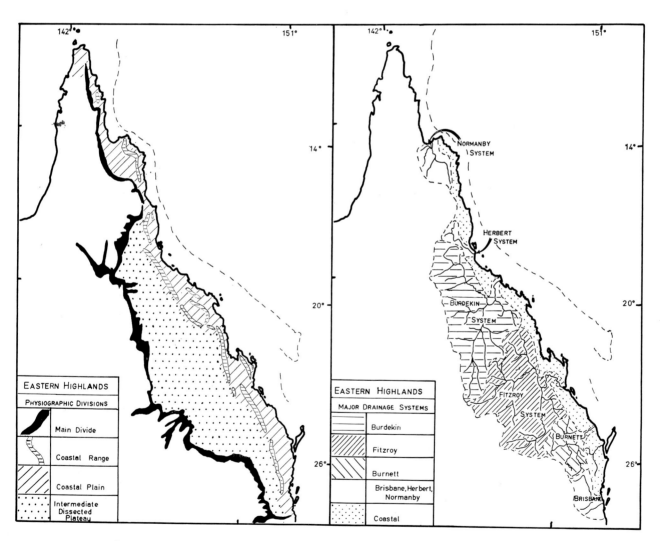

Fig. 12. The major physiographic divisions and the major drainage systems of eastern Queensland.

*25*

Tertiary basalts forming the northern and western segment and Carboniferous sediments and Lower Palaeozoic metamorphics forming the eastern third. Granitic rocks and Tertiary sediments are not abundant in the Fitzroy Basin. The Burnett River system drains predominantly granitic terrain with some Carboniferous and Mesozoic sediments and Lower Palaeozoic metamorphics. Each drainage basin has its own distinctive lithological character. The three rivers break through the Coastal Ranges and enter the sea between latitudes 19°30' and 25°S, a distance of approximately 400 miles (645 km). North of latitude 19°30'S, no major stream system opens into the sea, so that 600 miles (965 km) of the northern shelf is free from such discharge. The Coastal Plain and Coastal Ranges form a narrow strip less than 30 miles (48 km) in width, except for the area to the west of Cooktown, where it reaches 120 miles (193 km). As a result, no major stream system can develop and drainage is effected by short, fast flowing rivers. The rocks of the coastal strip are predominantly metamorphics of Lower Palaeozoic age with subordinate granite and Upper Palaeozoic sediments and, in the far north, Cretaceous sandstones. The extensive veneer of Quaternary sands, marine deposits and alluvium probably provides the greatest source of sediment.

The average annual discharge of the three major streams is of the order of 3.5 cubic miles (15.9 km³). Estimates of the coastal stream discharge average 0.8 cubic miles, (3.6 km³), so that the total land drainage of eastern Queensland contributes 4.3 cubic miles (19.5 km³) of water annually to the Great Barrier Reef Province, the water volume of which is of the order of 1,700 cubic miles (approx. 7,700 km³). The East Australian Current transport of 10 to 25 × 10⁶ m³/sec (WYRTKI, 1960, p. 31) moves 200,000 cubic miles (900,000 km³) of water annually, of which a proportion is from the reef province. From this it is evident that the contribution of land water is insignificant, and it may be inferred that its effect on the reef province is negligible.

## GEOPHYSICAL DATA

The main geophysical information (Fig. 13A, B) is provided by gravity surveys conducted by the Bureau of Mineral Resources (DOOLEY, 1959; GOODSPEED and WILLIAMS, 1959) and aeromagnetic surveys carried out by Aero Service Corporation (HARTMAN, 1962; JENNY, 1962) for Australian Oil and Gas Corporation Ltd. and Gulf Interstate Overseas Ltd, and aeromagnetic

surveys carried out by Australian Gulf Oil (ELLIS, 1966). Subsequent seismic surveys by petroleum companies involved in exploration of the Queensland shelf have not yet been released.

The aeromagnetic surveys have confirmed the northward extension of the Maryborough Basin and shown the existence of a parallel basin which may be named the Capricorn Basin and which appears to occupy the area of the Capricorn Channel and to extend northward into the Queensland Trench. Two basement highs, named here the Bunker and Swains Highs, border the Capricorn Basin. The Swains High is aligned with the guyots of the North Tasman Sea and the western part of the Coral Sea Platform. In the north, the seaward extension of the Laura Basin has been confirmed. Gravity data supports the interpretation presented in Fig. 11, which is based on aeromagnetic results, particularly with respect to the basement highs bordering the Laura Basin and the Maryborough Basin. Gravity contours in the north are suggestive of a basement swell trending north-eastwards through Cape Flattery, and possibly providing a southern limit to the Laura Basin.

## GEOLOGICAL CONTROL OF THE QUEENSLAND CONTINENTAL SHELF

An interpretation of the framework of the continental shelf and its evolution may be based on the four fields of evidence already presented, viz. the geological character of the adjacent land mass, the geomorphological character of both land and shelf, geophysical information and the regional trends that have been recognized in the South-West Pacific. The Queensland coastline, which has an overall direction of 330°, appears to transect the main geological trends of the land, trends which range from 335° to 355°. However, as BRYAN (1930) has indicated, the coastline is a composite of several dominant directions, some of which do reflect the geological grain. When allowance is made for the rounding of capes and infilling of bays by recent erosion, then it is possible to define the coastline with a series of nearly straight lines (Fig. 14), and on analysis of their directions, it is found that the coast is divisible into seven regional segments which, from north to south, have the following trends, A. 0°; B. 335°; C. 310°; D. 350°; E. 0°; F. 315°; G. 0°. Marked east–west displacements occur between segments A and B, and between segments D and E.

Comparison of Fig. 14A and B reveals a degree of correspondence between the distribution of major

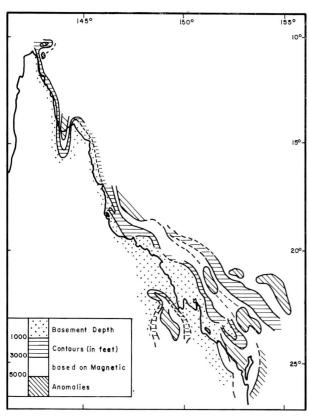

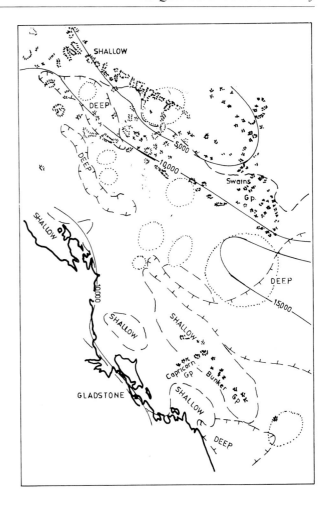

Fig. 13A. Tectonic framework of eastern Queensland based on the interpretation of aeromagnetic data of HARTMANN (1962) and JENNY (1962).
Fig. 13B. Tectonic elements of the Southern Region of the Great Barrier Reef based on aeromagnetic data. (After ELLIS, 1966). Contours in feet to estimated basement.

lithological groups and the directional segments. Segment A includes mainly Mesozoic and Tertiary sediments flanking a granitic axis and both geological and coastal trends coincide. Segment B contains mainly Lower Palaeozoic metamorphics with a grain of 340° that approaches the coastal direction of 335°. Segment C, trending 310°, transects terrain composed of granites elongated in 340° direction and metamorphosed Upper Palaeozoic rocks. Segment D includes Upper Palaeozoic sediments (limestone, greywacke and shale) of the Yarrol Basin and both geological and coastal directions are coincident at 350°. Segment E is the shortest interval and coincides with the main development of Lower Palaeozoic metamorphics and possibly Precambrian rock. Segment F is composite and includes Lower Palaeozoic metamorphics, granite and Mesozoic sandstones and shales. Its trend of 0° is discordant with the main geological grain of approximately 350°. Segment G of 0°, contains mainly Mesozoic and Tertiary sediments and both coastal and geological trends coincide.

It is evident that the main westerly to north-westerly

changes in the coast line are associated with granitic terrain (e.g., segments C and F), and that the main meridional trends are associated with Mesozoic and Tertiary sediments (e.g., segments A and G). The implication is that lithological character exerts an influence on the coastal direction, largely through differential erosion. Because of their weak consolidation and the general absence of oriented texture, the Mesozoic and Tertiary sediments yield uniformly along a line of erosion normal to the main wave fronts. The metamorphic rocks on the other hand, have a very definite grain of resistant and less resistant bands, of cleavage and of joints, and the line of erosion tends to follow this grain. The erosion of granitic terrain appears to be without direction, so that factors other than lithology must be sought to explain coastal trends in such areas. In addition to the directional relationship between lithology and coastline, there is a very significant relationship on the land between lithology and topography which may be extrapolated in order to aid interpretation of the shelf features. The highest areas of eastern Queensland have formed where Lower

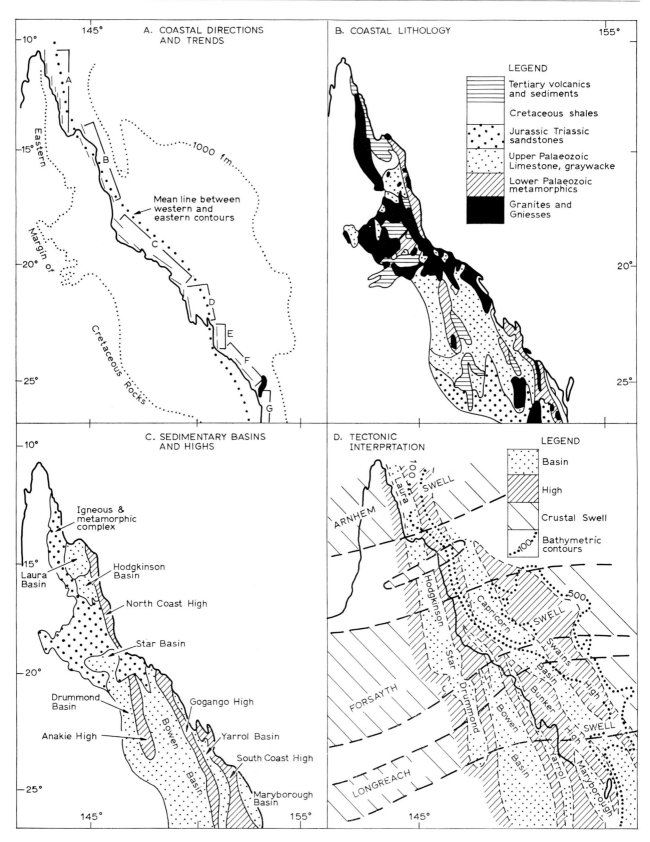

Fig. 14. Coastal trends, coastal lithology, sedimentary basins and tectonic framework of eastern Queensland and the adjacent oceanic area.

Palaeozoic metamorphics and Upper Palaeozoic sediments and volcanics, intruded by granite, are exposed. These occur in segments B, C, E and F. Except for the axial zone of the Cape York Peninsula, granitic terrain is generally low. Areas of Mesozoic and Tertiary sediment have the lowest topography of all. The more resistant Lower Palaeozoic belts might be expected to have a positive expression on the shelf, especially in the shallower regions where intensive subaerial erosion of granitic and young sedimentary terrain could have occurred during sea-level lows. The effect of their higher resistance to erosion should decrease seaward and ultimately no differential would occur between them and the softer rocks. The 20-fathom bathymetric contour reflects this relationship to some extent. It tends to parallel the grain of the metamorphics and to approach the shoreline in a random manner opposite granitic and sedimentary zones. Recent sedimentation in the reef areas tends to obscure this relationship.

While lithological character is significant in coastal and shelf developments, the distribution of lithological types is in fact a reflection of the tectonic framework of the region and this framework exerts the main control on the coastal and shelf configuration. The major Upper Palaeozoic and Mesozoic basins and the metamorphic belts are transected by the coastline, and the main projections of the coast form on the metamorphics. Trends of these tectonic elements are clearly evident on the land and they may be extrapolated seaward on bathymetric evidence. Further evidence from gravity and aeromagnetic data supports the interpretation of a northward convergence of the metamorphic belts and basins, and the existence of the submarine Capricorn Basin with its topographic expression in the Capricorn Channel and Queensland Trench. Bordering the basin are positive tectonic elements: the Bunker and Swains Highs which may be metamorphic, or less probably, volcanic in origin. The western margin of the Swains High can be aligned with the guyots of the Tasman Sea, and if these are volcanic, then a long, meridional fracture between positive and negative elements is probable. Such a situation prevailed in the Maryborough, Bowen, Esk and Yarrol Basins when large quantities of volcanic material were incorporated in the sedimentary sequences of these basins. The existence of the submarine basins and highs is also consistent with the tectonic evolution of Queensland. Meridional basins such as the Maryborough and Esk, appear to have developed as the continental margin warped upward in response to the main westward tilting of the Great Artesian Basin. These marginal

basins would seem to have formed when coastal upwarp had passed the limit of crustal strength. If the crustal thickness decreases oceanward, and there is strong evidence to support this view, then basin collapse may occur at an earlier stage in crustal upwarp of these marine regions. This may account for the less-pronounced, deeper basement in the Swains High reflected in the aeromagnetic results.

The effects of cross-trends on the semi-meridional features are quite marked and of real significance. Most obvious is the westward expansion of the Forsayth–Charters Towers granitic complex and the corresponding eastward development of the Coral Sea Platform. This is suggestive of crustal upwarp along an east-north-easterly axis and has been named the Forsayth Swell. The feature extends westward as the Euroka Ridge in the Great Artesian Basin and merges with the Mt. Isa Precambrian complex. It is the Forsayth Swell that accounts for the shoaling of the Queensland Trench and Capricorn Channel as they approach one another, and that accounts for the outer reef line transecting the basin trend. At the zone of transection there is a strong re-entrant on the shelf and an absence of reef, suggestive of a relict trench. If this interpretation is valid, then the original northern extension of the Swains Reefs would have been on to the eastern Coral Sea Platform. The marked difference in character between the reefs of the southern and central regions of the Great Barrier Reef Province may be due in part to tectonic factors such as this as well as the hydrologic factors mentioned in Chapter 2. Furthermore, the tectonic factor—the rising of the Forsayth Swell and its extension into the Coral Sea Platform—would exert a strong influence on the hydrology and bathymetry of the region. Thus, it may be postulated that the reactivation of the Forsayth Swell in sub-Recent, possibly Early Tertiary time, was one of the most important phases in the development of the Great Barrier Reef Province, and in conjunction with the subsidence of the Capricorn Basin, accounts for the separation of the Great Barrier Reef and Coral Sea Platform Provinces. When allowance is made for the Pleistocene sea-level lows, it is evident that the reef development could have occurred only on the Swains High and the Coral Sea Platform, and, therefore, the northern and central regions of the Great Barrier Reef represent younger developments.

The second cross trend, manifested in the Longreach Swell, is smaller, but equally significant. It includes the Longreach Spur in the Great Artesian Basin, the exposed southern end of the Anakie High, the Yeppoon-Cape Townshend peninsula and the eastern expansion of the Swains Reefs. The main effect of the east-north-easterly crustal swell on the progressively deepening shelf has been to produce an eastward shift and bending of the contours such as occurs around the Swains Reefs. Aeromagnetic evidence suggests that the southern margin of the swell may be defined by a major fracture. A third minor axis or swell is suggested by the gravity data, through Cape Flattery in the north. It may control the southern limit of the Laura Basin and also account for the sharp directional change in the bathymetric contours. Hypothetical stages in the tectonic development of the Great Barrier Reef Province are illustrated in Fig. 13.

# Chapter 4 | Bathymetry and hydrology of the Great Barrier Reef Province

## GENERAL CHARACTER

The region of the continental shelf occupied by the reef province extends from latitude 10°S to latitude 24°S, over a distance of more than 1,000 miles (1,600 km). The shelf width varies from a minimum 15 miles (24 km) in the north near Cape Melville, to more than 180 miles (290 km) in the south off Cape Townshend. East of Thursday Island in the far north, it again reaches a width of 120 miles (193 km). The shelf widens gradually northward and southward from Cape Melville. South of latitude 23°S, the shelf edge curves sharply south-westward and then resumes its southeasterly trend 50 miles (80 km) from the shore. Total area of the shelf is approximately 60,000 square miles (215,000 km²).

Two regional bathymetric gradients are evident. The first is the eastward decline from shoreline to outer reef zone, where the gradient reverts abruptly and then drops again towards the continental slope. The second trend is from north to south, and stages in this meridional trend permit the broad division of the province shown in Fig. 15 into Northern, Central and Southern Regions. The *Northern Region* extends northward from latitude 16°S, and is characterised by shallow water, mainly less than 20 fathoms (36 m). The *Central Region* extends from latitude 16°S to latitude 21°S on the coast and 20°S on the shelf edge, and except for a significant re-entrant towards the south, water depths of this region are generally less than 30 fathoms (55 m) but a great part is deeper than 20 fathoms. The *Southern Region* extends from latitude 21°S to latitude 24°S, and here much of the area is more than 30 fathoms deep. Thus the three major regions may be defined on bathymetric character (Fig. 16A–D)—shallow, intermediate, deep—and as will be seen, the bathymetric divisions correspond closely to the regional divisions (Fig. 17A–D) based on reef development, shelf width, submarine drainage patterns and water properties.

## BATHYMETRY AND PHYSIOGRAPHY

The *Near Shore Zone* (Fig. 18) extends from the coastal highwater mark to the 5-fathom (9 m) depth contour and ranges in width from 0 to 14 miles (0–22.5 km), with an average of 6 miles (9.6 km). Topographically, the zone is shallow, but extremely varied. Sand ridges, bars, banks, rock masses, reefal shoals, scour channels, rip current deposits, estuarine and deltaic features contribute to the complexity of its relief. It is also the zone of greatest energy. This is a consequence of shallow depth, broken topography, high tidal range, strong prevailing Trade Winds and associated south-easterly swell, and the frequent cyclonic depressions that develop in the summer. Proximity of the land and sediment source, energy of the sea and the narrow dimension of the zone result in sediment movement and reworking on a scale greater than that of any other zone. In spite of the varied and changing character of the near-shore topography, several persistent features can be recognised in the zone and these are significant in our understanding of the development of the shelf and reef province. One such feature is the steepening of gradient between the 2- and 5-fathom contours, particularly on the less protected areas of the Near Shore Zone. This steepening appears to be related to the distribution of sand which in turn is dependent more on the existence of ancient parabolic dune systems (WHITEHOUSE, 1963) than the present influx of sediment from rivers. The ancient dune systems (Fig. 29) developed during low stands of sea-level in the Late Pleistocene and Recent, and rose to heights estimated to exceed 400 ft. (120 m). The great aridity of the time, high velocity onshore Trade Winds and the prolific sand source in the Mesozoic sediments combined to provide the unusual situation under which such numerous, large systems could develop. With encroaching seas, the dunes were undercut and spread seaward as aprons and fringes, the margins of which provide the

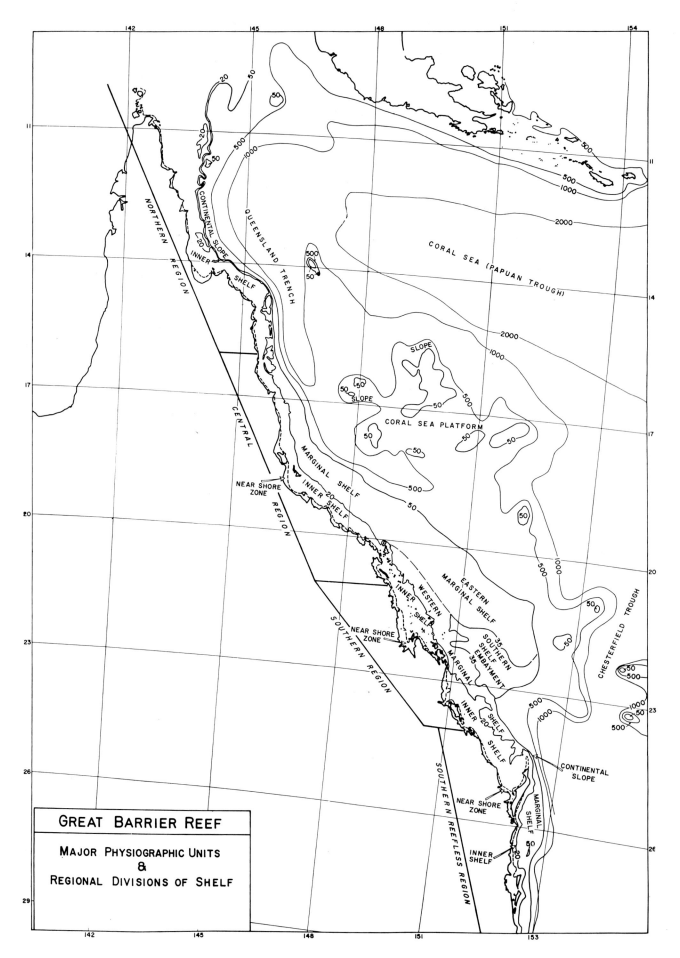

Fig. 15. The major physiographic units and the regional divisions of the Great Barrier Reef Province and adjacent area.

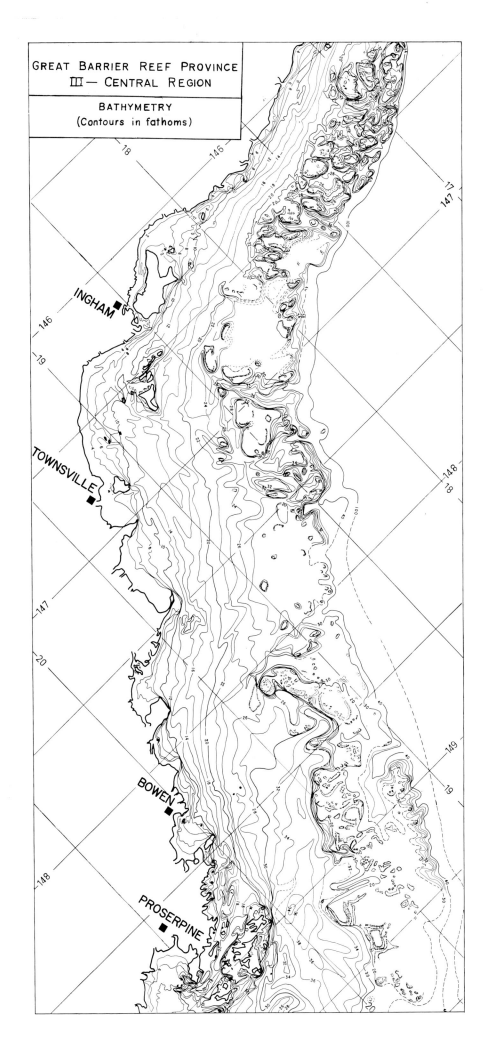

GREAT BARRIER REEF PROVINCE
III — CENTRAL REGION

BATHYMETRY
(Contours in fathoms)

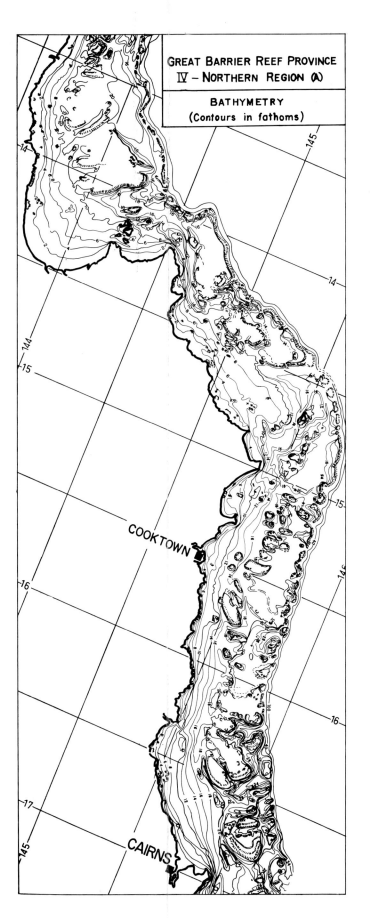

GREAT BARRIER REEF PROVINCE
IV — NORTHERN REGION (A)

BATHYMETRY
(Contours in fathoms)

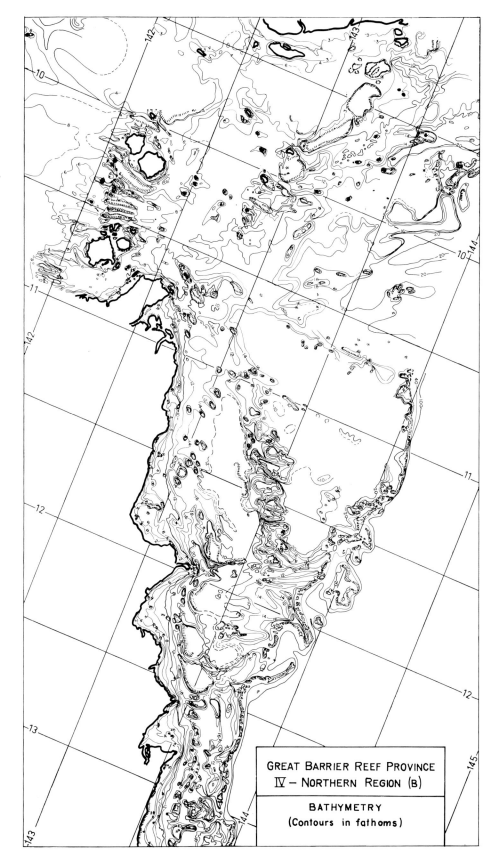

GREAT BARRIER REEF PROVINCE
IV — NORTHERN REGION (B)

BATHYMETRY
(Contours in fathoms)

Fig. 16C, D, E. Legend see reverse side.

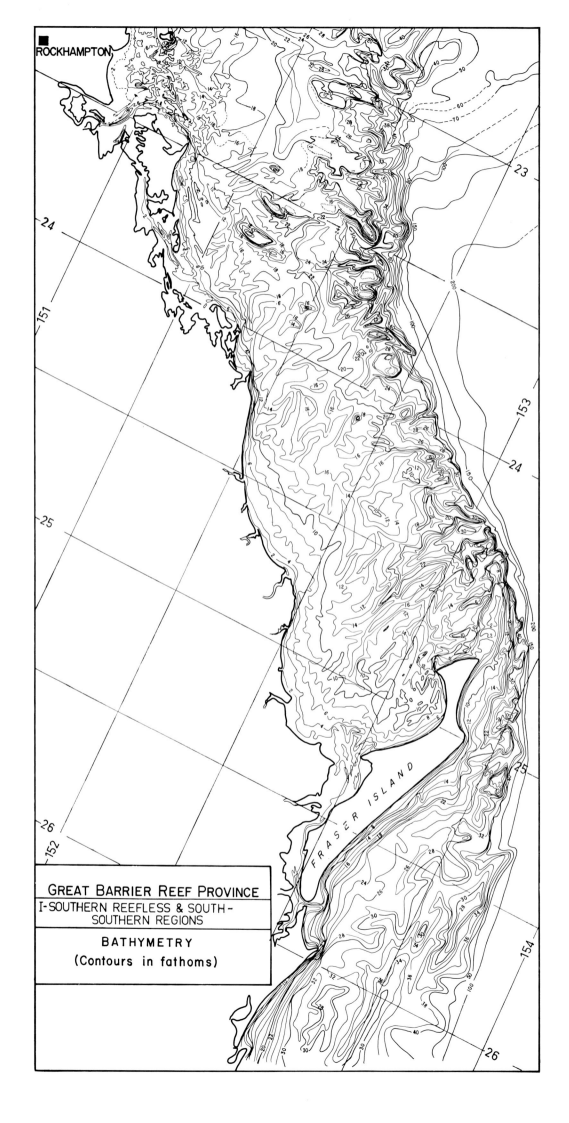

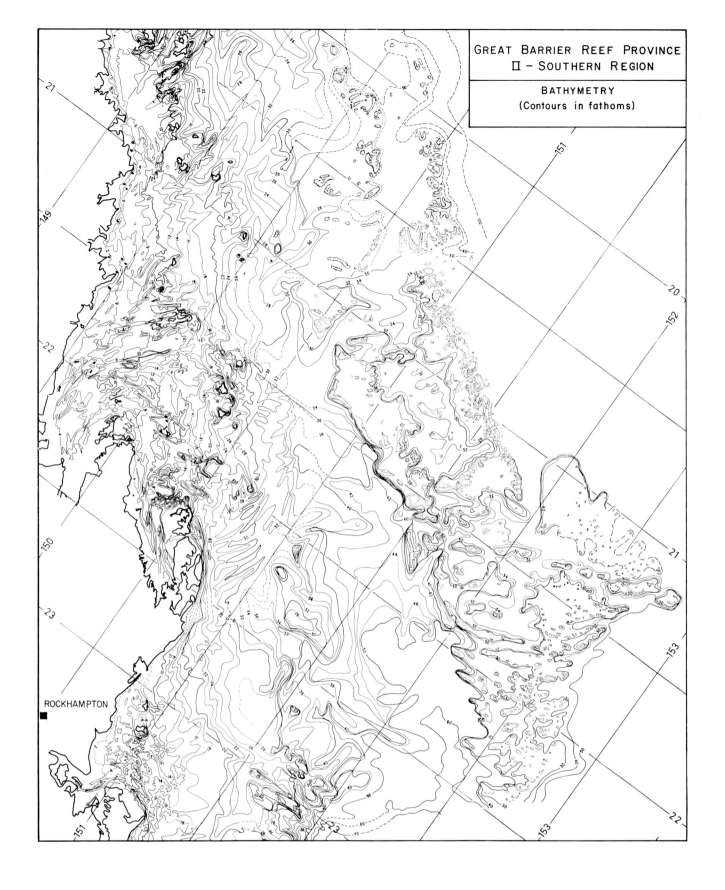

Fig. 16A, B, C, D, E. Bathymetric maps of the four regions—Southern Reefless, Southern, Central and Northern Regions of the Great Barrier Reef Province. (For Fig. 16 C, D, E see reverse side).

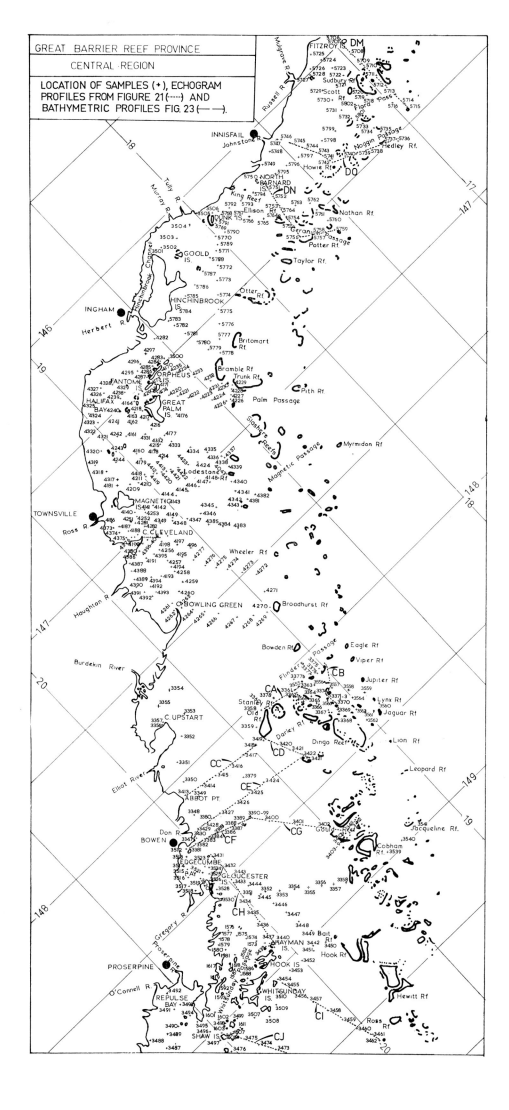

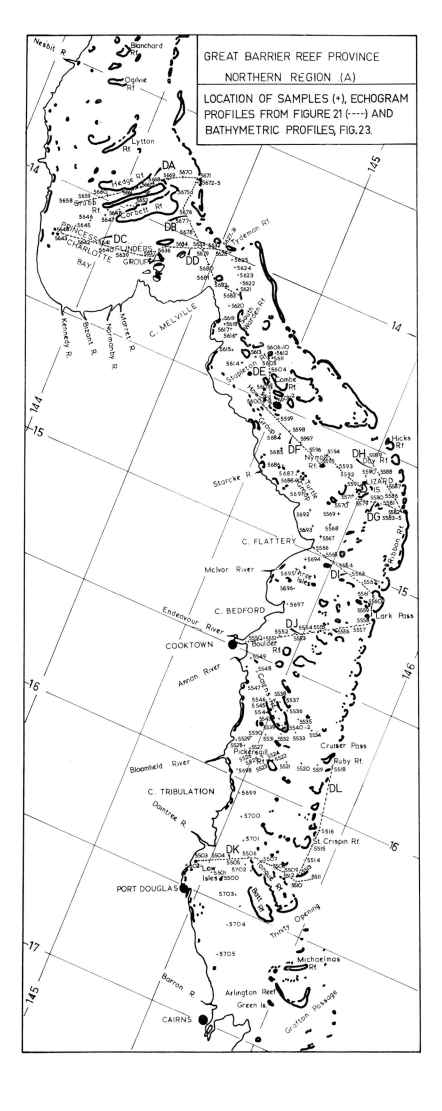

Fig. 17C, D. Legend see reverse side.

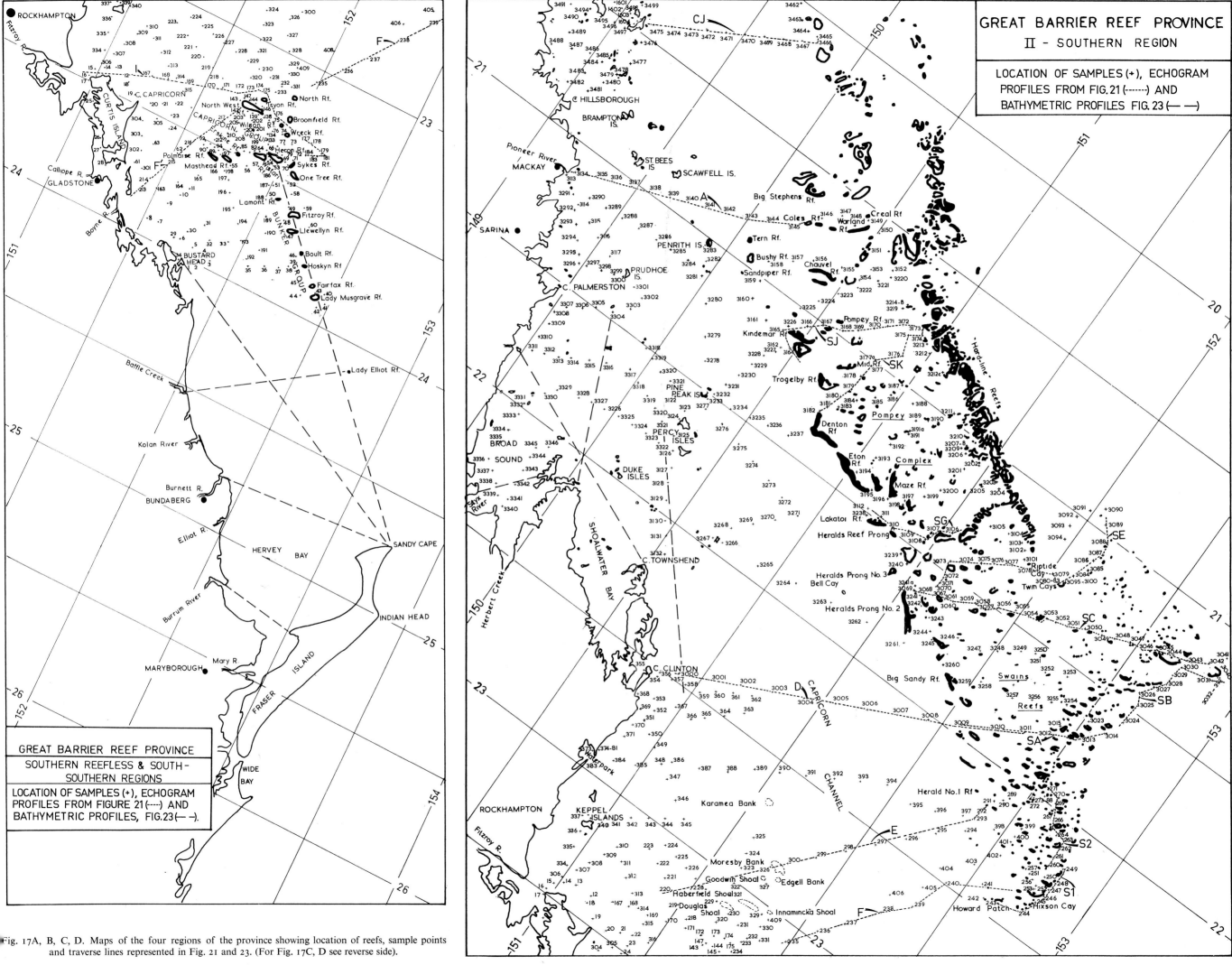

Fig. 17A, B, C, D. Maps of the four regions of the province showing location of reefs, sample points and traverse lines represented in Fig. 21 and 23. (For Fig. 17C, D see reverse side).

present steepened gradient. Similar undercutting at the present day is seen north of Water Park (Fig. 26). Erosion is still in progress and redistribution of the sands is facilitated by normal long shore drift and the strong rip current systems that develop on the more extended sections of coast exposed to the heavy south-easterly swell. Present stream contribution to the Near Shore Zone is almost negligible. As WHITEHOUSE (1964) has clearly demonstrated, in many cases the net movement of sand is probably from the sea into the

river mouths because of the Recent rise of sea level (and hence of base level), the high tidal range and the stream lag on the ebb tide. In large bays such as Princess Charlotte Bay (Fig. 31) Shoalhaven Bay and Broad Sound, the break in gradient has been obscured by the massive transportation of sand by long shore drift and tidal currents in the lee of large headlands.

A second feature of significance in the Near Shore Zone is the location of reefs, particularly in the Northern Region where much of the zone is narrow and the

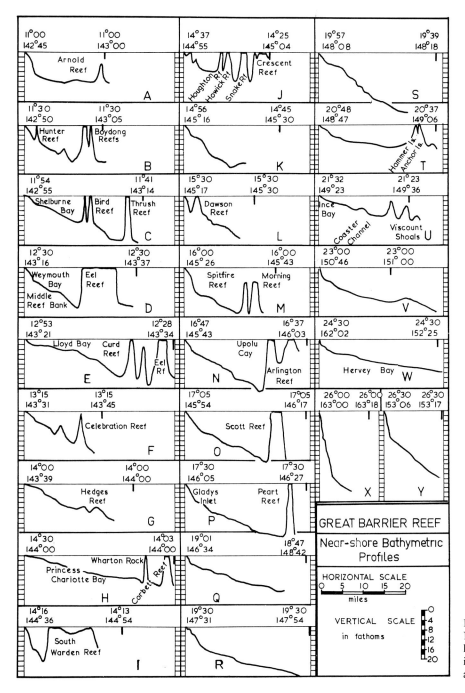

Fig. 18. Bathymetric profiles of the Near Shore Zone based on data from hydrographic charts. The profiles are in sequence from north to south at approximately half degree intervals.

*41*

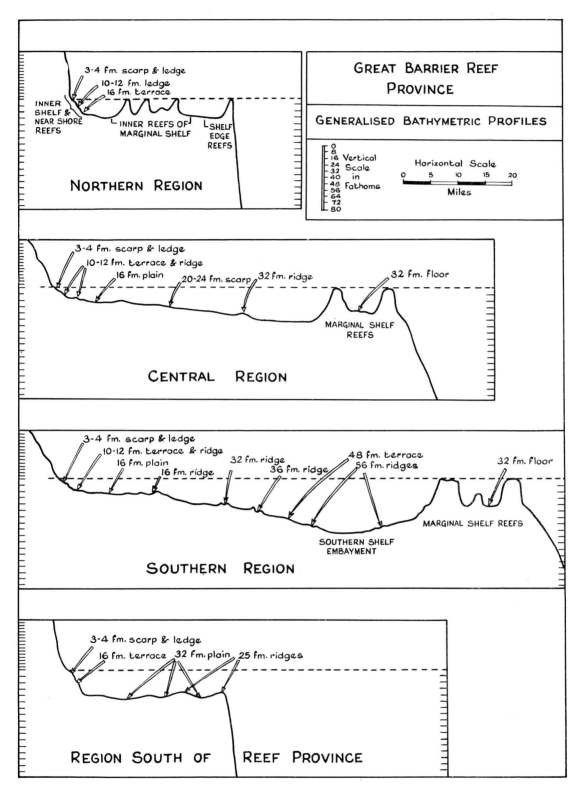

Fig. 19. Generalised bathymetric profiles of the shelf of each main region.

gradient extremely steep. The reefs appear to favour most of the rocky headlands and certain long, straight sections of the coast adjacent to deep water, thus suggesting that their existence, like that of the outer reefs, is dependent as much on the vigorous and plentiful supply of oceanic water as on bottom topography.

A third observation may be made on the occurrence

of reefs near the mouths of rivers and extensive mangrove swamps, e.g., Escape River, Pascoe River, and Mowbray River. This again demonstrates that the influence of terrestrial contamination may be far outweighed by marine factors when undepleted oceanic water is readily available for the reefs.

The final observation on the Near Shore Zone may be made on the occurrence of the long narrow sand ridges that have developed in the region of highest tidal range (more than 20–34 ft. or 6–10 m), viz. Shoalhaven Bay and Broad Sound. The ridges are parallel with the direction of the tidal currents and they extend seawards to the 10-fathom (18 m) contour. Similar banks have been developed in the present Fitzroy River mouth and adjacent area (Fig. 24, 25A). In both cases there has been a large sand source in the form of old dune systems already mentioned, and a constricted, funnel-shaped re-entrant in the coastline related to river effluence. The re-entrant has accentuated the tidal currents as well as controlling their direction. The large headlands of Cape Townsend and North Island have prevented destruction of the old sand ridge pattern by the prevailing south-easterly swell which characterises the rest of the Queensland shelf.

The *Inner Shelf* (Fig. 19, 20, 21) is delineated by the 5- and 20-fathom contours and it forms a band of relatively constant width, averaging 23 miles (37 km). In the far north where reef density is greatest, the Inner Shelf extends virtually to the Shelf Edge, possibly because of the shelf floor rising as a result of organic growth and bioclastic deposition. In part of the Southern Region, the Inner Shelf Zone also widens to 30 miles (48 km). This is in the area where maximum tidal range occurs (20–30 ft. or 6–9 m) and where there is extensive movement of coastal and near-shore sand. Also in the area, are numerous continental islands, suggestive of local warping of the shelf. It may be inferred that hydrologic, sedimentary and tectonic factors were all involved in the expansion of the Inner Shelf in this Southern Region. By comparison with the Near Shore Zone and the Marginal Shelf, the Inner Shelf is a zone of relatively even topography and uniform gradient. Sand ridges project into it from the Near Shore Zone in the Shoalhaven–Broad Sound area and adjacent to the Fitzroy River mouth, and long sand ridges are developed parallel with Curtis Island. Continental islands rise abruptly in the Central Region, but these and the sand ridges are the only major interruptions in an otherwise subdued relief. A persistent, though slight steepening in gradient occurs between the 10- and 12-fathom contour and along the greater part of the shelf, there is a recognisable change

at the 16-fathom line. The 16-fathom level is manifested in several ways: as a broad submarine plain forming the greater part of the Inner Shelf, bordered on the west by a rising, steeper gradient and on the east by slight depression, or as a low broad ridge (4–12 ft. high) or as a slight terrace on an otherwise steep gradient. Over much of the Central Region it has not been recognised. Nearer shore, a less persistent ledge is sometimes found at the 7-fathom line. Both the 7 fathom and 10–12 fathom terraces provide sites for the growth of Inner Shelf reefs. In the Northern Region where there are well defined reef zones, one zone generally occurs along the margin of the Inner Shelf, rising from depths of 20 fathoms and greater. On the Marginal Shelf, south of the Great Barrier Reef Province, a series of banks rise to 17 fathoms (e.g., Gardiner Bank off Fraser Island), and in the Central and Southern Regions on the deeper side of the Inner Shelf, a narrow zone of small ridges, rising to 17 fathoms, is sometimes present. These persistent bathymetric features are suggestive of old strand lines which must be taken into account in any analysis of the geomorphological development of the shelf.

The *Marginal Shelf* (Fig. 19, 20, 21) is the zone between Inner Shelf and Shelf Edge. As such, it may be defined by the 20- and 50-fathom contours. It is virtually indistinguishable in the Northern Region where the continental slope descends abruptly from the reef edge from depths of 20 fathoms and less. Large parts of the back-reef area of the outer reefs probably represent the infilled zone of the original marginal shelf. In the Central Region, it is developed as a definite physiographic unit, and it widens progressively southward from a minimum 12 miles to a maximum 60 miles. Its eastern margin rises sharply where the main reefs are developed and between them the eastern margin is deeply incised. These marginal channels and trenches are more abundant in the less populous Central Region than in the two other regions where reef growth along the shelf margin is more nearly continuous and more prolific. In the Southern Region there is a considerable expansion of the shelf as well as excessive deepening, and it is convenient to recognise both Western and Eastern Marginal Shelves, separated by the Southern Shelf Embayment.

The *Western Marginal Shelf* extends from the Inner Shelf to the Shelf Edge (50 fathoms) on the narrow southern part of the shelf, and to the edge of the embayment (35 fathoms) further north on the expanded shelf. The southern part has important reef groups—Capricorn and Bunker—and an incised shelf margin. No reefs develop on the Western Marginal Shelf where it

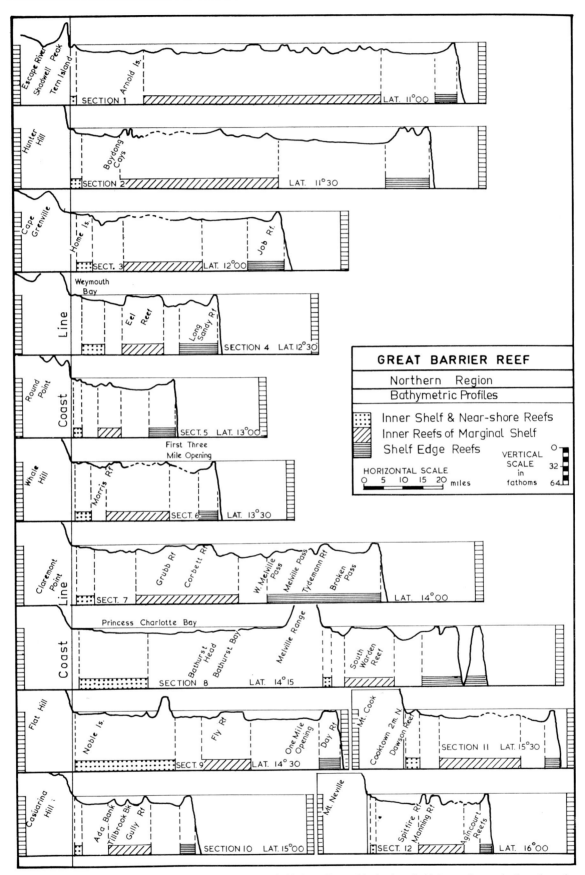

Fig. 20A, B, C. Bathymetric profiles of the continental shelf along lines of latitude at half degree intervals; based on data from hydrographic charts. Profiles are in sequence from north to south. Reef developments are indicated. (For Fig. 20B, C see pp. 45 and 46).

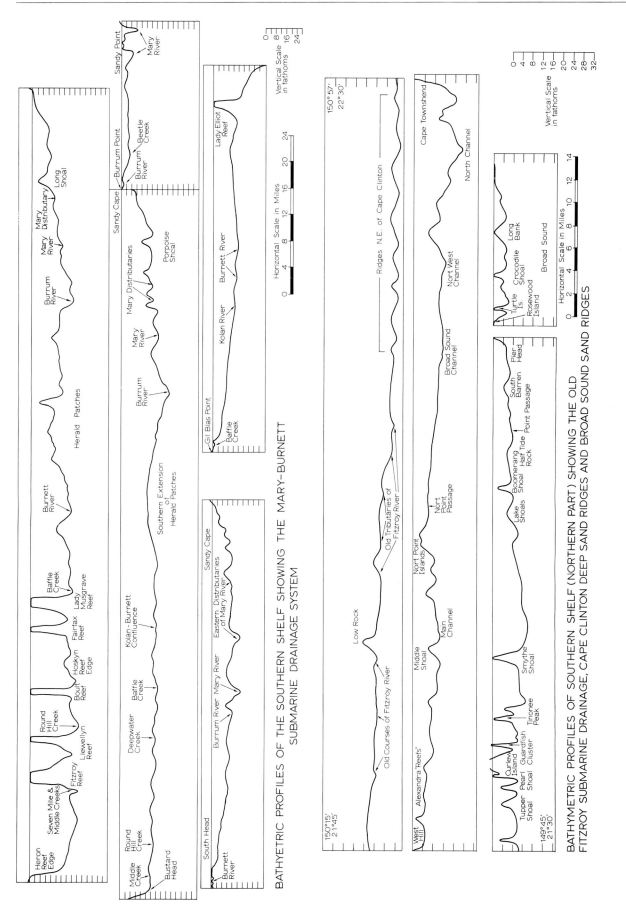

BATHYETRIC PROFILES OF THE SOUTHERN SHELF SHOWING THE MARY–BURNETT
SUBMARINE DRAINAGE SYSTEM

BATHYMETRIC PROFILES OF SOUTHERN SHELF (NORTHERN PART) SHOWING THE OLD
FITZROY SUBMARINE DRAINAGE, CAPE CLINTON DEEP SAND RIDGES AND BROAD SOUND SAND RIDGES

Fig. 23. Profiles of the southern part of the shelf showing the Mary-Burnett drainage system and the old Fitzroy system (locations indicated on Fig. 17).

A

B

Fig. 24. A. Aerial photograph of the lower reaches of the Fitzroy River showing the meandrine, dendritic drainage pattern and the extensive salt pans behind mangrove fringes. B. Low, mangrove-covered islands and sand banks in Broad Sound, the former outlet for the Fitzroy River.

pattern. The deeply incised submarine valleys of the southern streams imply either a longer history than the northern streams or a slower rate of sedimentation. Extensive reef development along the sides of the old courses near the shelf edge may be related to the development of ancient stream levees and sand bars.

GEOMORPHOLOGICAL DEVELOPMENT

Significant features that hold the key to the recognition of the sequence of geomorphological events include: (*1*) The two main groups of continental islands between latitudes 20°S and 22°S and between latitudes 18°S and 19°S.

Fig. 25. A. The coastal zone of Broad Sound showing the dendritic drainage pattern on the inter-tidal flats, the fringing mangrove forest and, at the base of the photograph, the shore line. B. Large inter-tidal sand flats and a refraction ridge joining Green Island to the mainland at Shoal Point near Mackay (latitude 21°S). The stream is Reliance Creek. Tidal range in this area is approx 20 ft.

(2) The submarine drainage patterns and the apparent recent changes in the stream courses.

(3) Changes of bathymetric gradient at the 56-, 48-, 36-, 32-, 20-, 16- and 10-fathom contours, and remarkably persistent surfaces at 32-, 20- and 16-fathom depths.

(4) The apparent difference in character between reefs of the Near Shore, Inner Shelf and Marginal Shelf zones, particularly in the Northern Region.

(5) The submarine ridges between 20 and 32 fathoms off Cape Clinton.

Fig. 26. Coastal features at Waterpark and Mackay. A. High dunes, lower terrace and nip north of Waterpark. B .View of beach and nip from the east. C. Aerial photograph of the extensive inter-tidal sand flats at the mouth of the Pioneer River, Mackay. Note the main development to the south of the river. A similar, though smaller development is seen on either side of the breakwaters of Mackay Harbour.

(6) The strong sand ridges of Broad Sound and Shoal-haven Bay.

(7) The dissected surface at 16 fathoms in the lee of the shelf-edge reefs of the Northern Region.

The occurrence of numerous continental islands in two groups aligned with the Forsayth and Longreach Crustal Swells, as well as the smaller group to the south-east of Princess Charlotte Bay in the Northern Region, and the closed submarine drainage pattern between the two main island groups as well as the changing courses of the Fitzroy System and the Kennedy–Escape System, may be regarded as evidence of comparatively recent crustal movement that has affected the continental shelf. Furthermore, the persistence of bathymetric features, particularly those at the 16-, 20- and 32-fathom lines, suggests that the crustal movement preceded the sea-level fluctuations which were responsible for the formation of these features and that any subsequent crustal movements were extremely localised. If this were not the case then correlation of the various levels throughout the

province would not be possible. It would appear that the main drainage pattern in the Southern Region consisted of the major Fitzroy effluence through Broad Sound and north-eastward across the shelf, entering the sea at the shelf edge just north of latitude 21 °S. Sea level at this stage was probably below the present 80-fathom mark. Further south, the Burnett and Mary River Systems flowed north-eastward towards Lady Elliot Island. Their deeply incised submarine valleys provide evidence of prolonged erosion and of stability of courses. In the Central Region, the Pioneer–Proserpine–Don River System and the Burdekin and Herbert River Systems followed east-north-easterly courses across the shelf. Further north, the submarine courses are less deeply incised, except for the old Kennedy–Escape system, and this may be suggestive of later stream development in the Northern Region.

Mild upwarp of the Longreach and Forsayth Swells, and possibly of the Arnhem Swell, slight subsidence of the Capricorn Basin and the beginnings of transgression may have opened the final phase of shelf development in Early Tertiary time, a phase that was controlled

Fig. 27. Shoreline features. A. Pine Peak Island, Southern Region, showing coastal terrace. B. Entrance to Waterpark showing low, rocky platform. C. Low platform surrounding small island, joined to Long Island in the Whitsunday Group, by a curved, inter-tidal gravel ridge formed through wave refraction. Small coastal terrace of Long Island in foreground.

largely by eustatic changes after the initial crustal movements had ceased. The diversion of the Fitzroy River from Broad Sound to the Water Park–Port Clinton area (from where it flowed north-eastward across the shelf into the subsiding Capricorn Basin and then southward), may have been caused by the up-warp of the Longreach Swell in the early part of this phase. Similar movement of the Forsayth Swell succeeded in isolating the Pioneer–Proserpine–Don System from both the major southern and northern systems: the Fitzroy and Burdekin respectively. The Burdekin System, located on the axial part of the Forsayth Swell, was not deflected by the crustal warping and persisted in its north-eastward course. In the Northern Region, it is possible that movement of the Arnhem Swell was responsible for the deflection of the Kennedy–Escape River System from its east-north-easterly course to the less deeply incised, easterly course that can now be recognized further south.

Strong and persistent topographic features at seven bathymetric levels are evident along the greater part of the shelf. Because of their persistence and constant depth they have been interpreted as old strand-line features formed after transgression and regression. Evidence indicating the sequence in which they were formed is difficult to obtain and far from conclusive. The deep, uniform dissection of the 16-fathom surface (Fig. 32) in the lee of the shelf-edge reefs of the Northern Region and its absence from a large part of the Central Region are suggestive of sub-aerial erosion after its formation, and this has been used as evidence for regression in what appears to have been a dominantly, though spasmodic, transgressive phase. The present interpretation (illustrated on Fig. 32) of this phase envisages transgression with still-stands at the present 56-, 48- and 36-fathom levels. With each pause in the rising sea-level, strand-line features developed in the form of wave-cut terraces, off-shore sand bars and coastal dune systems, which provided sites for subsequent reef colonisation. From the 36-fathom strand-line the sea rose rapidly to the present 16-fathom level where an extremely wide terrace and low coastal

*61*

Fig. 28. Shoreline features. A. Three levels above high tidal mark, carbonate beach on western side of Holbourne Island, east of Bowen. Higher terraces covered by vegetation and consisting of coarse darkly-stained coralline detritus and pumice. Rock outcrop on adjacent hill granitic in character. B. Eastern side of Holbourne Island, looking seaward over high berm of carbonate gravel, with slabs of old beach rock and cay rock in the foreground derived from formations to the west. In the bay in the background there is a strong reef development. C. Boulder beach in Puritan Bay on the mainland in the Whitsunday area. Boulders consist largely of andesitic material derived from Palaeozoic formations exposed along the coast. The higher, white sand and gravel is predominantly carbonate (foraminiferal). The person in the photograph is standing on an old terrace of boulders and coral debris, above the present beach. D. Coastal terraces on South Molle Island, Whitsunday Group.

plain developed, and reef growth continued on the older sites as well as on newer, near-shore features. This important still-stand was followed by regression to 32 fathoms. The coastal dunes and off-shore deposits of the 16-fathom strand-line possibly provided the huge volumes of sand which were carried seaward by the rejuvenated rivers to form sand ridges and bars similar to those found in the present Fitzroy mouth and Broad Sound. The ridges off Cape Clinton, between 20 and 32 fathoms may have originated at this time. Severe sub-aerial erosion of the previous coastal morphology as well as of the exposed reefs resulted in the cutting of the very extensive, very persistent 32-fathom terraces and benches. It is possible that remnants of the exposed, dead reef tops survived the erosive forces in much the same way as some of the high, near-shore reefs of the present day, and in this way preserved part of the old 16-fathom level. Follow-

ing the 32-fathom still-stand, there was spasmodic transgression to the 20- and 10-fathom levels and then to the high 10-feet level that is reflected in the raised coastal platforms of the present islands and mainland (Fig. 26, 27, 28). With each advance of the sea, new colonisation by reefs occurred. Finally, the sea retreated to its present level, exposed the reef surfaces and proceeded to erode the dead material. In the unprotected areas, this process has reached completion and new growth is occurring on the reefs. By contrast, many of the Near Shore and Inner Shelf reefs—the "high" reefs—still carry a thick veneer of dead reef material and sedimentary detritus which has yet to be removed.

The rate of sedimentation on the shelf was probably substantial only during the regressive stage from the 16- to the 32-fathom level. At this time, there was abundant material available from the exposed reefs and

Fig. 29A, B, C. Coastal dunes. Extensive sand-dune formation in the Northern Region between Cooktown and Princess Charlotte Bay. Arrows indicate true north. Note the extensive, inter-tidal sand flats on the leeward sides of the peninsulas. The higher, stratified hills consist of Mesozoic sandstones of the Laura Basin.

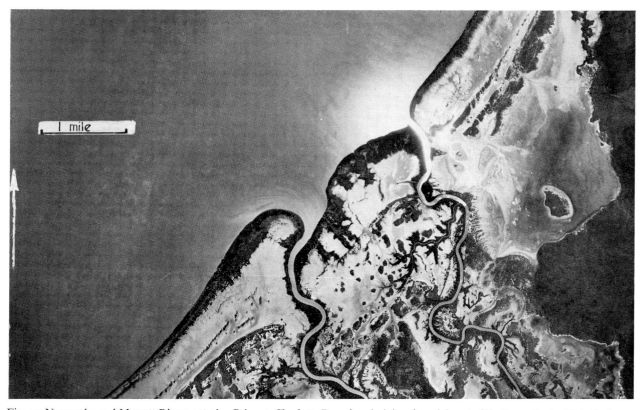

Fig. 30. Normanby and Marrett Rivers entering Princess Charlotte Bay after draining the axial part of the Laura Basin. Note the heavy fringes of mangroves, the old vegetated beach ridges to the north-east and the dissected remnants to the south-west. The hills in the eastern area consist of Mesozoic sandstones.

*63*

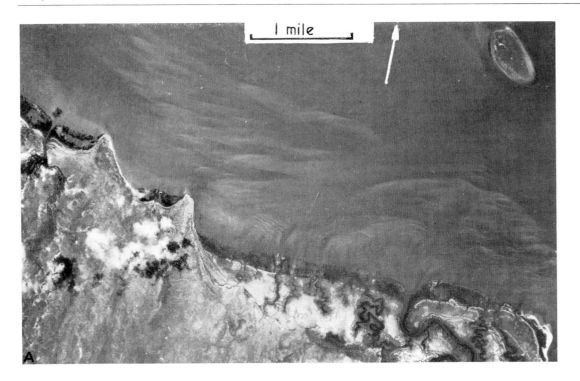

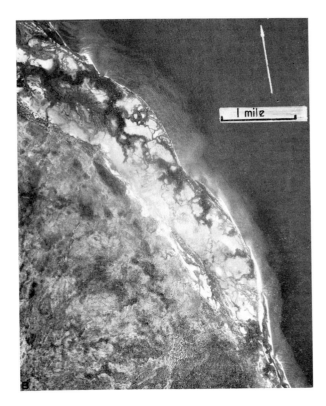

Fig. 31. Shoreline and inter-tidal features. A. Murdoch Point (latitude 14°35′S) showing sandy coastal strip fringing Mesozoic sandstone hills, and off-shore sand ridges; island in the north-east has marginal reef development. B. Wider coastal plain with small, meandrine streams and strongly ridged, sandy near-shore ridges; outer margin of coastal plain marked by en-echelon sand spits.

possibly an increase in the supply of terrigenous sediment from a rejuvenated land. During transgression, the reef contribution to sediment would be at a minimum, and terrigenous loads carried to the shelf by streams would also be reduced. However, transgression favoured the prolific expansion of reefs.

At some late stage in this final phase of shelf development, local crustal movement occurred in the Central Region where grabens such as that of Whitsunday Passage subsided (STANLEY, 1928; THOMAS, 1966), and on the adjacent mainland similar movement resulted in the formation of coastal corridors (SUSSMILCH, 1938)

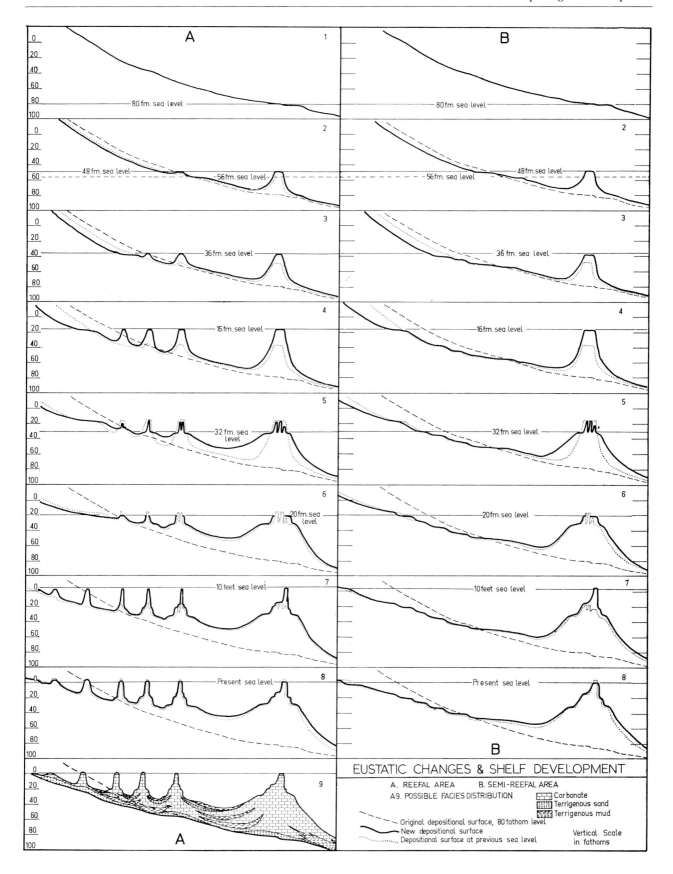

Fig. 32. Profiles illustrating the eustatic influence on the recent development of the Queensland shelf for both reefal and non-reefal areas, and the probable facies distribution resulting from regressive and transgressive phases.

of comparable magnitude. It is this type of adjustment which partly accounts for the absence of the 16- and 32-fathom features in the Central Region.

The differences in the character of the reefs of the Near Shore, Inner Shelf and Marginal Shelf Zones are undoubtedly the result of differences in the present hydrological conditions of each zone. But, in addition to the hydrological factor, it is very probable that the recent history of the reefs also exerts an influence that is less readily discerned. Because of their longer period of development and because sea-level changes could not lead to their total destruction, reefs of the deeper Marginal Shelf are normally robust structures, rising sharply from the 32-fathom floor. By contrast, those of the Inner Shelf in the Central and Northern Zones are frequently embayed, "corroded" relicts or clusters of small reef patches rising from large, submerged platforms that appear to be the truncated remnants of earlier reefs that were comparable in size to those of the present Marginal Shelf. The Near Shore Reefs have

their typical mantle of debris and dead coral that resulted from the last fall in sea-level. Both the Near Shore and Inner Shelf reefs were more sensitive to eustatic fluctuation, and because of their more recent establishment, more restricted foundation and closer proximity to the shore line, they were less capable of recovery than the seaward reefs.

## HYDROLOGY

### Tides and tidal currents

One of the most significant and distinctive features of the Great Barrier Reef Province is its tidal regime. Unlike the majority of reef provinces throughout the world, the Great Barrier Reef is situated in a region of unusually high tidal range. The minimum range of 7.7 ft. develops near its southern margin, the maximum of

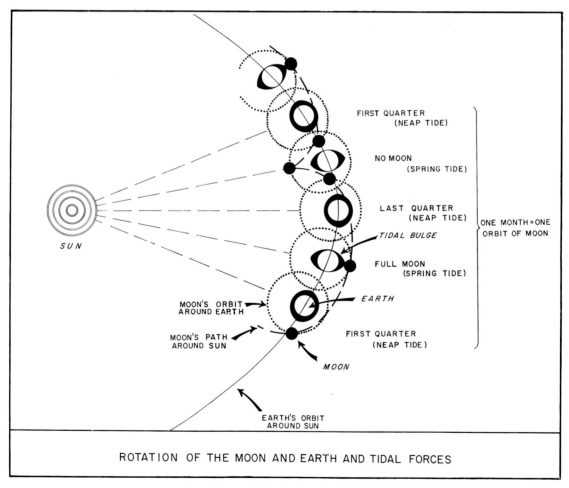

Fig. 33. Tidal diagram illustrating the effect of lunar and solar forces on tides.

34 ft. between latitudes 21°S and 22°S (Broad Sound) and an average range of 9–11 ft. through the rest of the province. Tides are semi-diurnal. This high tidal range is in contrast with those of the Pacific reef provinces where the semi-diurnal tides are less than 3 ft., with the Western Atlantic provinces where both diurnal and semi-diurnal tides rarely exceed this range, and with the Central and Northern Indian Ocean and Red Sea where tidal ranges are of the order of 1–5 ft. The only province where tidal ranges are comparable is in the Madagascar region. Since the tidal character of the Great Barrier Reef is almost unique, closer examination of tidal behaviour and effects may yield important evidence on the development of this reef province.

*Tidal theory*

The main tide-producing forces are the gravitational attractions of the moon and the sun, the latter exerting a force approximately half (46%) that of the moon (Fig. 33). The resultant movement of oceanic water in response to these forces is modified strongly by the distribution of the land masses, bathymetric variation, and the Coriolis force. To assess the influence of the astronomical forces one must first consider their effect on a completely water-covered earth. Because the plane of the moon's orbit (Fig. 34) is inclined to that of the earth's orbit, the moon passes over the equator twice in each of its revolutions and reaches points of maximum declination in the Northern and Southern Hemispheres. The maximum declination varies over a period of 18.6 years from 18°18′ to 28°36′, a variation which is symmetrical about the tropic (23°27′). Thus the main effect of the moon's tidal attraction should be manifested in the band between latitudes 28°36′N and S, and because of the earth's revolution this effect is manifested at any point on the earth's surface every 12 h 25.2 min (Fig. 35). Furthermore, this semidiurnal effect is strongest in the lower latitudes and weakest at the poles.

In addition to the moon's attraction, the attractive force of the sun (Fig. 33) augments the tidal effect when moon and sun are aligned (full moon and new moon), and decreases its effect when the two bodies act at right angles to each other (quarters). Thus, there is a progressive change from spring to neap tides as the moon moves through its monthly (29½ days) orbit, so that two periods of springs and two of neaps occur each month.

Tidal behaviour is further influenced by the varying distances that exist between earth and moon, and earth and sun (Fig. 36). Because of the elliptical orbits of both earth and moon, there is a time each month when the

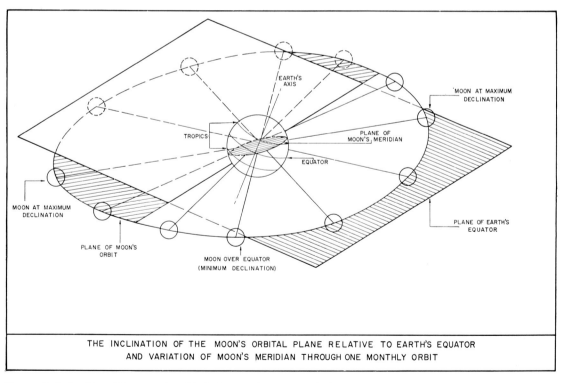

THE INCLINATION OF THE MOON'S ORBITAL PLANE RELATIVE TO EARTH'S EQUATOR
AND VARIATION OF MOON'S MERIDIAN THROUGH ONE MONTHLY ORBIT

Fig. 34. Relationship of the moon's orbital plane to the equatorial plane and the variation in declination through one monthly orbit.

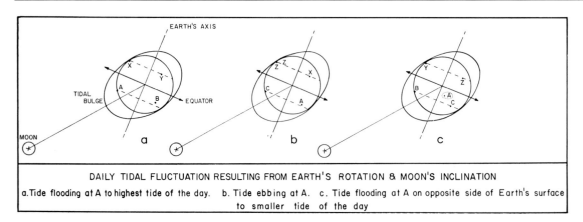

Fig. 35. The effect of the earth's rotation and the moon's inclination on semi-diurnal tidal fluctuation.

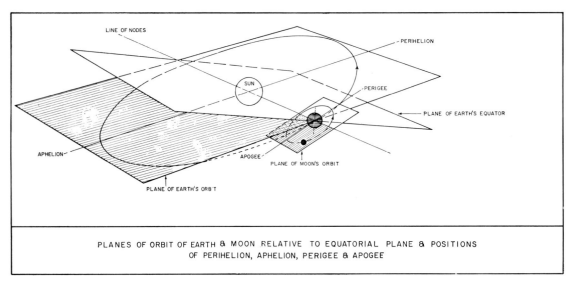

Fig. 36. Orbital movements of moon and earth relative to sun, and the significance of aphelion, perihelion, apogee and perigee.

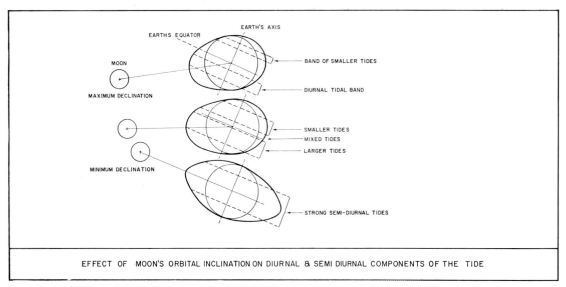

Fig. 37. Diurnal and semi-diurnal components of tides.

moon is closest to the earth (at perigee) and a time each year when the earth is closest to the sun (at perihelion). Perihelion occurs during the southern summer (December 21st). Thus, when the moon is at perigee and aligned with the earth and sun at or near the perihelion point, the maximum tidal force is exerted on the earth and abnormally high and low tides are experienced: the king tides.

Because of the earth's daily rotation, the moon's attraction tends to produce a tidal bulge which moves across the earth from east to west. If the moon's orbital plane were co-planar with the earth's equator then this would result in a tidal bulge nearest the moon and a corresponding, near-equal bulge on the opposite side of the earth so that there would be equal semi-diurnal (twice daily) tides. However, the moon's orbit is inclined to the equatorial plane (maximum declination 18°18′ to 28°16′) so that the situation for equal, semi-diurnal tides can develop only when it crosses the equator, which it does twice in its monthly orbit. The effect of the inclination of its orbital plane is manifested in the diurnal component of tides (Fig. 37), i.e., a point on the earth's surface that moves through the crest of the tidal bulge on one side of the earth will move through the lower flank of the opposite bulge as the earth rotates. Thus the point will experience two high tides of quite different magnitude: a very large one on the crest and a small one on the flank. Depending on the angle between the moon's orbital plane and the equatorial plane, the smaller tide may be completely suppressed thus resulting in a truly diurnal tidal fluctuation. Thus the diurnal component would be dominant in the middle and higher latitudes of a completely water-covered earth, and would merge with the semi-diurnal component in the lower latitudes to produce mixed tides. Three major factors interfere with this hypothetical model of the tides, viz. the distribution of the land masses, bathymetric variation and the Coriolis force. Only in the Southern Ocean is there a continuous belt of water around the earth, so that only in this region can tidal movements develop without interruption by the land masses. The bathymetric influence is equally important. It has been calculated (VON ARX, 1962, p. 49) that the minimum water depth necessary to permit the lunar tide to remain at the moon's meridian during the earth's rotation exceeds 22.5 km, which is much greater than the average oceanic depth of 4 km. Thus the model of the tidal bulge circumscribing the earth in phase with the moon must be modified drastically. The actual tides develop in response to the lunar and solar attractions as forced oscillations, the amplitudes and phases of which are controlled largely by the dimensions of the particular water body, whether it be a closed bay, shallow shelf or large, deep ocean. Thus the lunar and solar attractions provide the initial force necessary for the vertical tidal fluctuation while the other factors determine the manner in which this fluctuation is transmitted across the oceans and their marginal seas. Of the two groups of theories postulated to account for the tidal movement—the progressive wave theories and the standing wave theories—the latter appear to be substantiated best by observation of actual tidal behaviour. The standing wave theory postulates that the main tides result from stationary wave oscillations induced by solar and lunar forces. Since every body of water has a natural period of oscillation dependent on its dimensions according to the formula $p = 4\, l\, gd$ (where $l$ and $d$ are length and depth of the water body, g is the acceleration due to gravity), those water bodies whose natural periods of oscillation approach that of the lunar and solar forces, will be most susceptible to these tide-producing forces. Standing wave movement is of the kind observed in a tank when the water is set in motion by raising and lowering one end. The water oscillates about a neutral axis or nodal line across the middle of the tank. In the oceans, the oscillating wave is subjected to other influences, viz. Coriolis force, frictional drag of the sea floor and obstruction by land masses. The resultant movement then is as rotational waves which develop around nodal or amphidromic zones of negligible oscillation. In the Northern Hemisphere the rotation is generally counter-clockwise and in the Southern Hemisphere it is clockwise. By contouring localities where high tide is reached at the same time, a series of lines (co-tidal lines) can be obtained. These generally converge on nodal or amphidromic zones, of which more than 25 have been recognized in the oceans and marginal seas, as illustrated by DIETRICH (1963, chart 6). As DIETRICH (1963, p. 459) indicates, the distribution of the tidal ranges is closely related to the crowding of the co-tidal lines, the smallest ranges occurring at the nodal zones, the largest at the more distant points. This relationship is affected where the nodal zones are near land masses. As the tidal fluctuation moves into shallow water, the tidal range increases. Furthermore, if the natural period of oscillation of the shallow water body is similar to that of the ocean tide, the two augment each other. If on the other hand, there is a difference in their periods, co-oscillating tides develop.

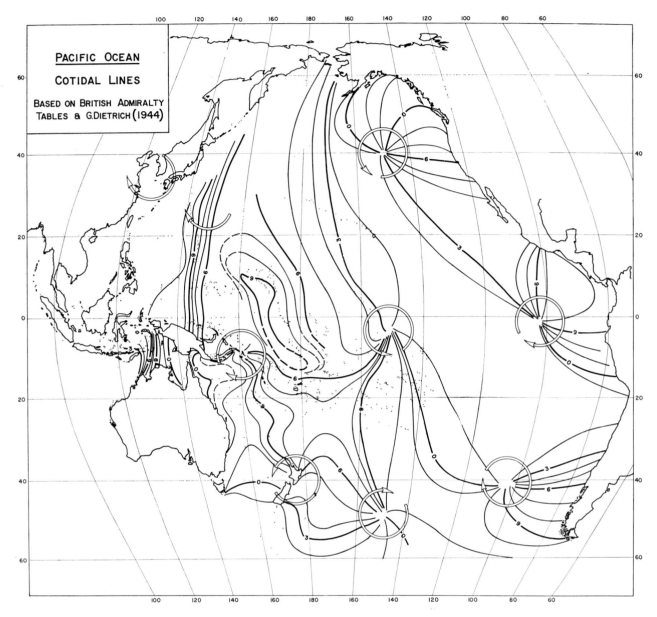

Fig. 38. Co-tidal lines and amphidromic zones of the Pacific. Numbers on lines represent hours. Note the westward advance of tidal lines towards the Australian coast and the opposing movement of lines from the Indian Ocean.

### Pacific tides

Tidal behaviour in the Pacific Ocean is best illustrated by the distribution of co-tidal lines and lines of equal tidal range as shown on Fig. 38 and 39. There are five nodal zones in the open ocean and at least four more adjacent to the land masses. In the Southern Pacific, the co-tidal lines normally rotate in a clockwise direction with the exception of those radiating from nodal zones near the equator (longitudes 155°W and 105°W) and these have an anti-clockwise motion typical of the Northern Hemisphere. The third nodal zone near the equator is adjacent to New Guinea and its co-tidal lines have the clockwise rotation normal for the Southern Hemisphere. In the open ocean, the opposing directions of rotation around nodes on opposite sides of latitude 30°S results in a general eastward progression of the tides from the New Zealand–Kermadec–Tonga line (i.e., the edge of the Eastern Plateau and Ridge System) into the deeper oceanic basin beyond. To the west of this line, the nodal zones of New Guinea and the South Tasman Sea have rotations which interact with each other and the shallower South-West Pacific floor and result in a semi-parallel advance towards the Australian land mass.

The clockwise component tends to bend the co-tidal

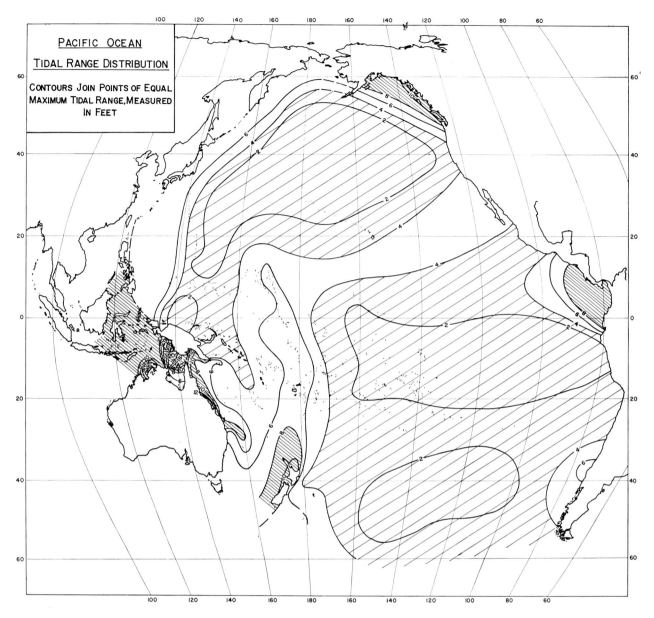

Fig. 39. Lines of equal tidal range for the Pacific Ocean; contour values in feet. Areas of maximum tidal range closely hatched, areas of minimum range sparsely hatched. Note the high range in the northern Australian region.

lines north-westward into the western Coral Sea and Gulf of Papua. From the western side of Australia, the rotating lines of the Indian Ocean node encounter the shallow, restricted Arafura Sea where the clockwise rotation is transformed into an easterly advance that continues as far as the shallow banks that extend northward from Cape York to New Guinea. Thus, in this shallow, epicontinental area, the western tides belong to a different system from those of the east and the two are seldom in phase. The tidal behaviour in this area is further complicated by the strong diurnal component about the New Guinea nodal zone.

The variation in tidal range across the Pacific is related to the location of the nodal zones and to the bathymetric character. From Fig. 39, it is evident that maximum tidal range develops along the Australian shelf and along the Eastern Plateau and Ridge System north from New Zealand to Fiji. East of the Plateau and Ridge System, the oceanic floor is almost 2,000 fathoms deeper, and the tidal pattern is related to two nodal zones, one near the equator at 155°W longitude, the other south-east from New Zealand. The general direction of the advancing tide is south-eastward from the Samoan region. West of the same system, the average water depth is 1,000 fathoms and the tide advancing westward and north-westward is governed by the nodal

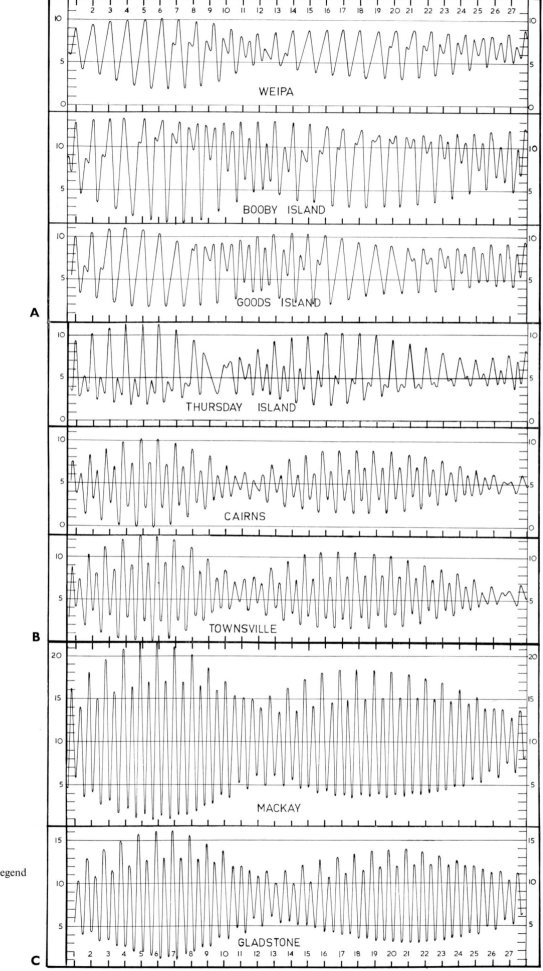

WEIPA

BOOBY ISLAND

GOODS ISLAND

**A**

THURSDAY ISLAND

CAIRNS

TOWNSVILLE

**B**

MACKAY

Fig. 40 A, B, C. Legend
see p. 73.

GLADSTONE

**C**

72

zone east of New Guinea. The belt of high tidal range (more than 6 ft.), occurs where the New Guinea and 155°W nodal zones augment each other and where the steep slope of the Ridge System rises from the deeper oceanic basin. As the influence of the 155°W zone decreases westward, so too the tidal range diminishes, until the bathymetric factor again becomes dominant on the Australian continental shelf and adjoining borderland. As the tidal front moves into the Great Barrier Reef Province it is restricted firstly by the reef development itself and secondly by the coastal configuration, particularly in the Gulf of Papua and further south in the Broad Sound area. Tides of the Broad Sound area are further augmented by the concerted influences of the New Guinea nodal zone which tends to force the water southward towards Broad Sound, and the Tasman Sea nodal zone from which water movement is directed northward. Thus two tidal movements converge near Broad Sound, resulting in an unusually large tidal range.

In the area between New Guinea and Australia, the tides progress eastward across the Arafura Sea into shallow, restricted water and ranges of 7–18 ft. occur. Because this tidal regime is unrelated to that of the Coral Sea east of Cape York, high and low tides may occur simultaneously on either side of the shallow sand banks that separate the two regimes. As a consequence high velocity currents (greater than 6 knots) develop in this northern region as water escapes from one to the other.

*Tidal behaviour in the Great Barrier Reef Province*

The tidal pattern of the Great Barrier Reef Province is best illustrated by the maps of co-tidal lines and lines of tidal range (Fig. 41, 42). The main factors influencing this pattern have been stated already, viz. (*1*) the converging effect of the two standing wave systems centred on the northern and southern nodes; (*2*) the interference of the western system of the Arafura Sea which is mostly out of phase with that of the Coral Sea; (*3*) the bathymetric character of the Queensland Shelf and forefront region.

Fig. 40A, B, C (p. 72). Tidal fluctuation over one month (February) for stations from the Gulf of Carpentaria and Torres Strait in the north to Gladstone in the south. Note the predominance of the diurnal component in the northern tides and its gradual transition to the semi-diurnal component in the southern tides. Maximum tidal range is recorded on the Mackay station. Tidal levels in feet.

Graphs of the tidal pattern at successive points northward along the Queensland coast (Fig. 40) illustrate the changing pattern of the tides and provide an indication of the manner in which these controlling factors interact. There is a progressive increase in tidal range as one moves northward from Brisbane (latitude 27°20'S) to the Broad Sound region (near latitude 22°S) where a maximum of more than 34 ft. has been recorded in the estuarine zone. Northward beyond Broad Sound, the tidal range decreases rapidly to 11 ft. near Bowen (latitude 20°S) and then more slowly to 9 ft. near Port Douglas (latitude 15°30'), a range that is maintained northward to latitude 16°S. North from this zone, the tidal range then increases into Torres Strait where maxima of 13 ft. and more have been recorded. The two regions of highest tidal range—Broad Sound and Torres Strait—are zones where tidal systems radiating from the Arafura, East New Guinea and Southern Pacific nodes converge, thus building up abnormally large bodies of water. These convergences then are partly responsible for the high tidal ranges. The other factor is bathymetry. The two South-Western Pacific systems sweep across the deep Tasman and Coral Seas and then encounter the shallow Shelf Zone of Queensland, with resultant interference. The very shape of the shelf, with its wide eastward expansion from the Broad Sound region to beyond the Swain Reefs—a distance of approximately 200 miles—accentuates the effect of tidal convergence by causing bottom interference in this region long before the other narrower parts of the shelf have been encountered. The arresting influence of the shallow shelf on wave movement generated in the deeper basins results in a greater build-up of water. A similar situation prevails in the northern area where deep Coral Sea water encounters the broad shelf between New Guinea and Cape York, and is then channelled through the narrow Torres Strait.

Tidal convergence and bathymetric variation thus combine to produce the unusually high tidal ranges that occur throughout the Great Barrier Reef Province. One of the obvious direct results of this is seen in the rapidly changing environment that oscillates semi-diurnally from subaerial to submarine, over enormous areas of the reefs and coastal belt. The intertidal and shallow sub-tidal zones are ones of high energy, efficient aeration, partial dessication and effective water exchange—factors that are especially conducive to the growth of reef communities. But in addition to this oscillation of environment, high tidal range results in significant secondary water movements: the tidal currents (Fig. 48, 50).

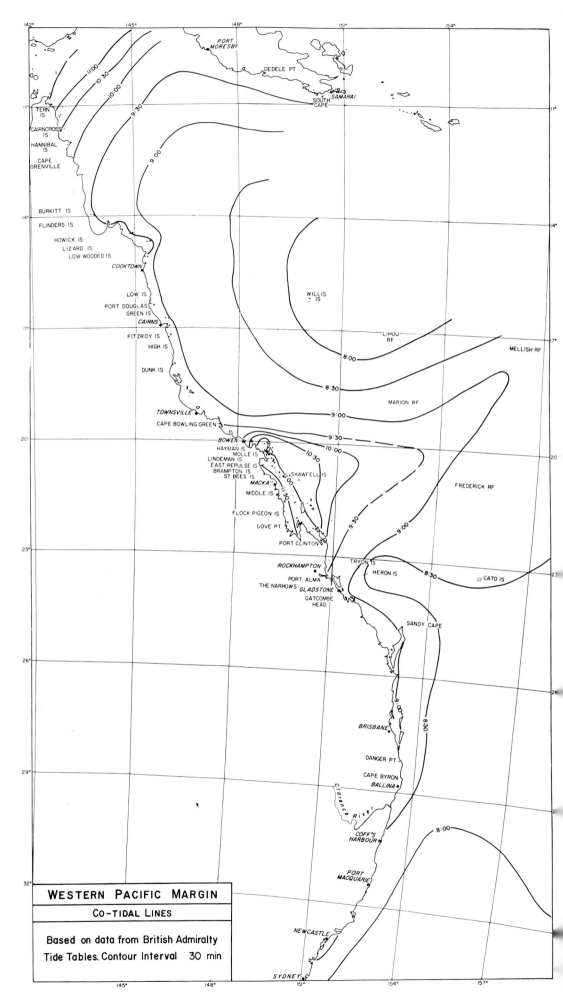

Fig. 41. Cotidal lines of Eastern Australian seas. Note convergence of tidal directions between Townsville and Gladstone, and divergence between Townsville and Cooktown.

74

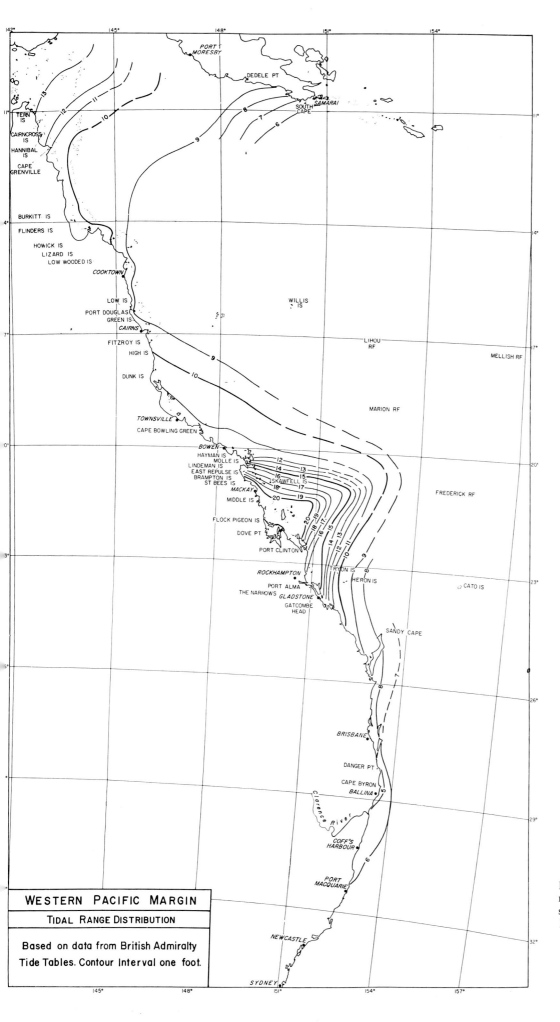

Fig. 42. Lines of equal tidal range in Eastern Australian seas. Note the maxima in the Mackay-Broad Sound and Torres Strait areas.

75

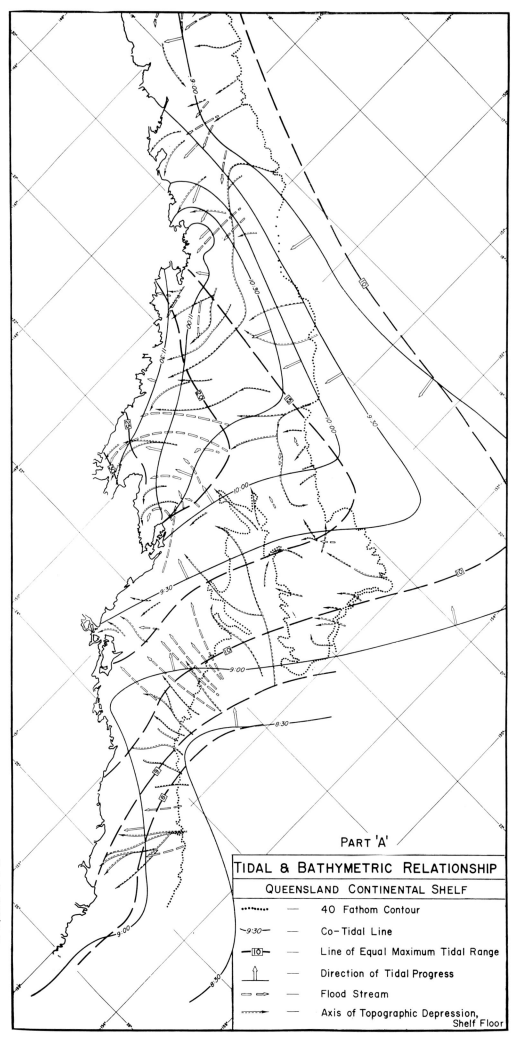

Fig. 43A, B. Maps relating tidal variation and bathymetric character for the Queensland Shelf. Note the parallelism between cotidal lines and the directions of the shelf edge in the Southern and Central Regions.

76

PART 'A'

## TIDAL & BATHYMETRIC RELATIONSHIP
### QUEENSLAND CONTINENTAL SHELF

| | | |
|---|---|---|
| •••••••• | — | 40 Fathom Contour |
| ~9:30 | — | Co-Tidal Line |
| ▢10▢ | — | Line of Equal Maximum Tidal Range |
| ↑ | — | Direction of Tidal Progress |
| ⇒ ⇒ | — | Flood Stream |
| ⇢⇢⇢ | — | Axis of Topographic Depression, Shelf Floor |

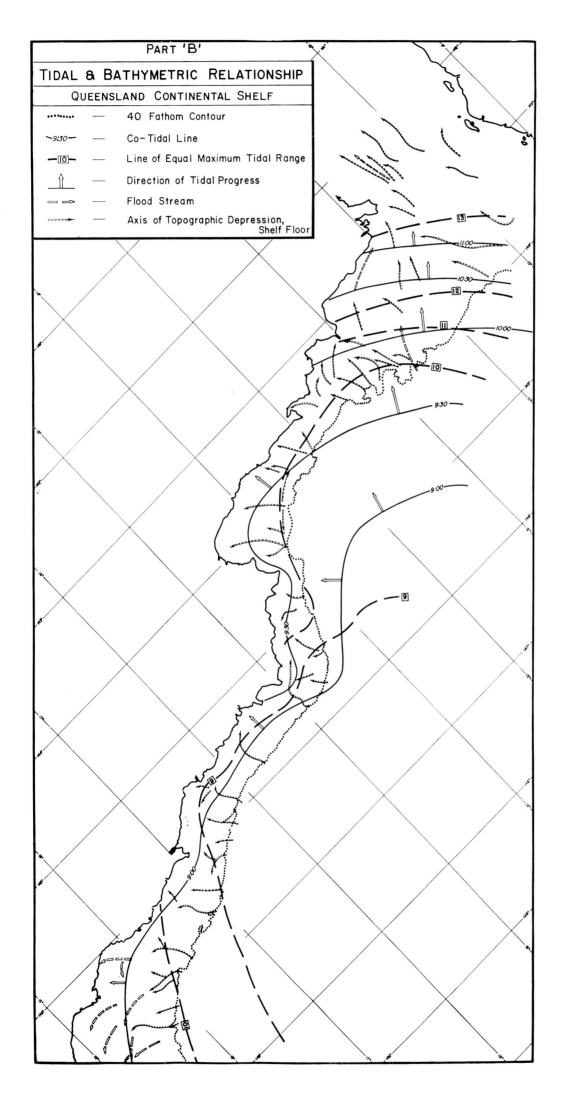

In the triangle extending from the coastline between Proserpine and Gladstone to the south-eastern corner of the Swains Reefs, an area of approximately 30,000 square miles, the tidal range varies between 12 and 34 ft., so that on the flood tide a volume increase of more than 1,000 cubic miles of water occurs on the shelf, the average water volume of which is of the order of 7,000 cubic miles. That is, there is a volume increase of approximately 15% between low and high tide. This volume must escape in the succeeding 6 h as the tide ebbs. In the coastal region the barrier islands (Curtis and Facing Islands), restricted inlets (Gladstone Harbour, Narrows, Port Clinton) and closely spaced off-shore islands (Whitsunday, Cumberland, Percy, Keppel Groups) effectively interfere with water escape. In the main belt of reef growth, similar restriction occurs. The result is the maintenance of considerable heads of water above the general level and swift currents develop between the restricted zones and the open sea. In many cases reverse flows occur with the next flooding tide. North of the Proserpine–Gladstone–Swains triangle, the tidal range, though smaller, still exceeds 9 ft. and gives rise to strong tidal currents. In the Torres Strait region, the eastern and western systems are frequently out of phase, and escape of water from one system at high tide may be facilitated by the low tidal level of the other system. It is in this region of tidal interaction, shallow bathymetry and narrow passages that the strongest tidal currents, with velocities of 6 knots, have been recorded.

Comparatively few measurements have been made of the currents on the Queensland Shelf, and because of the changing character of many of them any real understanding of their behaviour would require a major marine survey in which velocity and direction were studied over daily and seasonal cycles. In spite of the scarcity of current data, it is possible to derive a potential pattern from our knowledge of tidal data and bathymetry. Such a pattern is illustrated in Fig. 43.

The influence of tidal currents in the province is of very great significance. In the reef regions, the most prolific reef development occurs where the reefs are exposed to open water and vigorous surf action. This situation is best attained on the ocean side where the strong, persistent south-east swell encounters the reef zone, providing undepleted oceanic water and aeration in the surf. On the western side of the zone, similar though subdued and less persistent conditions arise under the influence of southerly and westerly swells which develop where the expanse of water between reef zone and coast is sufficiently wide. Where the marginal reef growth is such that ocean swell and surf

are prevented from reaching the inner reefs, tidal currents may provide the new water and carry away the depleted water so effectively as to permit the vigorous growth of these protected reefs. Examples of this influence are found behind the shelf edge reefs in the Southern Region (Fig. 47). Here, marginal growth is almost continuous, but where narrow breaks do occur and provide paths for strong tidal currents, extensive reefs develop along the sides of the current path, perpendicular to the main reef front. In the Whitsunday Group of off-shore islands, the main reef growth is in the lee of the islands where very fast currents flow through the deep Whitsunday Channel. On the eastern side of the islands, where the south-east swell provides a heavy surf, reefs are fewer and the beaches are composed of quartz sands derived from pre-Recent dunes now below sea level. Further north in the Central and Northern Regions, reefs have formed avenues perpendicular to the major breaks in the outer barrier. As well as affecting reef growth, tidal currents together with tidal overfall (which develops at the head of currents behind obstructions such as reefs and islands) result in extensive scouring of the sea floor (Fig. 44). Behind the outer reefs of the Southern Region and parts of the Northern Region, the scouring has been so effective as to produce a sediment-free zone approximately 4 miles wide. Where the currents pass through reef breaks or along channels between the avenues of reefs, very coarse, clean, reef detritus may be deposited, sometimes forming levees and banks (Fig. 49). In many cases these deposits consist almost entirely of one component, the most common being *Halimeda* and *Marginopora*.

In addition to their influence on reef growth, tidal currents play an important role in the Near Shore and Inner Shelf Zones. Here, they are responsible for the scouring and transportation of finer sediments from shallow to deeper regions. Their greatest effect may be observed in the areas of high tidal range and topographic restriction (Fig. 45, 50) such as occur in the Fitzroy, Broad Sound, Whitsunday, Princess Charlotte Bay, and Torres Strait regions. In these regions, the bottom topography is characterised by elongate ridges and channels and marginal expanses of subdued relief. Sands are generally restricted to the ridges, gravels to the channels and muds may occur in all three topographic zones, depending on the current velocities. It has been postulated by OFF (1963) that linear sand ridges such as those of Broad Sound have resulted from tidal-current deposition, but this postulate may well be questioned on several grounds. The main sand ridge development on the Queensland Shelf occurs in

Fig. 44A, B. Photographs of rough water and tidal overfall in the back-reef zone of the "hard-line" reefs of the Pompey Complex, Central Region. In Fig. 44B, there is a sharply defined contact between the turbulent water and the smooth water, in the background of the photograph.

Broad Sound, off Port Clinton and in the present mouth of the Fitzroy River. The three areas, which occur within a distance of 130 miles, have all been sites of effluence of the Fitzroy River during its post-Tertiary history. In the present Fitzroy mouth, the sand ridges are aligned with the stream course; in the Broad Sound area they are aligned with the ancient stream course, and off Port Clinton the same relationship appears to exist. Tidal-current directions in the Fitzroy mouth and Broad Sound approximate those of the stream courses, and in the Broad Sound are at 180° to the currents further off-shore. In the deeper Port Clinton area the directions are oblique to each other. One might conclude that the tidal-current directions in the shallow Broad Sound and Fitzroy mouth are controlled by the strong bottom topography developed by the river at different stages of its history, while the ridges off Port Clinton are too deep to exert any appreciable control on the water movement. Thus, the main effect of the tidal currents is to scour existing

channels, and in so doing to preserve the original topography. A second observation that might be made on the Broad Sound area is that two distinctive ridge types can be recognized. The first is the very elongate, curved shoal that appears to be unrelated to any island or rock mass. It is the more common. The second is the short, wide shoal that develops on the southwestern sides of numerous small islands and rocks. This may be caused by tidal-current interaction on the lee of the island or it may be the result of normal refraction of the wave fronts approaching the islands. In the more constricted part of Broad Sound, the high tidal range results in a tidal surge (Fig. 28E) which reaches a height of approximately 2 ft. Extreme turbulence, particularly along the margins of the Broad Sound scours the shallow floor and lifts considerable mud and sand into suspension.

In the Whitsunday area where strong tidal currents also develop, their main effect is to scour the deep meridional channels between the continental islands and the

Fig. 45. Photographs of small tidal bore in Broad Sound: A. Approaching wave. B. Turbulent water in the wake of the wave. Note the strong turbidity along the shore line.

Fig. 46A, B, C. Extremely turbulent water in the distance on Fig. 46A marks the strong tidal current that is flowing towards a reef opening in the Pompey Complex. Fig. 46B and C are photographs of algal slicks (*Tricodesmium*) taken from a boat and from the air. They reflect the movement of tidal currents and of surface wind.

mainland. The sediment of many of the channels is shell gravel. Some of the deeper channels contain mud. Sand and gravel shoals have developed parallel with the central line of islands between the coastline and the larger outer islands. In some cases, the shoals are in the lee of the islands, forming an extension of their axes. These appear to be the result of refraction of wave fronts, but may also owe their origin in part to tidal-current action. However, some shoals, e.g., Pigeon Island (Fig. 27C) have formed at right angles to the average tidal current direction and are almost certainly of wave origin.

In the far north, the ridges and channels of Torres Strait are controlled mainly by the pattern of reef growth and the distribution of the continental islands. Both tidal-current action and wave refraction are influenced by the reefs and islands, and both probably interact to scour channels and to build elongate shoals. On the wide shallow flats that occur along the Near

Shore Zone, mud deposition is dominant except for the section from Broad Sound to Repulse Bay, and the sections south and north of Princess Charlotte Bay, where prolific sand source and high tidal range combine in providing a comparatively mud-free zone. However, to the north and south of these areas, lower levels of tidal and wave energy permit the deposition of vast expanses of mud in the more protected parts of the Near Shore Zone.

In summary, it seems that tidal currents exert a significant influence on reef growth, particularly in areas that are normally protected from the oceanic swell. In the Inner Shelf and Near Shore Zones they are responsible for the scouring of channels and transport of muds to the off-shore areas. Evidence to support the view that they control the formation of sand ridges is not conclusive. It is believed that the directions of tidal-current flow, particularly in the shallow parts of the Inner Shelf, are controlled largely by the bottom topo-

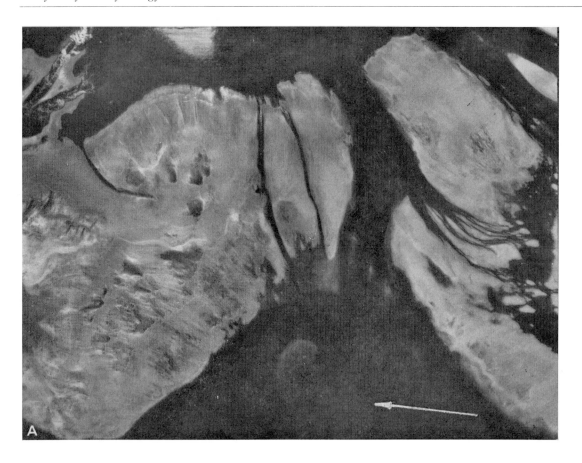

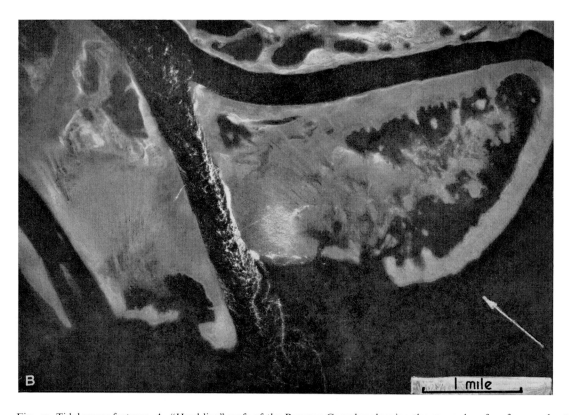

Fig. 47. Tidal scour features. A. "Hard-line" reefs of the Pompey Complex showing the scoured reef surfaces and extreme turbulence between plug reefs in the north-eastern corner. B. Current swept passage between reefs of the same complex.

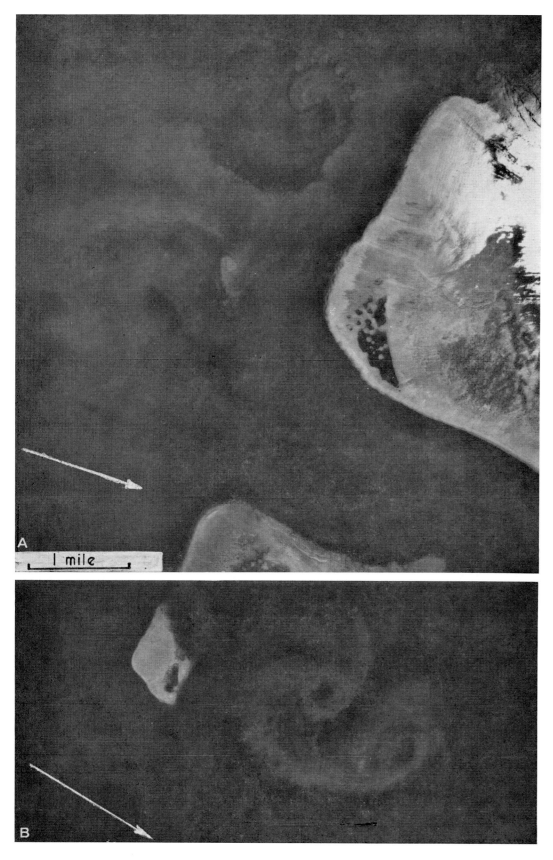

Fig. 48A, B. Strong current gyrals in the Pompey Complex on both leeward and ocean sides.

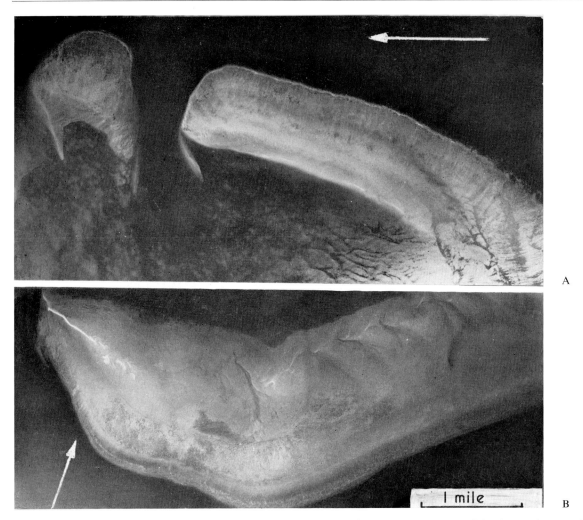

Fig. 49. Depositional features resulting from tidal current action. A. Sand levees between two reefs in the Northern Region. B. Large sand waves on northern side of reef surface, and sand spit on western side, due to current and wave action.

graphy, reefs and islands. This is especially obvious in the Broad Sound area where the current flow is at 180° to the direction of tidal currents further off-shore.

*Non-tidal currents*

In addition to the water movement induced by tidal forces and restrictive bathymetry, two other types of flow exert a strong influence in the province. The first include currents produced by the prevailing winds. The prevailing wind force is from the south-east, and the Trade Winds which are dominant and persistently strong from April to November, result in currents which set north to north-west along the shelf, through and behind the reefs. Current velocities range from $\frac{1}{2}$ to $1\frac{1}{4}$ knots. In many instances, the wind induced currents are opposed to tidal directions and this results in choppy seas and, in the shallower regions, much

turbulence. The net transport of water is from south to north. Long-shore drift results in considerable transport of Near-Shore sediment in the same direction. The second type of water flow is related to the main pattern of oceanic circulation. The Trade Wind Drift causes substantial penetration of the northern shelf areas by oceanic waters but current velocities resulting from this movement are modified by strong tidal fluctuation and the individual effects of the two regimes are impossible to determine. The Eastern Australian Current which diverges from the Trade Wind Drift in the Coral Sea, sweeps southward parallel with the central and southern shelf margins, and possibly invades the reef province only in the very south where there is an abrupt, eastward expansion of the shelf. As in the north, the oceanic current influence is complicated by flow induced by tidal forces.

The net surface movement of water in the Southern Region of the Great Barrier Reef Province has been investigated by Dr. Peter Woodhead and his initial results (personal communication, 1967) from float measurements reflect an extremely complex circu- lation south of the Swains Reefs. Elements of the East Australian Current are clearly evident along the zone between the Swains Reefs and Fraser Island to the east

Fig. 50. Current and sediment patterns in the Flinders Group and eastern part of Princess Charlotte Bay. Land areas consist of hori- zontally bedded Mesozoic sandstones.

of the shelf. However, westward from this zone, strong clockwise gyrals appear to exist at the southern end of the Capricorn Channel and in Hervey Bay. The effect of the first is to transport water northward into the Capricorn Channel, and westward through the Capricorn Group of reefs. The Hervey Bay gyral sweeps northward along the western shore and encounters south-westerly currents in the southern reefs of the Bunker Group. At this stage it is not possible to distinguish the various contributions from tidal currents, South East Trade Drift and the East Australian Current. However, there is a slight indication that the East Australian Current influences only the very marginal part of the Southern Region, while drift and tidal current are more dominant on the shelf proper.

Within the Great Barrier Reef Province and along the adjacent oceanic belt, there is clear evidence of vigorous water movement in the form of large vortices and zones of turbulence which can be seen from the air and from ships. Some of these features are illustrated in Fig. 43. The main areas of turbulence and tidal overfall occur in the Pompey Complex of the Southern Region and in the Northern Region behind the ribbon reefs. Further evidence of the vigorous water movement is seen in the tidal deltas and sand levees that develop on the ends of closely spaced reefs in the Northern Region (Fig. 49). Nearer shore, algal slicks (*Tricodesmium*) or "whale sperm" (Fig. 46), which are very common and very extensive, produce surface patterns that reflect both current and wind movement.

# *Chapter 5* | Climate and weather

GENERAL OBSERVATIONS

The Great Barrier Reef Province lies almost entirely within the tropics, extending from latitude 24°S to latitude 10°S. It forms a meridional belt between the Australian continental mass and the vast oceanic region of the South Pacific and, as a consequence, its climatic character is strongly influenced by both regions. In order to understand the complexity of its weather pattern one might first consider the general features of primary atmospheric circulation in the Southern Hemisphere.

Three primary pressure zones can be recognized (Fig. 51, 52). The first is the Equatorial Zone of low, uniform pressure where uniformity of surface-water temperature inhibits differentiation of air masses and where reduction of the Coriolis effect removes one of

that moves in from the summer and winter hemispheres. An intertropical front develops between the warmer and the slightly cooler air flows, and this front gives rise to local weather conditions that depart from the normal uniform pattern of the Doldrums.

The second pressure zone is the subtropical belt of high, uniform pressure. Its axis extends almost continuously along latitude 30°S in winter (July) and less continuously along latitude 40°S in summer (January), when it is interrupted by small areas of low pressure that develop over the continents. This is a broad belt, consisting of a series of anticyclones characterised by central areas of light winds and descending air. They result in calm, dry weather. The high-pressure belt gives rise to the South-East Trades along its northern margin and Westerlies along its southern margin. Between the anticyclone systems, north-flowing currents

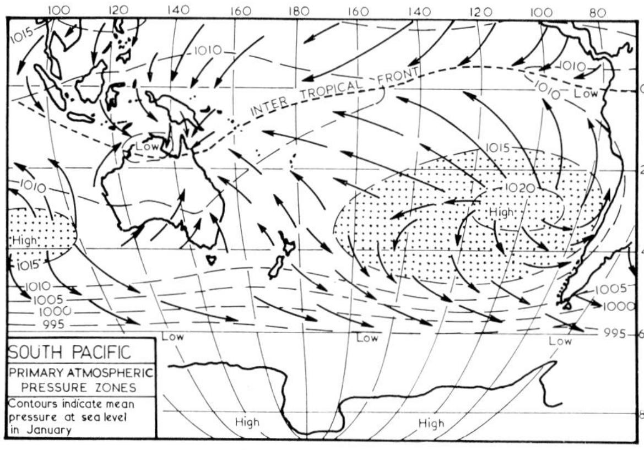

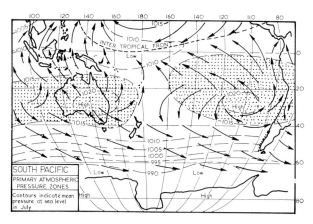

Fig. 51. Pressure zones and wind circulation in the South Pacific during January (summer).

Fig. 52. Pressure zones and wind circulation in the South Pacific during July (winter).

the main influences on wind development. This zone is characterised by hot, wet, calm weather. In January, the low-pressure systems move slightly southward and in July they move even further northward from the equator. Inflow of air into the systems from north and south results in a general upward convection of warm, moist air. However, the structure of this convection cell is complicated by the different character of the air

permit the invasion of cold, polar air masses into the inter-tropical region. The third pressure zone is the sub-polar low-pressure belt which flanks Antarctica and gives rise to the Polar Easterlies which move in from a high pressure area at the pole.

Because of the zonal distribution of the pressure systems, meridional pressure gradients induce air movement towards the low-pressure zones, and under the influence of the Coriolis force the winds are deflected from their meridional direction and become the South-East Trades, the Westerlies and the Polar Easterlies (Fig. 51, 52). In addition to these winds of the primary circulation pattern, a fourth important flow develops as a result of the summer low-pressure centres that exist over the continents. This is the Monsoon which moves southward from the cooler areas of the Northern Hemisphere and is deflected south-eastward by the Coriolis force, on crossing the equator. The South-East Trade Winds persist throughout the entire year, with only slight seasonal variation. They are modified near the continents because of the latter's displacement of the subtropical high-pressure belt. The Trade Winds consist essentially of warm, stable air which is moist from the sea surface to heights of 8,000 ft., and the resultant weather in the oceanic region is fair and clear. As the Trade Winds approach the Equatorial Low Pressure Zone, the air stability is reduced and storms become increasingly frequent. Similarly, as the warm, moist air of the trades passes from the ocean over the continental mass the stability is also reduced, with consequent precipitation.

The Monsoon develops as a result of winter cooling in Asia, southerly outflow over South-East Asia and the western Pacific and south-easterly deflection as it crosses the equator. Initially this air is extremely cold and as it moves into the tropical regions, it encounters warm maritime air and a cold front develops with all its complications. The Monsoon's influence is felt largely on the north-western and northern margins of Australia in the summer, when high rainfall occurs.

In addition to the main wind systems that develop in response to the zonal pressure belts, other atmospheric disturbances occur which have a marked effect on the weather pattern in the tropical region. Of these, perhaps the tropical cyclones or revolving storms are the most significant. They are much smaller than the low-pressure systems of the higher latitudes, but they have an intensity higher than any other type of storm. Their structure is deep, with an outer layer of strong downflow, an inner zone of strong rising currents and a calm centre of very low pressure. Wind velocities in these tropical cyclones may exceed 100 miles/h. The system generally moves slowly westward to south-westward, expanding in size and becoming less intense. On reaching the continent the low-pressure centre is rapidly filled and the storm dissipates. Cyclonic disturbances occur mainly in the late summer and early autumn (January–April). Their origin is in doubt, al-

though they appear to require potentially unstable air and a sea temperature exceeding 28°C. It has been suggested that they may form either as waves on the intertropical front in the equatorial zone or at points where several different air masses meet. Tropical cyclones bring heavy falls of rain which decrease outward from the central region of the disturbance. Their high wind velocities induce very rough seas.

Another disturbance that is less severe but possibly more effective in its total contribution to the intertropical weather pattern is the weak, low-pressure trough that develops as a wave in the Trade Wind stream and moves slowly westward. Such troughs occur mainly in the summer and, in some cases, they may grow into tropical cyclones, particularly when the wave moves into unstable air. Troughs are generally followed by extensive rain as they move westward.

The Great Barrier Reef Province is subjected to all the influences of the intertropical oceanic weather pattern. Perhaps the strongest influence is exerted by the South-East Trade winds. These reach maximum velocities in the spring (September). In the summer when the subtropical high pressure belt moves southward to latitude 40°S they become less persistent and weaker north of latitude 19°S. As the sun moves northward with winter, the high-pressure system migrates to latitude 30°S and the South-East Trades become effective from 24°S to the northern margin.

Although the summer Trade Winds are generally weaker, their long passage over the warm sea leads to high water-vapour content and this is released as heavy rain when the trades move into the unstable air masses of the Equatorial Zone and the continent. In the far-northern region, the Trade Wind influence is considerably reduced in summer although it is still the dominant wind. However, the high summer rainfall is maintained by a considerable contribution from the North-West Monsoon which brings moist unstable air from warm equatorial seas into the northern continental region and its marginal sea. The third feature of the summer weather pattern is the tropical cyclone and smaller low pressure centre which both contribute to the high summer rainfall, particularly of the northern part of the reef province. One of the main continental factors influencing the coastal weather is the persistent development of a trough that extends south-eastward from the Gulf of Carpentaria and causes considerable storm activity along the coastal belt and off-shore region.

RAINFALL

The main data on rainfall has been gathered from the mainland and little factual material is available from the reef province. However, examination of rainfall maps, both seasonal and annual (Fig. 53A, B) reveals a striking parallelism of the isohyets with the coastline so that one might extrapolate seawards with some reliability. Local variation in the coastal rainfall pattern is caused by high mountains which increase the orographic fall, and by sections of the coastline which are aligned with the main South-East Trade direction thus reducing the rainfall. There are two dominant rain influences: the northern summer one which is dependent on the trades, monsoons and tropical cyclones, and the southern winter influence dependent on the troughs and fronts that develop over the continent in the south. Between the two influences, there is a zonal belt of comparatively low rainfall extending along latitude 20°S.

The rainfall pattern of Queensland is marked by its great variability from year to year especially in the coastal strip within 50 miles of the sea (Fig. 54). As DICK (1958) has pointed out, this rainfall variability is probably responsible more than any other climatic factor for the main regional differences in climate in Queensland. The variability is due largely to the irregular generation of tropical cyclones and depressions which are short lived but which normally lead to extremely heavy rainfall. Such falls in reef areas have resulted in lowered surface salinities that have proved fatal for reef organisms. HEDLEY (1925) recorded the destruction of the Stone Island Reef near Bowen in 1918 by the heavy rain (35 inches in 8 days) that accompanied a tropical cyclone. Falls of 34 inches in one day have been recorded more recently (1958) in an adjacent area. DICK (1958) studied the relative variability of annual rainfall in Queensland and demonstrated that the areas of least variability include the coastal section north of latitude 18°S, while the section south of latitude 25°S is one of moderate variability. Parts of this same section show extreme variability during the summer.

If we are to extrapolate the continental data, then two features must be recognized as significant, viz. the zones of moderately high and very high rainfall and

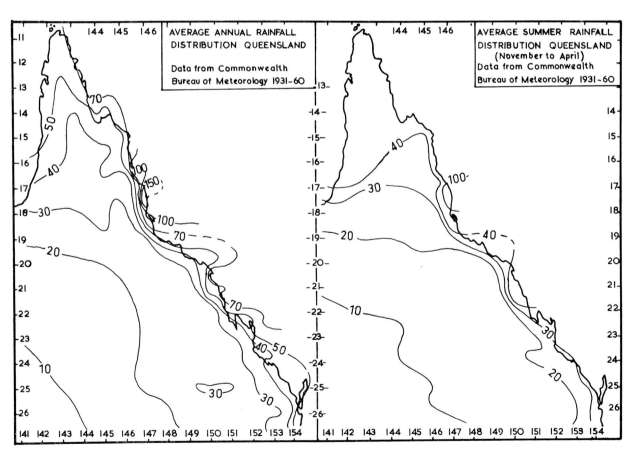

Fig. 53A  B. Average rainfall distribution in inches for the whole year and for the summer (November-April).

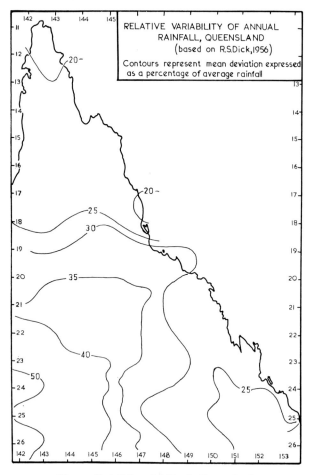

Fig. 54. Rainfall variability in Queensland.

the intervening belt of low rainfall and extreme variability. The far northern zone is subjected to monsoons, South-East Trades and tropical cyclones, and while the monsoonal effect decreases eastward, the trades and cyclones might be expected to cause rainfall only slightly less than that recorded on the coastal belt. In the north where the reef province narrows to less than 20 miles, there should be little change between the coastal and marine weather conditions. The semi-arid zone at latitude 20°S might also be expected to extend seaward although the more uniform conditions of the sea would reduce it rapidly. The southern coastal zone of moderately high rainfall is dependent largely on fronts and troughs that owe their origin to continental factors so that their influence further east should also decline.

In summary, the rainfall pattern of the reef province might be expected to resemble that of the coastal belt but there would be less variability in its distribution and generally smaller falls.

TEMPERATURE

Unlike the rainfall distribution, the temperature variation along the coastal belt of Queensland is gradual and is controlled almost entirely by latitude. Seasonal fluctuation in the tropical zone is extremely small, maximum temperatures occurring from November to January, minimum temperatures from June to August. The mean maximum temperatures range from 85° to 90°F in mid-summer over the entire coastal region. In mid-winter, mean maximum temperatures range from 70–75°F south of Cairns, increasing to 80–85°F northward to Cape York. Mean minimum temperatures range from 70–75°F in mid-summer to 50–65°F in mid-winter. Air temperatures decrease over the ocean from north to south and in general are higher than those over the coastal area. Night minima are considerably lower on the coastal strip.

# Chapter 6 | Morphology and distribution of reefs

An examination of the hydrographic charts or of aerial photographs of the Great Barrier Reef Province reveals an unusually wide diversity in the character of the reefs and reef groups that constitute the province. This diversity, illustrated in Fig. 55–59, is reflected in the reef population density, bathymetric level of the reef surface, size, shape, orientation, morphological zonation and central topography of the reef.

Central topography is extremely variable, and may be characterised by one of several distinctive features: deep lagoon, shallow lagoon, lagoon with large isolated remnant reefs, lagoon with small isolated patch reefs, lagoon with numerous reticulated reef systems, lagoonless sand flat, slight axial depression, marginal sand

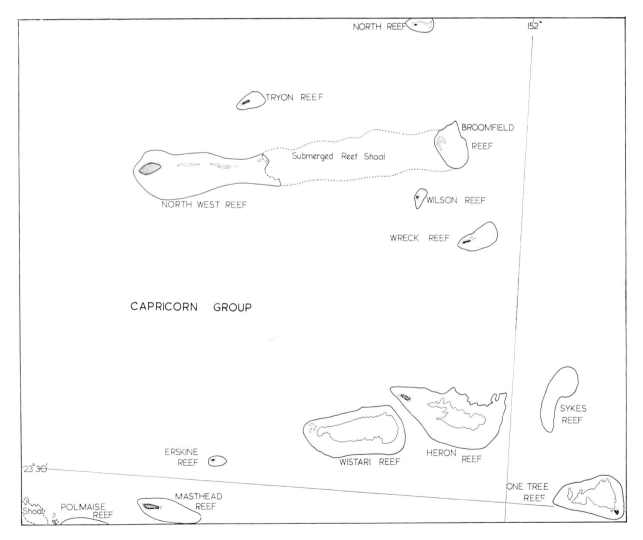

Fig. 55. Reef shape, density and distribution in the Capricorn Group, Southern Region. Western Marginal Shelf.

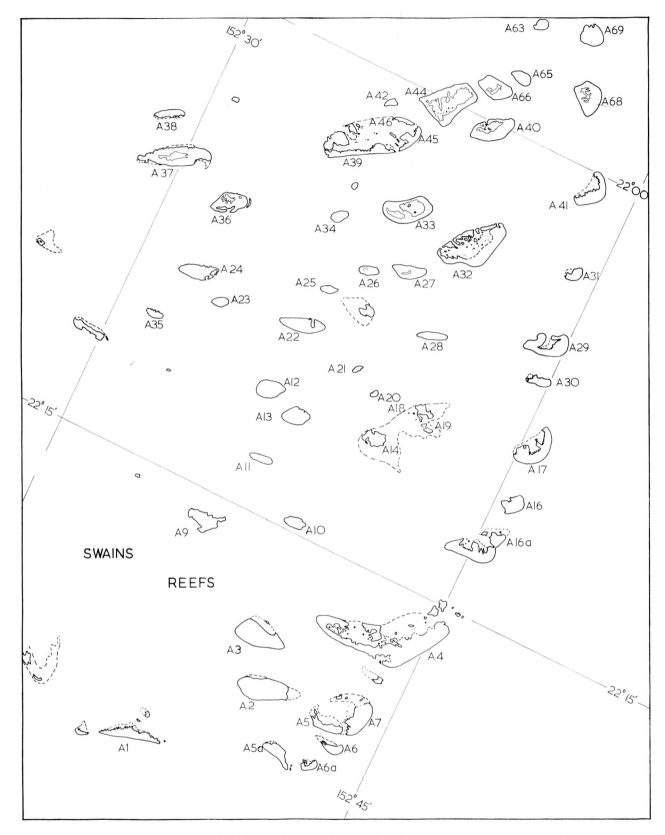

Fig. 56. Reef shape, density and distribution in the Swains Complex, Southern Region, Eastern Marginal Shelf.

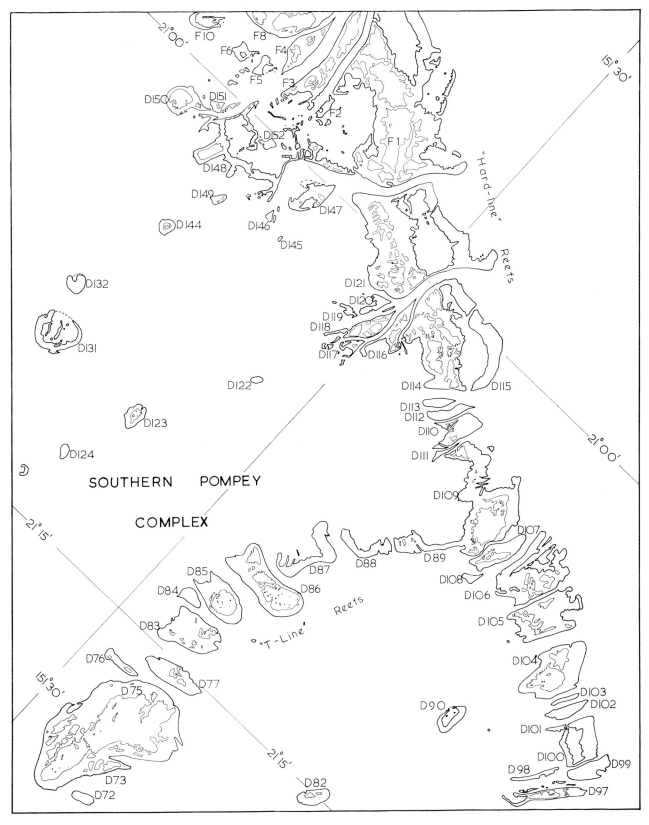

Fig. 57. Reef shape, density and distribution in the eastern part of the Southern Pompey Complex, Central Region, Eastern Marginal Shelf.

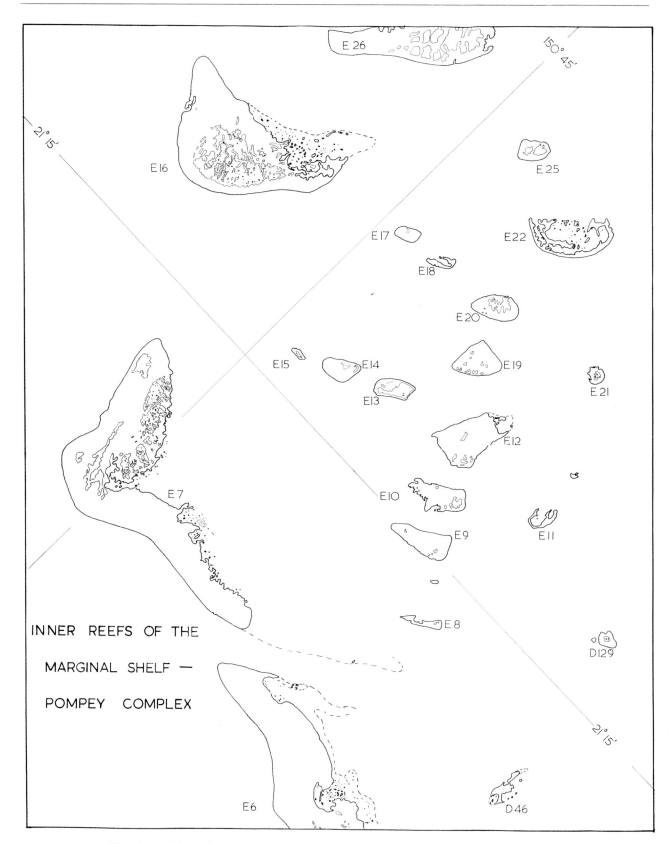

Fig. 58. Reef shape, density and distribution of the inner reefs of the Southern Pompey Complex.

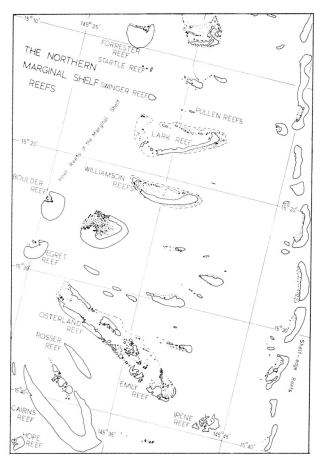

Fig. 59. Reef shape, density and distribution of the Marginal Shelf reefs of the Northern Region (southern part).

banks and gravel shoals, sand cay (unvegetated, grassed, or forested), mangrove swamps, rock platform, open lagoon or back-reef apron. Some of these features are clearly defined in Fig. 60–64.

Several attempts at reef classification have been made since DARWIN (1842) first proposed his theory on reef development in which he postulated the evolution of the fringing reef to the barrier and then to the atoll. Subsequent authors have tended to accept the fringing, barrier and atoll as basic types, although as defined by Darwin they represent stages in a reef history, stages that demonstrate the validity of his subsidence theory. The differences in the three stages are found, not in reef structure or shape, but in the degree to which a lagoon is developed, and when applied to oceanic reefs the terms imply a close genetic relationship. However, the fringing and barrier reefs of the oceanic province have a different genetic significance from those of the continental shelf. Fringing reefs along the continental shelf are unlikely to evolve into the closed rings that

form atolls. Furthermore, the majority of reefs designated as "barrier" on the shelf are so distant from the land mass to which they supposedly form barriers that the term as such loses all meaning.

It is perhaps advisable to consider the origin and subsequent usage of reef terminology that has become established, sometimes ambiguously, in the literature on organic reefs.

The term "atoll" was derived from the Indo-Malayan word of like sounding name, and European literature records its first usage by PYRARD DE LAVAL (1605). In the original Indo-Malayan sense and in the sense used by De Laval, it referred to the reefs with islands which occurred in the Indian Ocean. DARWIN (1842) used it for the Indian Ocean reefs and extended its usage to the Central Pacific. It is interesting to observe that in his outstanding work on the reef problem, Darwin examined only one atoll and this was the Cocos–Keeling atoll in the Indian Ocean.

Darwin and earlier writers, as well as authors who published shortly after Darwin (DANA, 1872; MURRAY, 1880; GUPPY, 1888; AGASSIZ, 1903) were concerned primarily with the origin of reefs in the Central Pacific and Indian Oceans, reefs which rose from the great depths of the ocean basins. They dealt with reefs whose structure, shape and growth pattern are controlled by the areal limitations of the topographic elevations on which they grow, by the unrestricted supply of oceanic water and by wind and water circulations that are unimpeded by continental masses. These are the reefs —whether fringing, barrier, or atoll—of the deep oceanic province, and it would seem reasonable to retain their names for this province alone.

By contrast, reefs of the continental shelf, and in particular, those of the Queensland Shelf, are favoured by topography that permits almost unlimited areal expansion, but in many cases they are restricted by adverse hydrologic factors resulting from the interference by the continent, of wind and water circulation. Furthermore, because of the wide variation in the hydrological factors throughout the shelf and the directional character imposed on them by the land barrier, there is a greater diversity of shape and structure as well as stronger directional features in the shelf reefs than are found in the oceanic reefs. It is important, then, to recognise the significant differences between the shelf and the oceanic provinces and to reduce ambiguity by restricting the term "atoll" to its natural province (the open ocean) and by minimising the use of "fringing" and "barrier" in connection with shelf reefs.

95

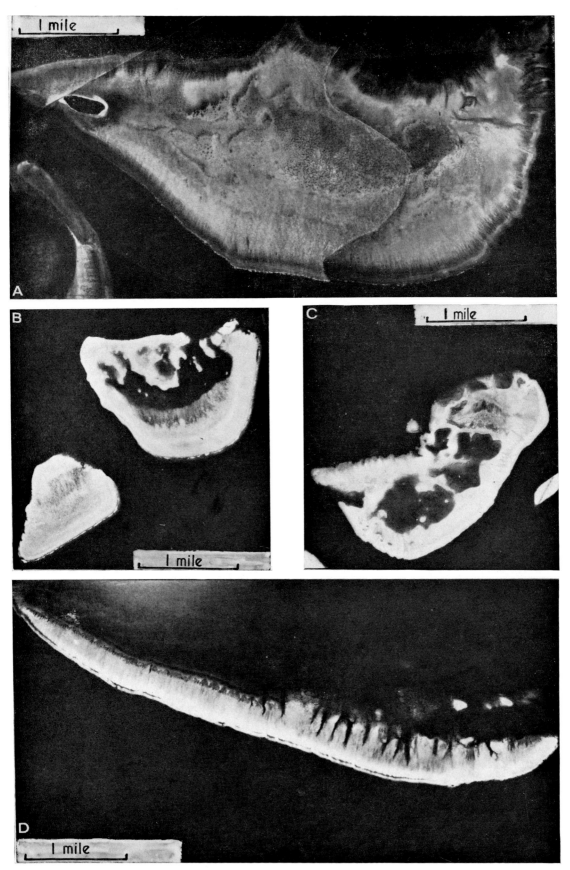

Fig. 60. Diversity of reef shape. A. Heron Reef—lagoonal platform type, approx. 5½ miles long; shallow, reef-studded lagoon, wide reef-flat; sand cay on western, leeward end; large shingle ridges on eastern and western margins. B. Shelf-Edge reef of Swains Complex; closed ring type; narrow reef flat, deep lagoon; sharp, irregular lagoonal margin, and small back-reef apron in lagoon. C. Central reef of Swains Complex; closed mesh type; narrow flat, deep lagoon, minor lagoonal reefs; irregular lagoonal margin. D. Reef on the inner edge of the Marginal Shelf, Swains Complex; wall type; deep grooving on leeward side; no lagoon; slight back-reef apron. (All reefs are oriented such that the vertical plate edge is directed northward.)

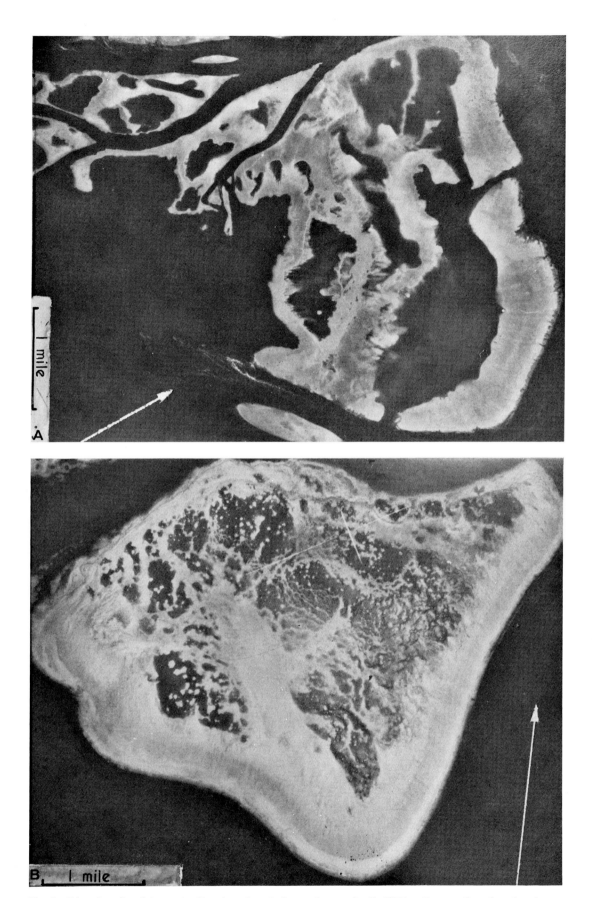

Fig. 61. Diversity of reef shape. A. Closed mesh and plug reefs near the Shelf Edge, Pompey Complex; deep lagoons, narrow reef flats; high reef density; strong currents between reefs evidenced in white-capped water. B. Closed mesh reef of the inner side of the Marginal Shelf, Pompey Complex; dense lagoonal meshing.

97

## CLASSIFICATION OF REEFS

If the broad division of reefs into oceanic and shelf groups is accepted, one is still faced with the problem of nomenclature of reef types within each group. The broad division into two groups is essentially genetic, although a purely descriptive criterion may be used to separate them, viz. depth of off-reef floor. Oceanic reefs rise from depths greater than 100 fathoms, whereas shelf reefs have surrounding depths which are much less. Subdivision of each group is somewhat arbitrary and is based on the more readily recognised features such as shape, morphological zonation and central structure. Undoubtedly, detailed biological analysis would provide a more reliable basis for reef classification and yet it is interesting to speculate that such analysis might well provide evidence to support the more arbitrary divisions derived from these grosser features.

It is apparent that a reef may originate in an area where bathymetric and hydrologic conditions are favourable and where coral planulae or other similar organisms are available for colonisation. Once the embryonic reef colony has been established, it will expand according to the forces (physical, chemical and organic) that are prevalent. Such development may be symmetrically or asymmetrically outwards (radial or multi-directional), symmetrically elongate (two opposite directions) or asymmetrically elongate (unidirectional). With subsequent development, the balance of controlling forces may be modified and directional trends in reef growth may change accordingly, leading to more complicated patterns of shape and structure. The many patterns that have been observed in the Great Barrier Reef Province provide the basis for the classification presented in Fig. 65. The gradational nature of the patterns lends support to the view that they represent various stages in reef development, stages which are defined in the classification. Other modifications resulting from eustatic changes and deterioration of hy-

Fig. 62. Near-Shore and Inner Shelf reefs. A. Near-Shore reef around South Island of the Lizard Group, Northern Region. Very wide reef flat, shallow back-reef area. B. Near-Shore reef near the delta of the Mowbray River, Northern Region; reef development irregular and discontinuous. C. Near-Shore reefs at Cape Tribulation, Northern Region; similar to B. D. Inner Shelf reef—Three Isles, Northern Region; strong development of shingle ridges, sand cay and mangrove swamp; very broad, poorly differentiated reef surface.

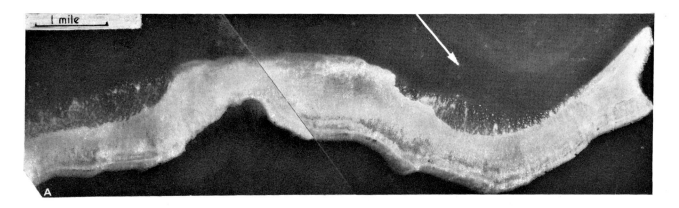

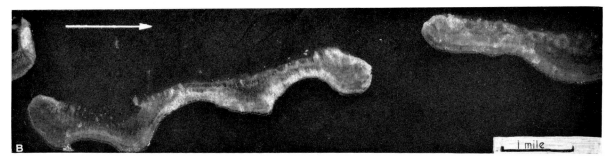

Fig. 63A, B. Shelf-Edge reefs. Extended wall reefs, known as ribbon reefs, Northern Region.

drological conditions may be imposed on these basic reef types.

The observation which is fundamental to this classification, and in fact lends its significance, is that organic reefs, once initiated, will expand in directions controlled by the hydrologic–bathymetric–biological balance. Where this balance of factors exerts an influence that is nearly equal from all directions, expansion should be approximately radial and the *platform* reef type should result. Evidence to support this deduction is found in the widespread occurrence of the platform type throughout the province, but particularly in areas where bottom topography favours growth in all directions, where hydrologic conditions—wave action (due to wind stress), tidal currents, and water composition—are similar on all sides, and where species of organisms are similarly distributed in near-concentric zones. The Shelf Edge and Near Shore Zones preclude this symmetry of balance, and so one finds the platform reef best developed in the middle Shelf region, behind the main line of Shelf Edge reefs. Where continued radial expansion of the platform type is favoured, again in the middle zone, *lagoonal platform* reefs develop because the central area of the reef becomes more sheltered from surf and wave action and can no longer support the colonial organisms—coral and algae—that are so dependent on aeration from the surf and nutrition from the open sea. The lagoon of

such reefs represents the dead heart of the reef colony. Where bathymetry restricts radial expansion, elongation of the platform reef may occur and this is generally accompanied by reduction of organic growth along the axial zone which results in slight axial depression and extensive sand deposition. The *elongate platform* reef does not develop a true lagoon; its axial depression is merely an extension of the sand flat.

Along the shelf margin or along the coast line, bathymetric and hydrologic conditions are markedly asymmetric so that reef growth is restricted to one or two directions. This results in various types of linear reef development. The *wall* reef represents an early stage of such growth and it may evolve into the *cuspate* reef where the reef ends curve leeward and border the passages between adjacent reefs. Alternatively, the wall reef may develop irregular buttresses or prongs normal to its axis in both leeward, and to a smaller degree, seaward directions. The *prong* reef is more common along that part of the shelf margin where high tidal range and the near continuous line of reefs cause strong tidal currents through the narrow reef passages. The prong or buttress development appears to be the reef's response to this unusual supply of turbulent, aerated, oceanic water that finds its way into the back-reef zone. By extending such buttresses, greater surfaces of the reef are exposed to more favourable hydrologic influences.

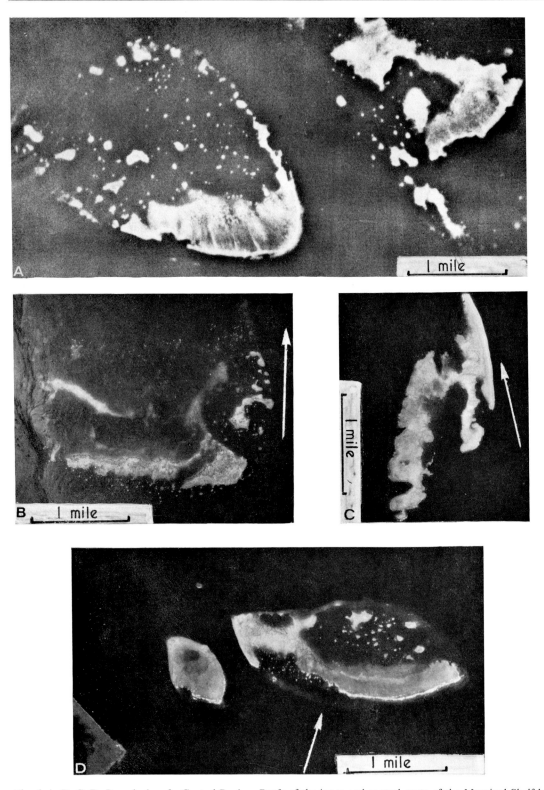

Fig. 64A, B, C, D. Resorbed reefs, Central Region. Reefs of the inner and central parts of the Marginal Shelf between latitudes 18°S and 20°S. Typical are the embayed margins, the dispersed reef segments and the larger submarine platform (clearly visible in D) from which the reefs rise.

Under conditions of persistently strong wave attack, there may be a rapid, abundant production of detritus, some of which is swept across the reef into the back-reef zone, between the cusps or prongs, where it extends as an apron. Scattered coral growth on the apron helps to raise its bathymetric level and the *composite*

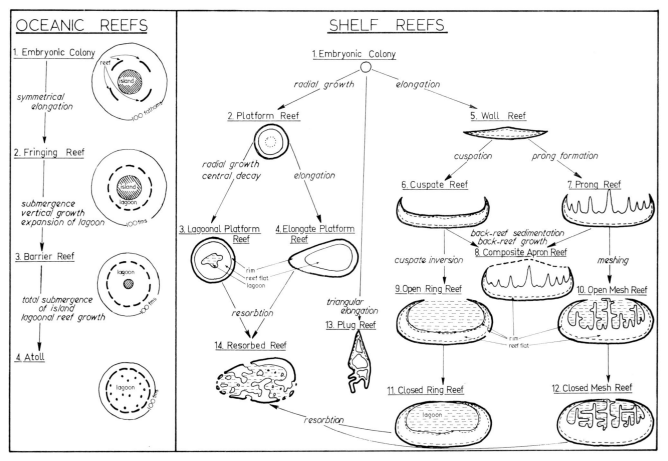

Fig. 65. Classification of reefs.

*apron* reef so formed may approach the platform type in shape. However, the lack of a true algal rim and coral zone on the lee side distinguishes the composite apron reef.

Further leeward growth of the cuspate and prong reefs may be restricted by bathymetry and this leads to re-curving of the cusps and prongs to produce the *open ring* and *open mesh* reefs respectively. Merging of op-posite cusps and branching of prongs lead finally to the *closed ring* and *closed mesh* reefs. Evidence sup-porting the view that lagoonal platform reefs are of different origin from the similar ring and mesh reefs is found in the morphological–biological zonation. In some of the ring and mesh reefs, algal rims are de-veloped around the lagoon margins as well as around the seaward margin. This suggests that the lagoonal margin was at one stage open to the sea. The second algal rim never develops on lagoonal platform reefs where the lagoon is a late stage feature formed through degeneration of the central area. Differences in algal-rim development are illustrated in Fig. 66–71. Another distinction is found in the lagoon depth: that of the lagoonal platform generally being much less than that

of the closed reefs. The lagoon margins are also dis-tinctive. That of the lagoonal platform reef is normally simple whereas the lagoonal margin of the ring and mesh reefs is irregular because of prong development. As further outward growth becomes more restricted, especially by bathymetry, the ring and mesh reefs tend to grow inwards until a balance is reached between inner growth and the supply of undepleted, aerated oceanic water to the central area. Such a situation is found in the shelf-edge reefs of the Pompey Complex where inward growth has resulted in enormous reef-surface areas, some of which are illustrated in Fig. 98–100.

An unusual type of reef found mainly in the Southern Region where dense reef development occurs along the shelf edge and where high tidal range results in strong currents, is the *plug reef*. It is a small, triangular form that grows with its apex pointing oceanward through openings between the linear shelf-edge reefs. Its outline is analogous with that of the sand ridges formed in the lower reaches of large rivers.

The reef types which have been described above are difficult to recognise in the Inner Shelf and Near Shore

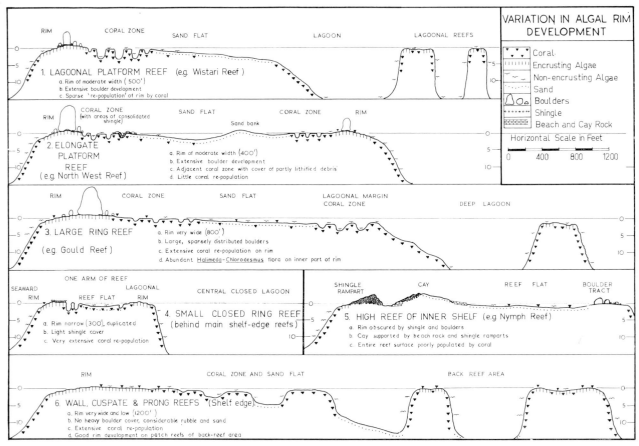

Fig. 66. Variation in development of the algal rim of the different reef types.

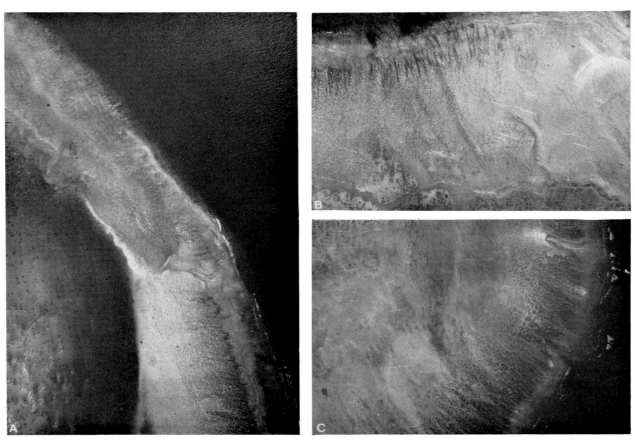

Fig. 67. Legend see p. 103.

Fig. 68A, B. Photographs of the rim of North West Reef showing the prolific epi-rim coral fauna and grooves and surge channels into the rim.

Fig. 67. (p. 102) Photographs of the algal rim of Heron and Wistari Reefs. A. Eastern side of Wistari Reef with strong shingle ridges on the rim, lineated coral zone and smaller sand flat; eastern end of lagoon clearly obvious. B. Northern side of Wistari Reef showing algal rim free of ridges; coral zone poorly developed; sand flat very wide; lagoon margin visible on southern edge of photograph. C. Eastern end of Heron Reef showing the algal rim and reef flat with large shingle ridges and lineated coral development; sand flat is extremely wide.

0.1 mile

Fig. 69. Algal rim, reef flat and sand cay of Tryon Reef (Capricorn Group) showing poor differentiation of the surface zones; lineation of coral is striking.

Fig. 71A, B. (p. 105). Reefs in the northern part of the Pompey Complex, behind the Shelf-Edge reefs The reef flat, slightly depressed is bordered by a seaward and a lagoonal rim. No strong boulder development is evident.

Fig. 70. A. Aerial view of Nymph Reef and Cay showing boulder and shingle zone on northern rim and the almost complete masking of the reef by the vegetated cay and surrounding debris. B. View of Nymph Reef from the north showing the strong boulder zone, narrow reef flat and vegetated cay. C. Northern end of Ribbon Reef viewed from the back-reef zone across the reef flat to the seaward edge marked by line of breakers. There is no strong boulder zone. D. Underwater view of the rim of Ribbon Reef showing the relatively fine boulder material.

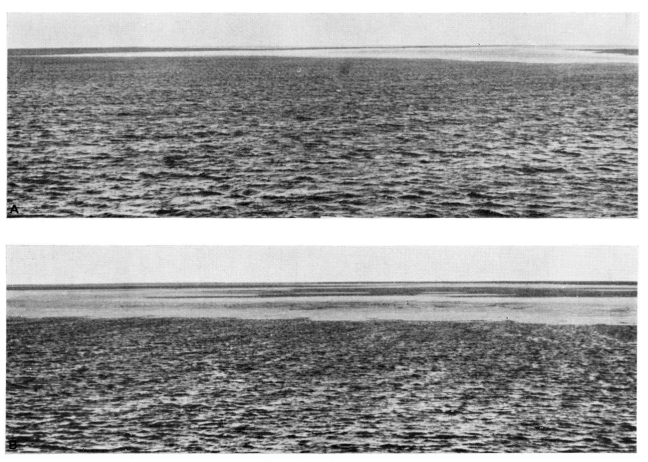

Fig. 71. Legend see p. 104.

Zones because of the heavy detrital blanket that covers most reefs of these zones, giving them a very distinctive appearance. During the time of highest sea level, reef surfaces grew to heights 6–10 ft. above the present high water mark and with recession of the sea to its present level, the reef surfaces died and were eroded. The reefs of the Marginal Shelf, poorly shielded from oceanic attack, were stripped of their dead cover. Those of the Inner Shelf and Near Shore Zones were more protected and most of the surface detritus remained and is represented today by extensive boulder zones, shingle banks and sand cays. Much of the material has been cemented to form large raised platforms of cay rock. Much of it has been spread over the lower surfaces of the reefs where it has stifled organic growth and contributed to the lithification of large tracts of these surfaces, producing "cellular" zones of reef rock. The high sand cays and boulder tracts have been vegetated in many cases by grasses and trees while the lower surfaces have been invaded by mangroves. Earlier writers have distinguished these high reefs (not to be confused with the "high" or continental islands of

STEERS, 1929, p. 244) from the clean, low reefs that make up the greater part of the province. The protected high reefs are essentially platform and wall types in which the original surface zonation has been obscured by residual detritus and in which surface lithification has reached an advanced stage. Typical of these are the reefs of the Turtle Group in the Northern Region. The differences between the high and low reefs were recognised by the early workers. JUKES (1847) distinguished the outer linear reefs from the more protected inner reefs. SPENDER (1930, p. 27) recognised a third type, the island reefs, the true high reefs of the Inner Shelf and Near Shore Zones. Spender emphasised that reefs such as the Capricorn and Bunker groups (Marginal Shelf reefs) were not of this kind. FAIRBRIDGE (1950) followed Spender in his recognition of these reef types and further refined the classification of island reefs.

Another unusual reef development is that which has been termed the *resorbed* reef in this work. Typical examples of these are illustrated on Fig. 64 and 73B. They are characterised by their embayed margins and by the numerous, isolated patches of reef that are

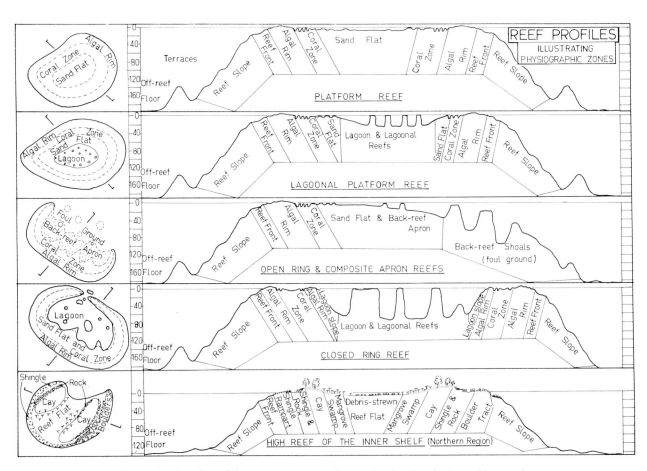

Fig. 72. Reef profiles of the more common reef types showing the physiographic zonation.

closely distributed about the main mass. Frequently, resorbed reefs rise from larger, submerged platforms, some of which are visible on aerial photographs (Fig. 64, 104B). These features are suggestive of restrictive growth and in some cases of degeneration of the reef mass, caused through unfavourable conditions developed after a low stand of sea level. In the case of those rising from submerged platforms, it seems that the platforms represent the planed surfaces of earlier reefs, and that with rising sea level, new hydrologic conditions prevailed that prevented the same degree of growth. In other cases, it appears that new hydrologic conditions have reacted against existing reefs causing the extinction of reef organisms and the progressive resorbtion of the reef mass. This same process is probably responsible for the *remnant patch* reefs of the lagoons which will be discussed later.

### GENERAL REEF STRUCTURE AND ZONATION

All reefs have a basic pattern of morphological and biological zonation. Depending on the growth stage

### Off-reef floor

In the Great Barrier Reef Province, reef masses rise fairly abruptly from the shelf floor in depths averaging 16–32 fathoms. On the Inner Shelf depths are much less, whereas along the northern shelf margin the reefs border the Queensland Trench which descends sharply to depths greater than 1,500 fathoms. Whatever the depth, the zone immediately surrounding a reef is named the *off-reef floor*.

In many areas, particularly in the Swains and Pompey complexes, the individual reefs are separated from the main floor by comparatively high submarine ridges, the composition and structure of which are not known. Such ridges are seen on the echogram traces of Fig. 73. They may represent organic structures or they may be scree deposits from the reef, related to strong tidal currents and down-slope avalanching from the reef. In most cases where they have been observed these ridges are more strongly developed on the lee side of the reef. Fig. 74 shows the off-reef floor in the Capricorn Group at depths of 20 fathoms. Well defined ripple marks and

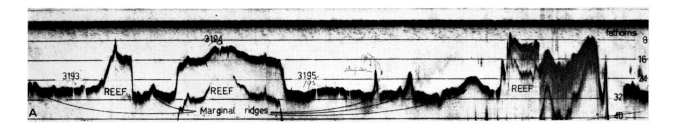

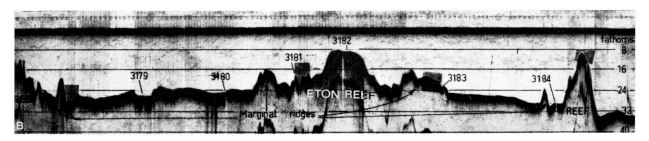

Fig. 73A, B. Echogram traces in the Swains and Pompey Complexes showing marginal ridges adjacent to the main reef developments.

and size of a reef as well as on local conditions, various zones may be exaggerated, others may be almost suppressed. In the case of the "high" reefs of the Inner Shelf and Near Shore Zones the original zonation has been obscured by excessive detritus from the older, dead surface. The normal zonation is best demonstrated diagrammatically and for this purpose four profiles have been presented in Fig. 72, each one showing the zones of a particular reef type.

oriented gravels provide convincing evidence of current action on the floor.

### Reef slope and terraces

The face of the reef rising from the floor is the *reef slope* and this varies in gradient with different reefs as well as at different levels on the slope of an individual

Fig. 74. A. Off-reef floor. Photograph at 110 ft. showing the sand and gravel with strong current furrows and cross ripples, algal clumps and non-calcareous algae; off the north-east side of Wistari Reef; scale is 1 ft. B. Off-reef floor at 110 ft. Similar sand and gravel, and clumps of *Halimeda*; scale is 1 ft.

Fig. 77. A. Terrace at 30 ft. on northern side of Heron Reef, with abundant *Acropora* and *Chlorodesmis*.
B. Same terrace with abundant *Acropora hyacinthis*.

isms invade the reef-ward side of the spur-and-groove system and grooves are gradually roofed over, particularly when the algal genus *Lithothamnion* is abundant. This results in sub-reef tunnels which extend backward from the 2-fathom terrace and grooves, well into the reef mass. One consequence of such tunnels is the formation of "blow holes" on the reef flat, where fountains of water and spray gush as successive waves force water along the restricted passage of the groove and through the narrowing tunnel to its terminal opening in the reef flat.

### Algal rim

Behind the reef front, the main reef surface or reef top begins. The outer part is the *algal rim* (Fig. 66–71) which rises gradually from the reef edge and frequently culminates in a low ridge—the *Lithothamnion ridge*—that forms the most elevated part of the reef top.

The algal rim varies enormously in width and may attain dimensions greater than 500 yards.

It consists of a stepped pavement of encrusting coralline algae, predominantly *Lithothamnion* and *Porolithon* which encroach seaward over the main coral fauna of the growing spurs. The algal pavement provides a hard, resistant surface which bears the main force of the attacking waves and reduces their destructive power before they sweep into the zones of coral on the reef flat behind the rim. The algal pavement is itself populated by small, isolated colonies of coral—the epialgal fauna—as well as by numerous, small echinoids (*Echinometra*) and various species of the green algae *Caulerpa*, *Halimeda*, *Chlorodesmis*, and *Acetabularia*. On some reefs, particularly those of the Pompey complex, the green-algal species appear to be restricted in their distribution across the rim and form weakly defined zones. *Chlorodesmis* and *Caulerpa* are dominant in the outer part of the rim, whereas *Halimeda* becomes more abundant towards the flat. Foraminifera, particularly *Baculogypsina*, *Calcarina*, *Alveolinella*, and *Marginopora*, occur in abundance, many of them adhering to the algae. A vigorous molluscan population also thrives on the algal rim.

Fig. 78. Terrace at 50 ft. on north-western slope of Heron Reef showing extensive sand and shingle cover, much algae and little coral.

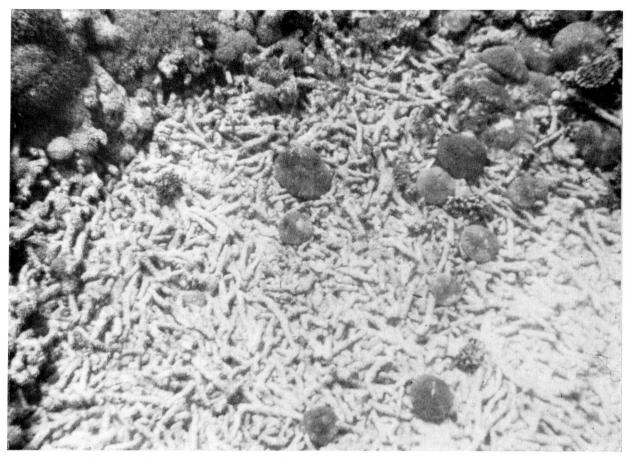

Fig. 79. Fungiid community on *Acropora* shingle on terrace at 25 ft.; north-west slope of Heron Reef.

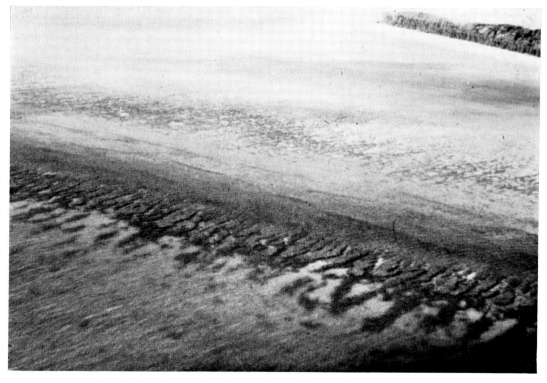

Fig. 80. Aerial view of northern reef front, Masthead Reef, showing spur-and-groove structure.

*113*

Because of their exposure to rough seas, the rim and reef front are constantly under attack. Very little fine sediment is retained on the rim's surface, but on many reefs extensive banks of shingle or coral gravel (generally composed of "sticks" of *Acropora*, 3–5 inches long) and considerable tracts of large boulders (niggerheads or negro heads; several inches to several yards in dimension) are found. Several authors have assumed that the shingle and boulder accumulations represent material torn from the reef front and slope and carried upward on to the rim during severe storm-wave activity. However, this assumption may be challenged. Boulder tracts and shingle banks are most poorly developed on the Shelf Edge reefs where wave attack is strongest and most persistent and where one would expect greatest destruction and accumulation of coarse reef material. Furthermore, where they do occur on such reefs (e.g., Tydeman and Stapleton Reefs in the Northern Region), their maximum development is on the western, leeward sides. By contrast, the Inner Shelf and Inner Marginal Shelf reefs support the largest boulder and shingle accumulations, many of which are on the leeward sides of the reefs. Frequently, the larger boulders have been sculptured above low-water mark into pillar-like masses (probably by the numerous boring lamellibranchs and by solution) that expand baseward into broad, irregular flanges which merge into the present reef surface. Smaller, loose boulders

may have been derived through the break-up of the larger pillars. The origin of the boulder tracts and shingle banks is most probably related to the destruction of the old, higher reef surface that was exposed after the last fall of sea level. Their occurrence on the present windward sides of reefs is not necessarily a reflection of present reef destruction but a consequence of the more intensive coral growth on those sides at the time of higher sea level. With subsequent exposure and erosion the less resistant materials (sands of the reef flat and smaller skeletal debris) were removed more readily and the stronger coral framework survived.

In cases where the accumulations occur on the leeward side the intensive coral growth of the previouphase was possibly the result of effective current activity rather than of surf action, and when erosion occurred at lower sea level, the leeward structure survived. The fact that such accumulations are greatest on the protected Inner Shelf reefs further supports the view of their residual rather than depositional origin. At the same time there is probably a minor contribution of shingle from the present coral. However the contribution of boulder material is almost certainly negligible. The bulk of this material when formed by present wave destruction probably moves down the reef slope. It is under the boulders of the rim that an abundant molluscan fauna is found, while large colonies of

Fig. 81. Distal end of spur-and-groove system grading on to submarine terrace at 15 ft.; floor of groove sand-covered; south-west side of Heron Island.

oysters encrust the boulders and numerous boring lamellibranchs infest them. Constant movement of the smaller boulders by wave action results in their grinding into the algal pavement, with consequent production of generally coarse sand and gravel, much of which is eventually swept down the reef front on to the terraces below.

## Reef flat

The *reef flat* extends backward from the algal rim and is divisible into three distinctive zones (Fig. 82) which are readily recognised in Fig. 83–85.

First, there is the *zone of living coral and coral pools*, in which dense populations of *Acropora*, *Pocillopora* and *Seriatopora* thrive in the protective lee of the algal rim and are nourished by the subdued surf and oceanic water that surges up the grooves and tunnels beneath the algal rim. The zone of living coral is extremely variable in width, ranging from 50 to 500 yards, but it is present on all reefs. In some its surface is encrusted to varying degrees by coralline algae, but around the pools where coral growth is most vigorous, algal encrustation is negligible. A common inhabitant of the coral pool is the black, long-spined echinoid *Diadema setosa*. The main corals include *Acropora hebes*, *A. pulchra*, *A. aspersa*, *Favites*, *Goniastraea*, *Goniopora*, *Seriatopora* *Pocillopora* and the red *Tubipora*.

The transition from the living coral to the *dead coral zone* is comparatively abrupt and is marked by a slight increase in the depth of the reef surface, as well as by a marked increase in the amount of sand. The massive brain corals—*Favia*, *Platygyra*, and *Lobophyllia*—are generally most common in this transition region between the two zones, and not as one might expect in the reef front where their greater strength would equip them well to resist destruction by wave forces. On many reefs the brain corals rise above the level of the adjacent fauna and form a discontinuous belt of rounded

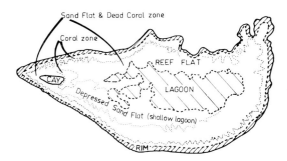

Fig. 82. Zonation of reef surface, illustrated by Heron Reef. (After MAXWELL et al., 1964).

clusters. In the dead coral zone the dead material consists largely of the broken branches of *Acropora* species from the adjoining living coral zone. This material is generally coated with brown algae. The zone becomes progressively more sandy as one proceeds across the reef flat, and it merges with the third zone, the sand flat.

Typical of the *sand flat* is the microatoll which is formed by one of several species of coral that grow radially in the horizontal plane and produce a flat-topped mass that is circular in outline or consists of several merging circles. The top of the microatoll is encrusted by calcareous algae and the living coral survives mainly around the margins and outer face. The coral *Porites* forms the compact, purple and brown microatolls which are possibly the most common. The blue *Heliopora* and grey *Goniopora* are also responsible for compact microatolls, while more open structures, generally yellow and pale green in colour, are produced by certain branching species. In addition to the microatolls, small clumps of coral are sparsely distributed over the sand flat and include *Acropora cuneata* and *Acropora hebes* as well as small massive forms such as *Goniastraea benhami*. The sand flat also supports a varied fauna of burrowing molluscs: *Conomurex luhanus* and *Strombus gibberulus*, the clam *Tridacna*, and abundant black beche-de-mer: *Holothuria*.

All three zones of the reef flat are characterised by a marked radial pattern of sand channels and discontinuous organic ridges, the orientation of which clearly reflects the direction of wave translation across the reef. Radial elements are most obvious on the smaller platform reefs such as Tryon, Hoskyn and Fairfax in Fig. 83, 85, 88, where wave action is strong across the entire flat.

In the case of Inner Shelf reefs where there is extensive development of boulder tracts, shingle banks and cays with rock formations, the reef flat may be covered by coarse sand and shingle, boulders and large slabs of transported cay and beach rock. Furthermore, the slightly higher, outer part of the flat may have a "cellular" zone of partly lithified material (reef rock) and sparse clumps of small coral, surviving on a predominantly sandy substrate. The cellular zone probably formed through cementation of the reef material before the old, dead reef surface was eroded away. During this interval, fresh water on the exposed surface would have taken carbonate into solution and reprecipitated it at deeper levels on diffusion with salt water. Generally, the zones of living coral, dead coral and sand flat that are so clearly defined on most reefs, cannot be distinguished on these high reefs.

*115*

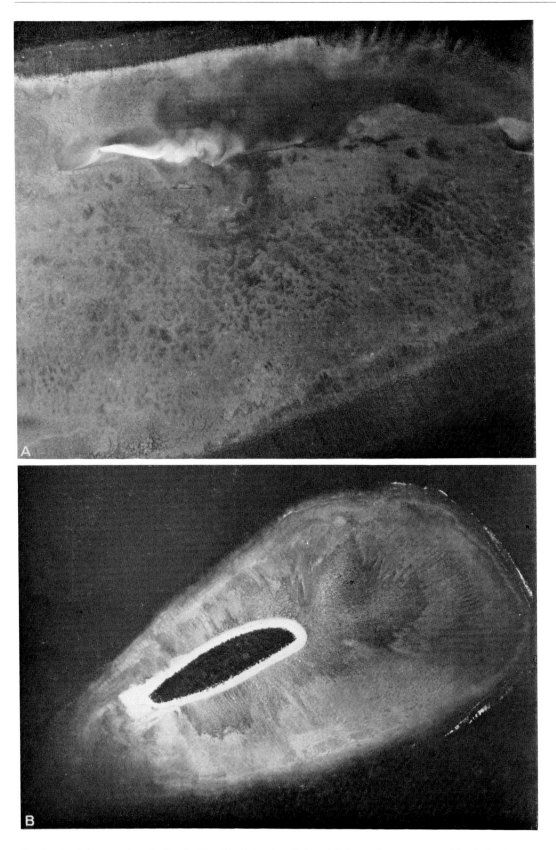

Fig. 83. Reef flat zonation. A. North West Reef showing slight axial depression, strong sand bank development on northern side and irregular coral distribution. B. Tryon Reef—aerial view of entire surface showing strong radial lineation of coral on northern and eastern flat, and increasing sand invasion in the south and west.

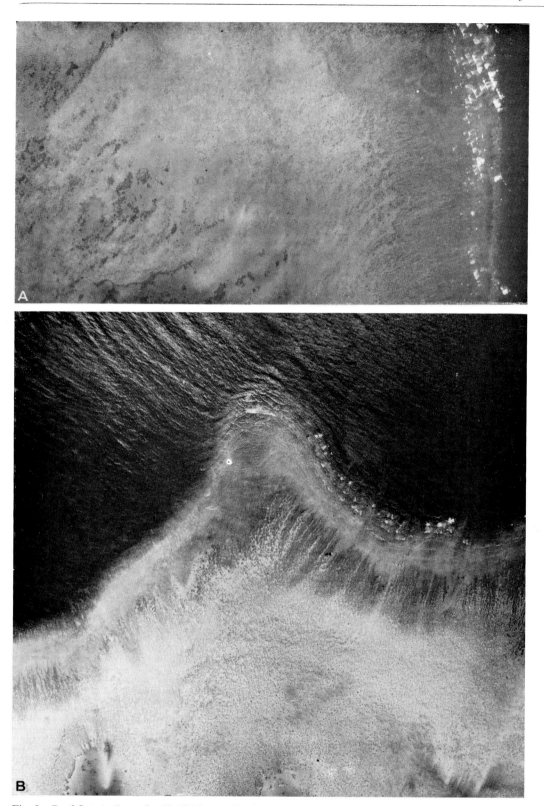

Fig. 84. Reef flat. A. Part of a Shelf-Edge reef in the Northern Region showing broad coral zone and sand flat and deeper back reef apron. B. Northern side of Heron Reef showing the wide reef flat extending from the rim to the lagoon; the radial lineation of the coral zone is normal to the refracted wave fronts that are evident, and parallel with the spur-and-groove structure of the reef edge; the lagoonal margin of the sand flat has stronger coral growth than the central part of the flat.

Fig. 85. Reef flat. A. Aerial view of part of Hoskyn Reef showing well differentiated coral zone, sand flat and sand cay; the strong radial pattern in the coral zone and the directions of wave fronts are clearly obvious. B. Lady Musgrave Reef showing the radial pattern in the coral zone and wave front directions.

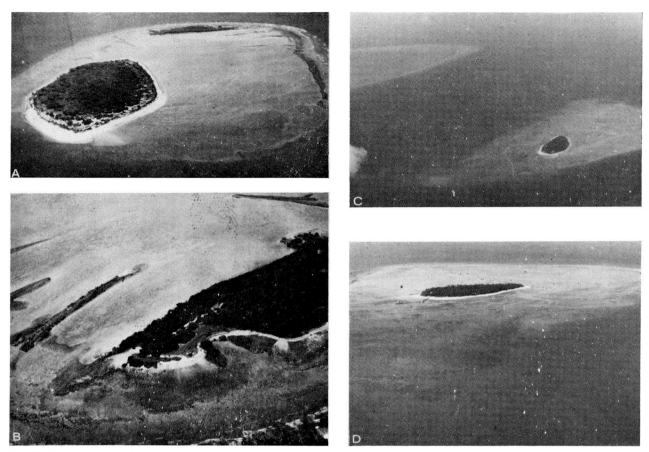

Fig. 86. Sand cays of Inner Shelf reefs, Central and Northern Regions, showing extensive sediment cover and paucity of coral on adjacent reef flats. A. Two Isles Reef with vegetated cays and shingle ridges. B. Closer view of smaller cay in A, from the south. C. Green Island and reef from the south-west. D. Green Island and reef from the south.

Fig. 87. Sand cays of Inner Shelf and Western Marginal Shelf reefs. A. Vegetated cays of Low Isles Reef, Central Region (mangrove dominant). B. Vegetated cay of Heron Reef (*Pisonia* dominant). C. Vegetated cays of Fairfax Reef (*Casuarina* dominant).

*119*

Fig. 88. Sand cays of the Capricorn-Bunker Complex. A. Vegetated cay of Masthead Reef. B. Barren cay on Fairfax Reef.

Fig. 89. Sand and shingle cays. A. Low Isles (smaller cay). B. Nymph Islet, mainly shingle. C. Mangroves growing on shingle, Low Isles Reef. D. Heron Island—sand cay.

Depending on the type of reef, as one proceeds further across the reef flat one may encounter (*1*) a sand cay or (*2*) the dead coral zone of the leeward flat, or (*3*) a lagoon or (*4*) the back-reef apron and foul ground which falls away to the leeward off-reef floor.

### Sand cay

Sand cays (Fig. 86–92) occur most commonly on the platform, elongate platform and lagoonal platform reefs at the inner edges of the leeward and windward sand flats. They are generally situated towards the more protected end of the reef. They never occur in the lagoon. Their formation depends on the convergence of opposing bodies of water.

Convergence of opposing water bodies can be caused by wave refraction around the reef and the approach from opposite directions of two main wave fronts, particularly when the reef tends to be elongate. Such a situation is illustrated in Fig. 83 where the refracted wave fronts can be seen sweeping across the flat towards the sand cay of Tryon Reef. Because the conditions which result in wave movement from several directions are those which also favour platform-reef growth, then it is not unexpected that sand cays are more commonly found on platform reefs, and rarely on the linear reefs. Another type of convergence is caused by tidal currents moving from opposite sides of the reef top towards the same opening in the reef rim, through which the water escapes as the tidal level outside the reef falls. Such currents may develop in any type of lagoonal reef where a water body of sufficient size can build up behind the rim. Thus cays of this origin are found on various reef types, but are less common than those formed by converging wave fronts. In both cases, the converging translatory waves or converging tidal currents lift sediment from the reef surface and carry it forward until water velocity is reduced abruptly in the area of convergence. The coarser material is then deposited. With low tide, the deposit is exposed to wind action that can result in the further building of dunes which ultimately stand emergent at high tide. Sand banks such as these (Fig. 106) may not survive unless they are stabilised by vegetation. Development of beach-rock also helps to preserve the sand cay.

Most emergent sand banks are invaded by bird populations early in their development and the appearance of grass (*Thuarea involuta*, and *Sporobolus virginicus*)

Fig. 90. Vegetation of cays. A. High *Pisonia* forest, North-West Island. B. *Casuarina* forest and low scrub and dry grass, Nymph Islet. C. Sparse weed and grass cover, Stapleton Reef.

*121*

Fig. 91. Carbonate rock formations. A. Beach rock on south-western side of Heron Island. B. Looking eastward along the Heron Island formation; uniform joint pattern and zonation into inner, central and seaward units are obvious. C. Old lithified reef surface on Nymph Reef; rock is strongly corroded; bedding is horizontal; rock surface is higher than that of Heron Reef. D. Beach rock on the southern side of Green Island showing the same uniform jointing and topographic zonation as is found at Heron Island.

is a natural consequence of the bird invasion. Further expansion of the flora occurs with the growth of forests of *Pisonia grandis* (the dominant species), *Ficus opposita*, *Pandanus tectorius*, *Pipturus argenteus*, *Casuarina equisetifolia*, *Scaevola sericea*, and *Messerschmidia argentea*. In the Northern Region of the Great Barrier Reef Province, some cays of the Inner Shelf reefs are bordered by comparatively large mangrove swamps in which the species *Rhizophora mucronata* (red mangrove) and *Avicennia officinalis* (white mangrove) are common In most cases the sand cay is assymetric in profile, with a steep windward face rising 10–12 ft. above the beach to the cay top which then slopes gradually leeward and merges with the leeward beach without marked change in gradient. Permanent, vegetated sand cays generally have beach rock formed in the lower intertidal zone on the windward side and, less frequently, on the leeward side. Extensive beach rock formations on Heron, Nymph and Green Islands are shown in Fig. 91. On some cays erosion has almost completely removed the beach rock, on others the sand cay has encroached

over the beach rock while in still others the beach rock appears to be forming and expanding. It has also been found on sand banks that are submerged at high tide, and on small, non-vegetated bird-infested shingle banks of the outer reefs.

Again, the Inner Shelf reefs are distinctive in their cay and rock development. Typical examples are Nymph Reef (Fig. 93, 94) and members of the Turtle Group in the Northern Region. In all cases, the reef flat is covered by shingle, boulders and rock slabs. Lithified remnants of the old reef flat are extensive, and form horizontally bedded platforms of rock consisting largely of *Acropora* sticks, large *Tridacna* valves and finer, sand-sized reef detritus. Second cycle material derived from the rock platforms is spread over the lower surfaces of the reef. The sand cay is flanked in part by the rock platform, in part by younger beach rock and in part by banks of shingle of various ages. The older, higher shingle is generally darkly stained and more corroded. Inside the shingle ridges, the main sand accumulation occurs. This is terraced and may have cay rock de-

Fig. 92. Beaches and spits. A. Aerial view from western end of Heron Island showing strong development of western sand spit beyond the beach rock formation; the spit has resulted from convergence of tidal currents and wave fronts. B. Large inter-tidal sand flat on the north-eastern side of Heron Island; this flat carries a thin algal veneer. C. Steep beach of the western spit, Heron Island, showing beach rock in the background.

Fig. 93. High reefs and islands. A. Shingle ridges of Nymph Islet, with coarse, dark shingle derived from disintegrating rock surface, occurring just above the low tide level. B. Close-up view of second cycle shingle of A. C. Orientation of *Acropora* shingle; long axes perpendicular to strand line; Nymph Islet. D. Succession of shingle ridges along the north-eastern side of Nymph Islet.

Fig. 94. Shingle and boulder developments of the Inner Shelf reefs. A. Large residual boulder bank on the northern margin of Grubb Reef; submerged at high tide. B. View along axis of the same bank showing heavy, corroded boulders and finer shingle. C. View along the leeward margin of bank showing small sand ridge on crest of bank and very shallow, barren, sandy reef flat to the right. D. View across the reef flat between the curved arms of the boulder bank, with shallow sand ridges in the central part of the flat.

veloped on its higher parts. The leeward side of the cay generally descends into a mangrove swamp. Mangroves are also extensive in the lower areas between the rock platforms and boulder tracts.

Where sand cays are not developed, the windward sand flat may be continuous with the leeward flat, and this is the case with the majority of platform and elongate platform reefs.

Features of similar appearance to the sand cay but of quite different origin and location are the *shingle bank* and its coarser equivalent the *boulder tract* (Fig. 93, 94). They occur on both the exposed, windward sections as well as the leeward sides of reefs.

*Boulder tracts* consist of heavy concentrations of very coarse reef material that is probably residual from an older, higher reef surface. The power of waves is greatly reduced after breaking at the reef margin and incapable of carrying the coarse boulders across the reef surface for any great distance. Boulder tracts are more common on the smaller, Inner Shelf reefs, where reduced wave action from several directions is less effective in removing the heavy boulder material.

The *shingle bank* is comparable in origin, but in this

case the detritus that is concentrated in low deposits consists of finer material, generally 2–6 inches in maximum dimension and composed mainly of fragments or "fingers" of the branching staghorn coral *Acropora* (Fig. 93). Because of its smaller size, the shingle may be carried some distance reefward by the incoming waves, and is sometimes deposited across the outer and middle reef flat. On the Inner Shelf reefs it is largely residual in origin, but the banks of the Shelf Edge reefs are probably being formed by the destruction of living *Acropora* and transportation of the shingle so derived. On Heron Reef (Fig. 67) shingle banks form long ridges distributed radially around the southeastern and eastern outer reef flat, where the most severe wave attack takes place, and on the less exposed western tip. On the adjacent One Tree Reef (Fig. 96) the shingle bank has risen above sea level and been vegetated and is now a permanent reef island. This shingle may have multiple origins. It is interesting to note that unlike the other islets of the Capricorn and Bunker groups, One Tree Islet is situated on the windward south-eastern corner of the reef, an area where sand banks would not survive. In the northern Swains

124

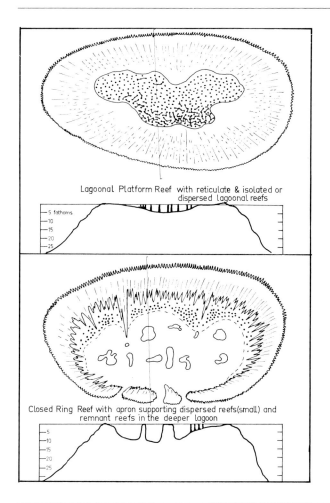

Lagoonal Platform Reef with reticulate & isolated or dispersed lagoonal reefs

Closed Ring Reef with apron supporting dispersed reefs(small) and remnant reefs in the deeper lagoon

Complex, Twin Cays Reef has two unvegetated, bird-infested shingle banks that are located on the two ends of a horse-shoe-shaped reef. They are the result of heavy wave action as well as strong tidal-current movement. In general, it may be said that, with the exception of the Inner Shelf reefs, shingle banks are found on both windward and leeward ends of reefs whereas sand cays form only on the leeward ends.

*Lagoon*

Where lagoons are developed as in the lagoonal platform reef and the ring and mesh reefs (Fig. 96–106), three situations are possible.

With the lagoonal platform reef there is an increase in gradient along the inner margin of the sand flat and the floor descends to depths of 15–20 ft. to form the lagoon. Lagoons of this type are comparatively shallow with simple margins (as illustrated in Fig. 95) and they contain small reefs which may be widely dispersed, as in Fig. 103B of Heron Reef, or they may be closely developed and connected to form a reticulate pattern such as that found in One Tree Reef shown on Fig.

Fig. 95 Plan and profile of two main types of reef, illustrating different lagoonal development.

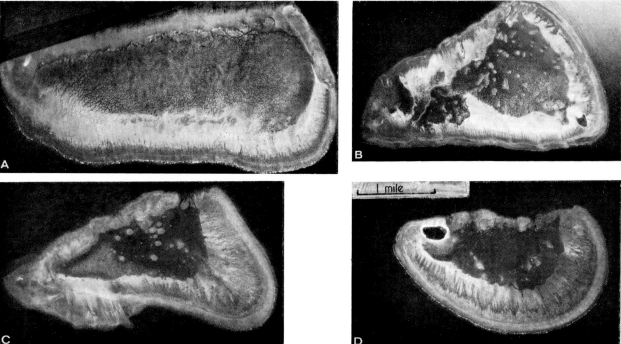

Fig. 96. Lagoons. A. Wistari Reef—lagoonal platform type; shallow lagoon with numerous reticulate reefs. B. One Tree Reef—lagoonal platform type; shallow lagoon with reticulate reefs and coarser remnant reefs. C. Boult Reef—closed ring type; deeper lagoon with marginal apron in the south-west, and remnant reefs in deeper part. D. Lady Musgrave Reef—closed ring type; deep lagoon with less numerous remnant and dispersed reefs.

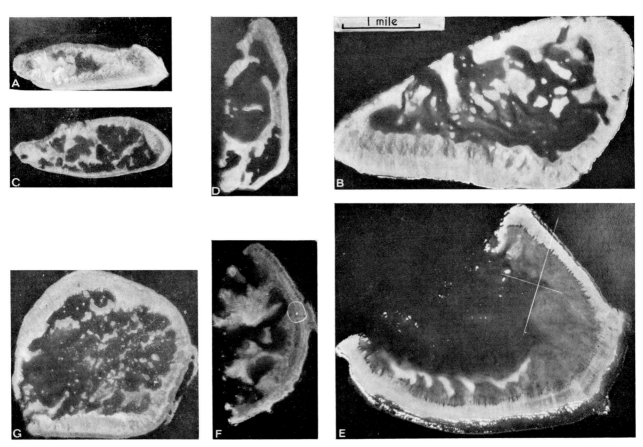

Fig. 97. Lagoons of Swains Reefs. A. Lagoonal platform reef—small, very shallow lagoon; Shelf Edge. B. Closed-mesh reef, inner side of Marginal Shelf, Swains Complex; strong scour channels and sediment banks through lagoon to breaks in reef margin; large remnant reefs. C. Closed-mesh reef, near outer edge of Swains Complex. D. Open mesh reef, adjacent to C. E. Open-ring reef at the most easterly corner of the Great Barrier Reef; strong back-reef apron and sand waves encroaching deep, open lagoon. F. Open-mesh reef, central part of Swains Complex; strong prong development; deep, narrow lagoonal channels. G. Closed-mesh reef, near western margin of Swains Complex; large lagoon, numerous remnant reefs.

103A, 96D. The small reefs of this type of lagoon are remarkably uniform in size, ranging from 20 to 40 ft. in diameter. On the leeward side, the lagoon floor abuts against the near-vertical, embayed face of colonial organisms which form the inner margin of a much-reduced sand flat or coral zone.

In the second situation—ring and mesh reefs (Fig. 95) —the lagoon may grade down rapidly from the windward sand flat, but more commonly, the third situation prevails where the lagoon drops off abruptly from the inner algal rim which is frequently present. Where the lagoon floor grades, as in the second case, the lagoon represents an enclosure of what was originally a gently sloping back-reef area, possibly even a back-reef apron, such as occurs behind cuspate, prong and composite apron reefs.

The third type represents a recurving of linear reef that has been exposed to similar hydrologic conditions on both sides so that the initial reef was symmetrical in its zonation about the reef axis, i.e., it has the zonal charac-

ter of an elongate platform reef, but it has grown subsequently in converging directions, resulting in the enclosure of off-reef floor, thereby producing a deep lagoon.

The two kinds of ring-reef lagoons are illustrated in Fig. 97b, 99. In both types, patch reefs may occur, which are larger and more variable in size and less numerous than the reticulate and dispersed patch reefs found in the lagoonal platform reef. In some cases their irregular size and distribution (Fig. 65C, 66B, G) are reminiscent of the submerged reefs that occur in the "foul ground" of certain back-reef areas, and it is quite possible that they represent the relics of foul ground that was surrounded by the converging ends of the ring or mesh reef. In other instances they appear to be the remnants of an old prong system that has degenerated as the lagoonal area was sealed off by marginal growth. Because of their appearance they have been termed *remnant reefs* (Fig. 104, 105). In the deeper type of ring reef lagoon, the lagoonal margin

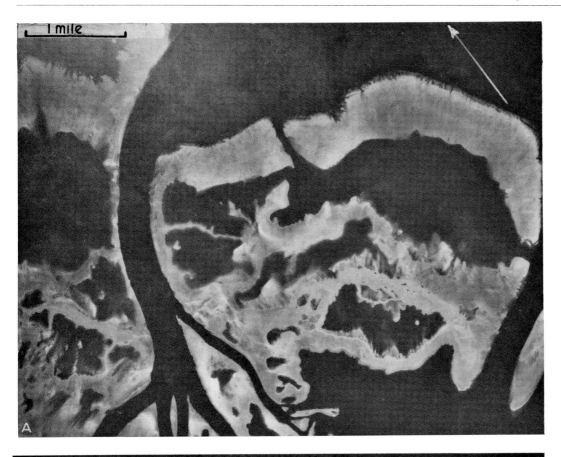

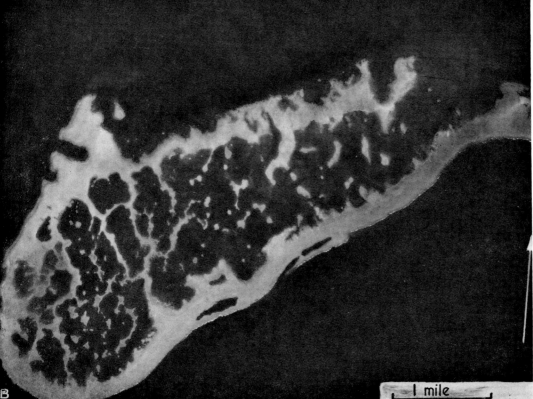

Fig. 98. Lagoons. A. "Hard-line" reefs of Pompey Complex, showing extensive and deep lagoonal development of composite, mesh, wall and plug reefs. B. Closed-mesh reef along the southern margin of the Pompey Complex, central part of Marginal Shelf; remnant reefs decrease north-eastward near the reef opening.

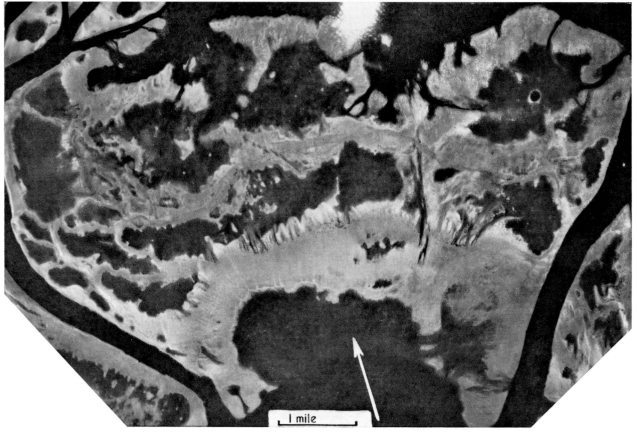

Fig. 99. Shelf-Edge reef development of the Pompey Complex showing diversity in lagoonal character.

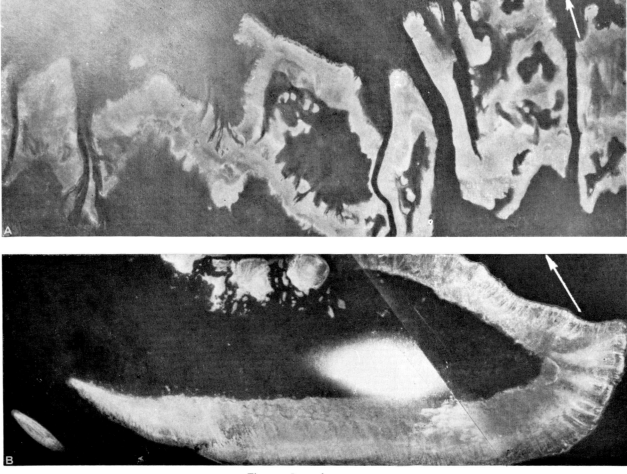

Fig. 100. Legend see p. 129.

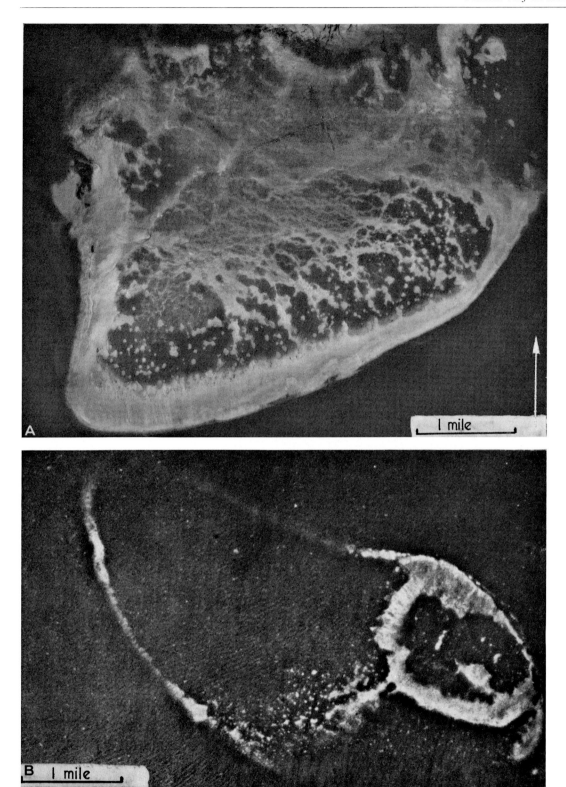

Fig. 101. Lagoons. A. Strongly reticulate lagoonal reef system in Big Stephens Reef, western side of Northern Pompey Complex. B. Resorbed reef, north-east of Townsville, showing numerous remnant reefs and exposed lagoon.

Fig. 100 (p. 128). Lagoons. A. "Hard-line" reefs of Pompey Complex showing deep lagoons with scoured margins and few lagoonal reefs; some lagoons reduced by expansion of reef flat. B. Cairns Reef, Inner Shelf of Northern Region; this is a composite-wall reef, disintegrating in the north-west; few lagoonal reefs; lagoon comparatively deep.

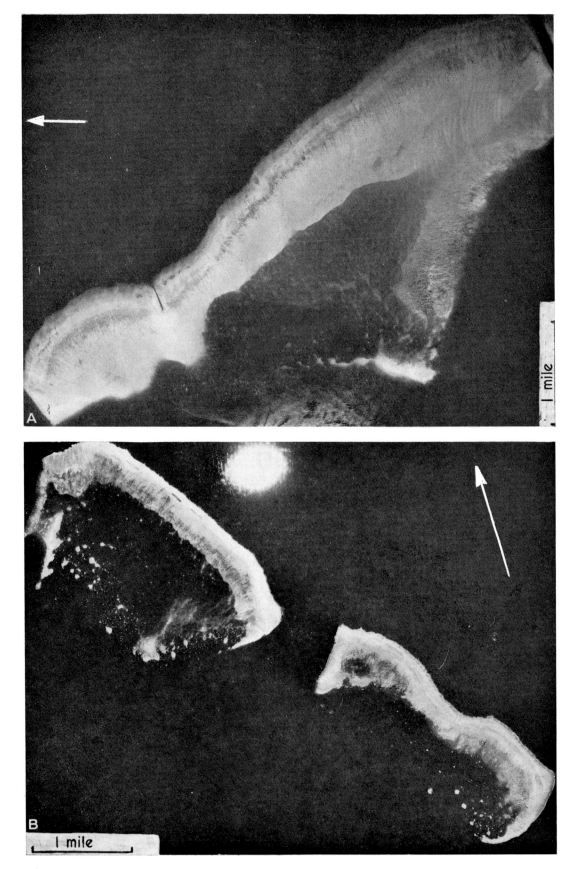

Fig. 102A, B. Wall (Ribbon) reef lagoons, Northern Region.

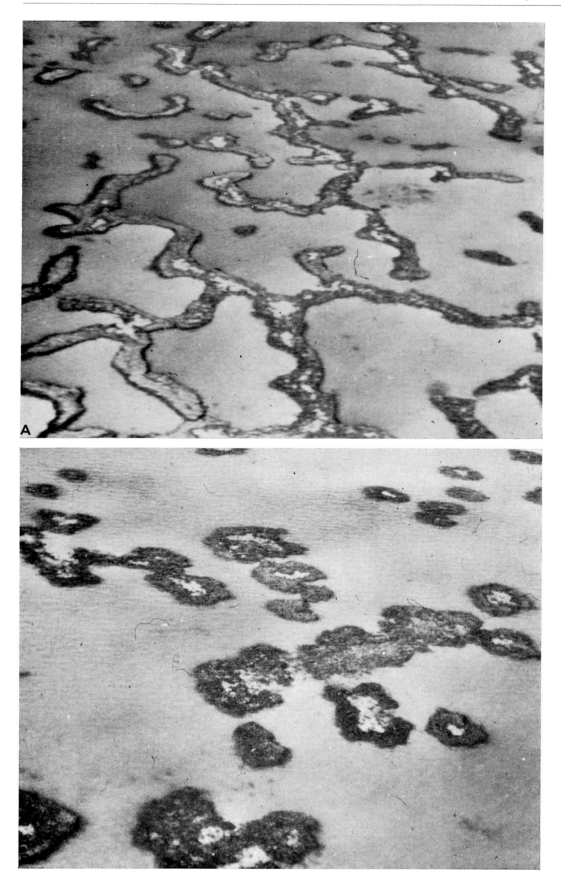

Fig. 103. Lagoonal Reefs. A. Reticulate reefs, One Tree Reef lagoon. B. Dispersed reefs, Heron Reef lagoon.

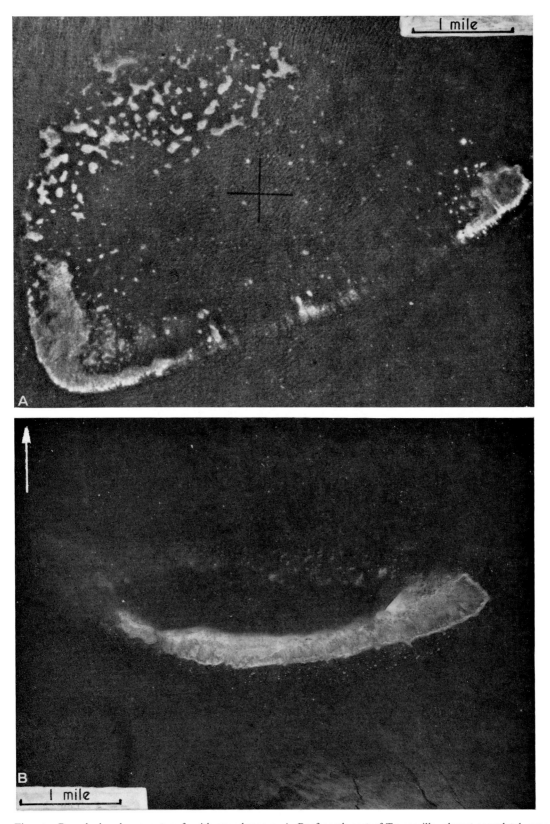

Fig. 104. Resorbed and remnant reefs with open lagoons. A. Reef north-east of Townsville, almost completely resorbed. B. Williamson Reef in the Northern Region showing resorbtion effects and submarine platform on which remnant reefs are situated.

may exhibit a reduced prong system similar to the spur-and-groove of the outer reef margin, and this, too, may be regarded as a relict from the time when the reef had not completed the enclosure of its back-reef area. Depths in both types of ring reef lagoon exceed 40 ft. and in the deeper one, they may even reach 80 ft.

### Open back-reef

With reefs of the linear group—wall, cuspate and prong—the sand flat gradually descends into the *open back-reef zone* which may be extremely wide (2 miles) and which supports large, scattered reef clumps that

dominant after a platform or lagoonal platform reef has reached an advanced stage of growth. In such cases a composite reef form results in which an open or closed ring lagoon has developed after the main radial expansion of the platform has ceased. Alternatively, a section of a ring or mesh reef may initiate an outward growth that will progress towards a platform stage and may even develop the shallow central lagoon of this type. In other cases, it becomes difficult to determine whether a reef is an elongate platform type or a wall reef in its early stage of growth. Generally, the difference in the two types is reflected in size, the elongate platform tending to be much larger than the young wall reef.

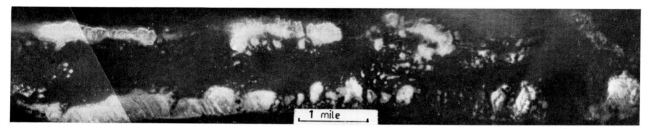

Fig. 105. Osterland Reef, Northern Region, showing resorbtion effects.

are always submerged (Fig. 63, 102). At low tide they may be covered by less than 3 ft. of water and are a real hazard for navigators, who have labelled such back reef areas "foul ground". The submerged reef clumps are referred to commonly as "bombies" by reef fishermen. Foul ground such as this generally ends abruptly where the floor descends steeply into the off-reef floor. In the Northern Region large, shallow, back-reef areas are formed, e.g., Corbett Reef (Fig. 106) and Grubb Reef (Fig. 49), which are characterised by extensive sand bank development along their inner margins and very irregular distribution of remnant reefs near the open water.

### REEF SHAPES AND ORIENTATION

### Shape differentiation and transition

When the outlines of the many reefs of the Great Barrier Reef Province are drawn and compared, it becomes evident that the classification based on shapes does accommodate the majority of reefs, although there are those that are transitional or even composite in character. The same factors that induce cuspation and prong development in the linear reefs may become

### Basic control factors

Reef growth and consequently reef shape depend on the initial establishment of reef organisms and their subsequent nourishment in an environment where bathymetric conditions will permit expansion. Factors controlling expansion include the availability of nutrient and carbonate-rich water, oxygenation, the suitability of temperature and light penetration. These, in turn, depend on latitude, bathymetry and water circulation. Nutrients are more abundant in the zones of high organic productivity, zones which have access to waters rising from greater depths where nutrient elements have been replenished. The same water, with its low temperature—high salinity range, is favourable to carbonate build-up. A continental shelf or island margin may provide the bathymetric situation for adequate light penetration, while the adjacent slope may help to induce upward movement of deeper water. Thus the shelf on the western sides of the oceans, subjected to the warm surface currents moving out from the equatorial zone and the deeper, westward moving water pushed up along its slope, is ideal for reef colonization. Another possible factor is vulcanicity and this may exert a significant influence, particularly in the oceanic province. Submarine vulcanicity introduces

*133*

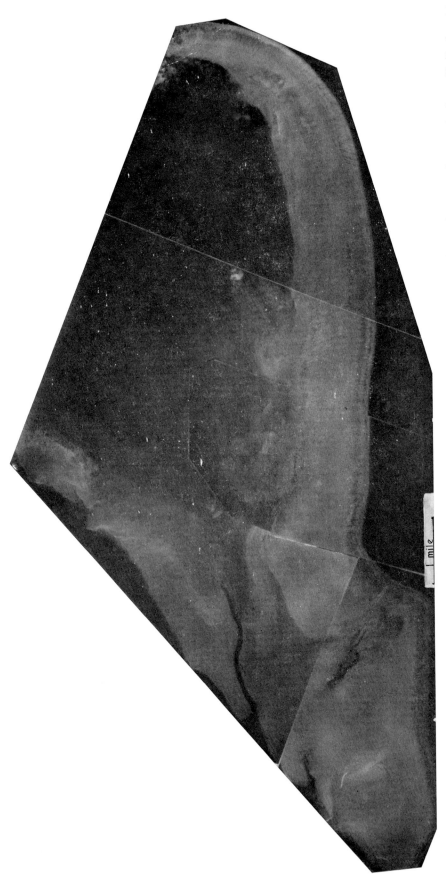

Fig. 106. Corbett Reef. One of the largest reefs of the province, Corbett occurs to the north-east of Princess Charlotte Bay and extends eastward across the Inner Shelf, almost to the Shelf-Edge reefs. It has a large, sediment covered surface, with negligible coral fauna. The lagoonal area is shallow and sparsely populated. Sand banks and sand waves are found along its northern margin.

carbon dioxide into sea water, thus permitting greater carbonate solubility. At the same time, the basic lava and ash deposited above sea level provide a considerable lime source on weathering. Thus the association of reefs with volcanic islands and with shelves where mainland vulcanicity has been active, may not be entirely fortuitous.

### Shelf edge and steep slope

Along the Queensland Shelf, the general pattern of surface currents is augmented by the westward trend of the tidal cycle, the unusually high tidal range and the persistent easterly swell that builds up under the influence of the South-East Trade Winds. Thus, the zone of vigorous reef growth is found along those parts of the Shelf Edge bordering comparatively steep slopes where the main surface current flow is westward and south-westward, where tidal range is high and tidal currents strong. Reefs on sections of the shelf facing steep slopes are so aligned that their maximum surface is exposed to the open sea, to the westward moving currents and to the oceanic swell that rises under the prevailing South-East Trades. Their eastward expansion is restricted by the deepening floor of the continental slope, their westward expansion by the partial insulation of the back-reef areas from open oceanic water. Such conditions are conducive to elongation of the reefs parallel with the shelf margin and normal to the main directions of water movement. However, this directional growth is arrested as the ends of adjacent reefs approach one another and the passages between successive reefs are narrowed. Continued growth can occur only where bathymetric and hydrologic conditions are favourable and this results in the backward projection of the reef ends. They extend marginally along the current-swept passages as cuspate projections. In areas of high tidal range where cuspate growth has resulted in the narrowing and attenuation of inter-reef passages, the tidal forces build up greater pressures and currents penetrate further into the back-reef area, between, around and beyond the cuspations. One result of deeper penetration is the invigoration of back-reef growth in those parts newly exposed to current activity. Such back-reef growth is manifested in the recurving of cuspations or the extension of prongs and the final enclosure of lagoons.

The manner of growth is dependent on both the nature of the current movement (its magnitude and persistence), and the relief of the adjacent sea floor. In some cases, the frontal attack on the linear reef by oceanic waves results in considerable production and transport of reef detritus towards the back-reef. Shallow talus aprons form and provide suitable sites for colonisation by reef organisms when subsequent changes in the current pattern permit the entry of oceanic water into these areas. In other cases, the sea floor is sufficiently shallow to allow extensions of the reef to develop wherever hydrologic factors are favourable. The sea floor of the Swains Complex rarely exceeds 32 fathoms, a depth that is so constant as to suggest that the floor is an ancient wave-cut terrace. It is also conceivable that many of the ridges and depressions on the terrace are relics of older reefs and erosion channels formed at times of lower sea level, as well as features of tectonic origin. Whatever the cause—depositional, erosional or tectonic—the topographic character of the floor surrounding the reefs exerts a significant influence on the shapes that the reefs assume. The spur-and-groove structure which characterises the reef front of all linear reefs reflects the manner in which reef-building organisms seek maximum advantage from the nutrient, carbonate-rich oceanic waters. Once irregularities develop in the reef front, they are accentuated by certain species that populate the distal ends, species presumably that thrive in the vigorous surf conditions that characterise this zone. Proliferation of such species leads to spur-and-groove structure which continues to expand seaward until excessive depth prevents further advance. A balance is then achieved between organic growth, wave destruction and faunal density.

The same trends are seen in the back-reef area when favourable hydrologic conditions develop as a result of tidal-current activity. The prongs and cusps are manifestations of this trend. However, the density of such projections never approaches that of the reef front, and the greater variations in depth and hydrologic conditions result in more irregular development of the projections. Thus we find that prongs in the back-reef area (Fig. 63) are generally represented by a few large projections and many smaller ones. As the prongs grow they too interfere with the current pattern and bring good water into previously unsuitable parts of the back-reef where new growth is initiated. Ultimately a state of equilibrium should be approached whereby the density of the reef fauna is in balance with the available supply of nutrient and carbonate, and with the rate of destruction by waves. If bathymetry prevents such a balance being reached through its restriction on outward growth, one might expect a tendency for denser population of the lagoon and inner parts of the reef flat. This appears to have occurred in the outer reefs of the Pompey Complex (Fig. 47, 61, 99, 100).

In addition to its influence on the elaboration of linear reefs, current activity in areas of high tidal range is probably responsible also for the development of the rather unusual reef shapes that have been called the *plug* type (Fig. 61A, 98A, 100A). Growth of the plug reef occurs along its two sides, parallel with the tidal current, and it expands towards the back-reef zone. As it enlarges, there is increased interference with water movement and consequent diversion. The leeward end of the reef responds with intricate growth patterns that presumably take advantage of the diverted flows of incoming oceanic water. On the falling tide, outflow of the back-reef water is hindered by the plug reef. This has two important effects. The first is extreme turbulence or "overfall" (Fig. 44) which results in the scouring of the floor and the removal of almost all sediment. The second effect is the retention of apparently depleted water in the back-reef area and this seems to prevent reef colonization of a zone, 5–15 miles wide, immediately behind the Shelf Edge reefs. The zone is recognised by fishermen as "dead water" because it supports a sparse fish population, possibly as a result of the nutrient depletion suggested above.

Linear reefs and accessory plug reefs attain their best development where the shelf is bordered by a steep slope and where surface currents, nearby divergence and upwelling contribute to the vigorous growth of reef faunas. Under optimum conditions, a near-continuous wall is formed, broken by the narrow passages which lead to the back-reef complexities and barren zones already described. Under different bathymetric and hydrologic conditions, such as those described below, other reef types become dominant.

### Shelf Edge with gentle slope

There are large sections of the shelf where the adjacent slope has gentle gradients, the oceanic water circulation has been modified by the Coral Sea Platform and the areas of current divergence are remote. On such sections the reef population is more dispersed, possibly because hydrologic conditions are inadequate to support the density of growth found opposite the steeper slopes. Linear reef types are subdued and widely spaced. Cuspation begins before much elongation has occurred, and the recurving cusps frequently enclose reef flat rather than off-reef floor, resulting in shallow ring or composite apron reefs. The forms so produced have many of the features of the platform reef: the outline is circular, tear-shaped or oval, and the central structure is usually too shallow to form a lagoon. However, the cuspate ends seldom merge with each other and a re-entrant may extend into the reef centre. Furthermore, the leeward arm of the reef is narrower than the main, windward section. Because of the lower reef density along the shelf edge, movement of oceanic water into the province is not hindered by narrow passages, neither are tidal currents of extreme velocity generated. There is a more uniform distribution of oceanic water and the response to this is a uniform distribution of similar, rather simple reefs. Plug reefs are not found and intricate back-reef patterns are rare. Behind the outer series of scattered reefs, which are mainly short, cuspate masses with thickened windward sections and occasional small open lagoons or re-entrants, the most common types are the small platform, elongate platform and lagoonal platform reefs. The platform reefs are oval or tear-shaped, with maximum dimension ranging from $\frac{3}{4}$ to $1\frac{1}{4}$ miles. Elongate platform reefs range from 1 to 2 miles in length and from $\frac{1}{3}$ to $\frac{2}{3}$ miles in width. Lagoonal platform reefs have similar dimensions and their lagoons generally occupy less than a quarter of their surface area. In the Swains Complex and in the Central Region of the Great Barrier Reef Province, many of these reefs are elongated in the same direction, a direction that is consistent with the flow of tidal currents and normal to the prevailing wind and swell. Furthermore, many are aligned in belts, most of which are parallel with the directional elongation of the individual reefs. When outlined on the hydrographic charts, the belts have the appearance of a "mega" spur-and-groove structure, and it might be inferred that their orientation is controlled by the same factors that result in normal spur-and-groove growth, viz. by currents, availability of oceanic water, strong frontal wave action and bathymetry.

### Inner edge of the Marginal Shelf

Separating the main region of reef development from the continental mass is the Inner Shelf, a zone that has been defined in Chapter 4 as extending shorewards from the 20-fathom line. In the Northern Region, it is extremely narrow and in the south it expands for more than 30 miles and is joined by the Southern Shelf Embayment which reaches a maximum width of 55 miles. Both the Inner Shelf proper and the Shelf Embayment are areas of predominantly terrigenous sedimentation,

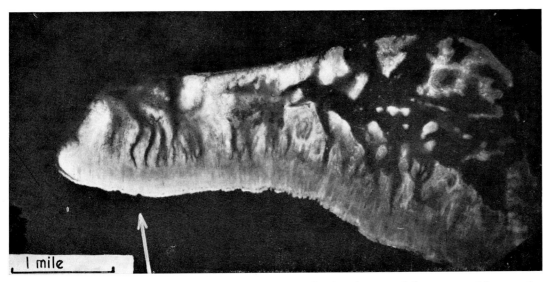

Fig. 107. Big Sandy Reef, western margin of Swains Complex, showing the strong influence exerted by westerly winds and waves on reef orientation and structure; the deep scour channels and lagoonal apron are typical of these western reefs.

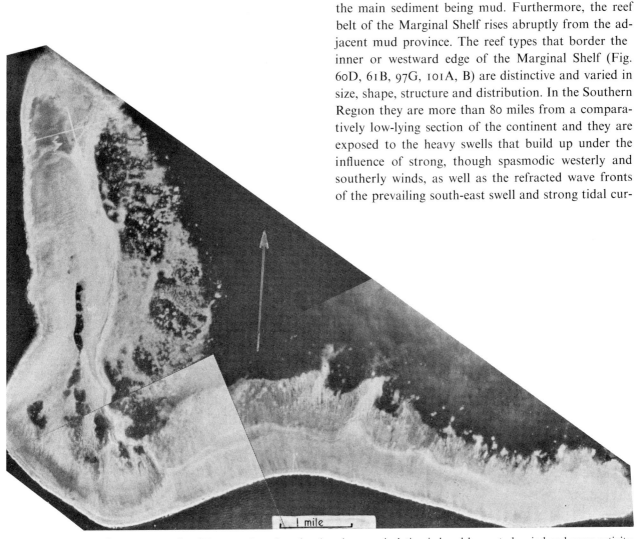

the main sediment being mud. Furthermore, the reef belt of the Marginal Shelf rises abruptly from the adjacent mud province. The reef types that border the inner or westward edge of the Marginal Shelf (Fig. 60D, 61B, 97G, 101A, B) are distinctive and varied in size, shape, structure and distribution. In the Southern Region they are more than 80 miles from a comparatively low-lying section of the continent and they are exposed to the heavy swells that build up under the influence of strong, though spasmodic westerly and southerly winds, as well as the refracted wave fronts of the prevailing south-east swell and strong tidal cur-

Fig. 108. Denton Reef, western margin of Pompey Complex, showing sharp geniculation induced by westerly wind and wave activity and tidal currents and southerly wind influence; strong back-reef development behind small platform lagoon.

*137*

rents. Further north where the land mass has higher, coastal mountains and the shelf is narrower, the westerly and southerly influences are reduced and the inner border of the Marginal Shelf is less distinctive in its reef character. However, along the entire inner margin, the reefs reflect the varying and decreasing influence of the easterly and south-easterly factors that dominate the Shelf Edge reefs (Fig. 113).

The strong, though spasmodic westerly and southerly winds blow for 3–4 months of the year, mainly in the winter, and they generate heavy seas on the Inner Shelf. The inner Marginal Shelf reefs have responded to this influence in a manner that one might have expected: elongation normal to the wind-wave direction, some cuspation, strong boulder residuals on the western and southern rims, and the spreading of backreef aprons. In addition, the eastern sides of the reefs still come under the somewhat reduced influence of the South-East Trades and, depending on the effectiveness of the Shelf Edge reefs in decreasing the penetration and wave roughness of the oceanic water, the eastern sides may show varying degrees and types of growth. Furthermore, tidal currents of considerable velocity are developed in the Southern and Central Regions where tidal range is large, and they exert a third powerful influence on the manner of reef development.

In areas where the westerly influence is dominant and the south-easterly factor negligible, such as that where Big Sandy Reef is found (Fig. 107), wall, prong and composite apron types are most common. Modification of these may be caused by strong tidal currents which foster growth parallel with the current flow. A common result of such growth is the geniculate or L-shaped linear reef. Geniculation is encouraged further when the new reef arm is so aligned as to encounter wave and wind fronts that also stimulate reef growth. A situation of this kind is found in Denton Reef, illustrated in Fig. 108. Continued growth of reefs under two-directional wind influence as well as that of tidal currents may result in a form such as that assumed by Herald's Prong No. 2 Reef (Fig. 109). It is a composite reef in which the parent is an elongated ring reef that has developed an additional "dead" lagoon of the platform type on its western arm, and a northern prong extension which has allowed a back-reef apron to form. Heavy boulder concentrations on the western rim are evidence of the westerly dominance, which also resulted in initial cuspation that was ultimately turned by

Fig. 109. Herald's Prong No. 2 Reef, western margin of Swains Complex, showing composite features of wall, lagoonal platform and prong reefs.

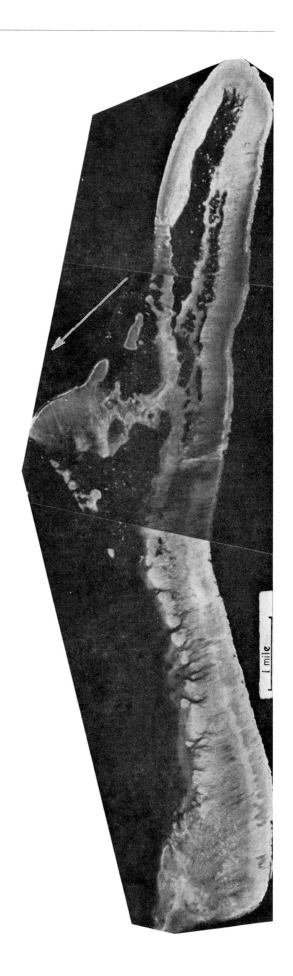

1 mile

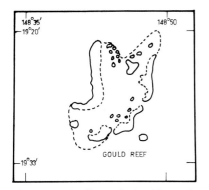

Fig. 110. Outline of Gould Reef, Central Region, western side of Marginal Shelf.

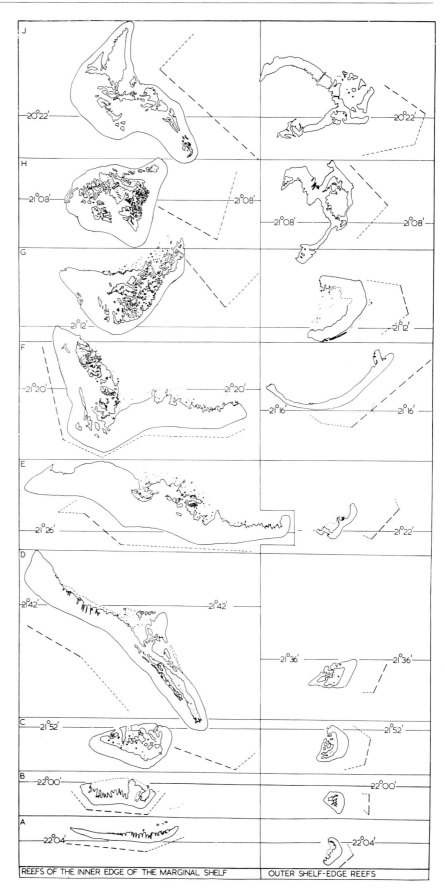

Fig. 111. Orientation of reef axes of the inner and outer edges of the Marginal Shelf of the Southern Region. Heavy dashed lines indicate main axes, lighter dashed lines indicate minor axes.

REEFS OF THE INNER EDGE OF THE MARGINAL SHELF | OUTER SHELF-EDGE REEFS

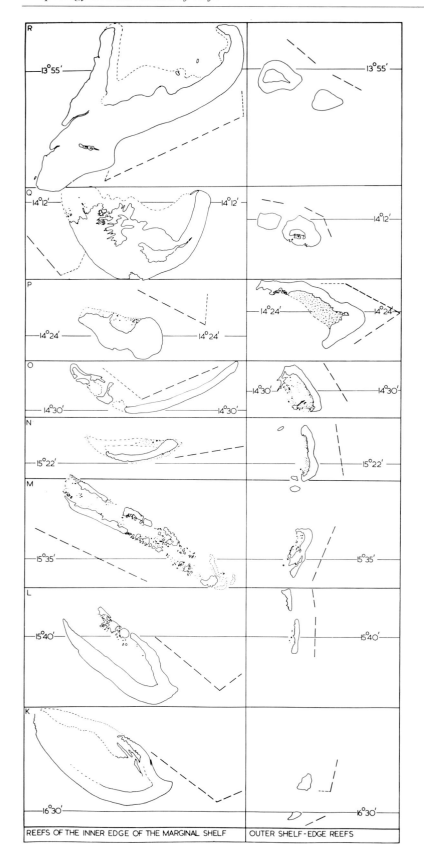

Fig. 112. Orientation of reef axes for reefs of the Central and Northern Regions.

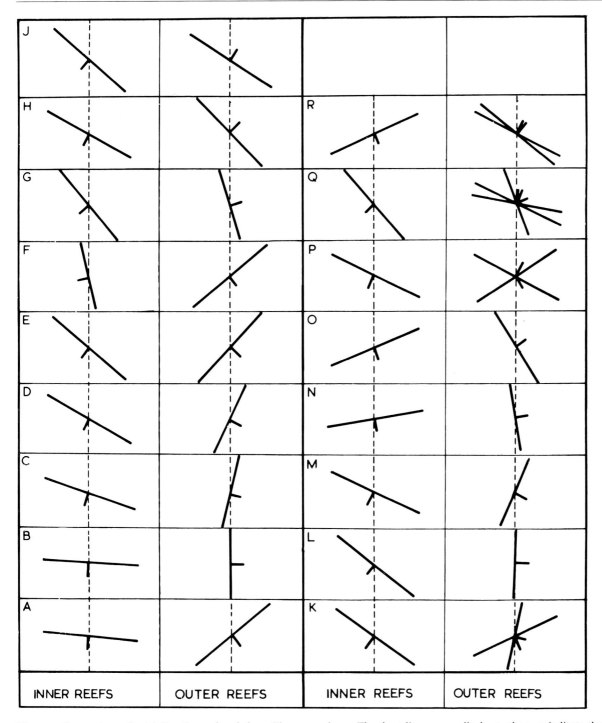

Fig. 113. Comparison of axial directions of reefs from Fig. 111 and 112. The short lines perpendicular to the axes indicate the direction of growth of the reef fronts.

the weak though persistent South-East Trade influence. Closing of the ring lagoon under this influence deprived the western reef flat of its open-water supply and led to its degeneration into a "dead" lagoon. Further expansion of the reef was favoured by the shallow bathymetry to the north and resulted in prong development and accompanying apron deposition. One might specu-late that a future growth stage will witness the re-curving of the northern prong and enclosure of the apron to form a mesh lagoon.

On the southern part of the Marginal Shelf, the inner edge has long, narrow wall and prong reefs such as that illustrated in Fig. 60D in which the axis is east–west. The direction of elongation is the result of southerly wind influence in part, but the dominating controls appear to be the original east–west bottom topography and the strong tidal currents.

Further north, where the westerly influence is weaker, rather symmetrical ring reefs have formed, such as Old Reef and Gould Reef illustrated in Fig. 110. Their main growth surfaces appear to be on the south-west and south, where the algal rims and reef flats are extremely wide and boulders are large and numerous. Their lagoons are also wide and very deep. Reduced spur-and-groove or prong structure is typical of the lagoonal margin. In the case of Gould Reef, there is evidence to suggest that it formed by the coalescence of individual wall and cuspate reefs and not by the cuspation and recurving of a single reef.

The changing influence of the various factors involved in reef growth and orientation is readily observed in the Inner Marginal reefs and in the reefs to the east of them. Related dominance of winds from west, south and south-east as well as the tidal-current effect are well demonstrated by the western Swains and Pompey Complexes which have been illustrated in Fig. 111 and by the reefs of the Northern Region in Fig. 112. In the first figure many of the reefs are geniculate and cuspate. If the axes of the main arms of the reefs are plotted (Fig. 113) then one can observe a marked difference in the orientation of the inner and outer reefs and an almost progressive rotation of the axial directions as one moves from south to north. The degree of rotation is generally greater for the western Marginal Shelf reefs than for those of the central Marginal Shelf where less severe wind influences and more variable tidal forces permit greater opportunity for varied growth patterns. When the directional character and the rotation of the inner Marginal Shelf reefs are considered it would seem that from south to north there is a decreasing westerly influence and an increasing south-east to easterly influence. The former may be due to closer proximity of higher land as one moves north and consequently a smaller fetch for the westerly winds. Throughout, there seems to be a recognisable, though minor, southerly influence which becomes dominant in the very south. North of latitude 19°S, both westerly and south-easterly winds are less persistent. The South-East Trades subside as the high pressure belt moves southward in the summer and, in the winter, westerly winds which reach considerable strength in the south have little effect on the narrow, northern shelf. On the other hand a strong, northern component may exert itself in the summer in the northern region and this may account for some of the rotation of the reefs as one moves northward. However,

other factors such as tidal currents, bathymetry, narrowing of the shelf and increasing reef density tend to obscure this effect.

*Inner Shelf and Near Shore reefs*

The Inner Shelf and Near Shore reefs include the small, isolated platform reefs that occur between the shore-line and the main reefs of the Marginal Shelf, as well as the numerous diverse reefs that border continental islands and the main coastal strip.

The Inner Shelf reefs are comparatively rare except in the Northern Region. Perhaps the best known and certainly the most studied of these is Low Isles Reef (Fig. 114) which was the site of the Great Barrier Reef Expedition of 1928 (YONGE et al., 1928) and of later expeditions (STEPHENSON and WELLS, 1956). Fig. 87A is an aerial view of Low Isles Reef and a map of the main physiographic zones based on that of STEPHENSON et al. (1931) is presented in Fig. 114. Low Isles Reef, and other platform reefs of the Northern Region, are distinctive in their physiographic character as well as in their faunal and floral constitution. The major zones defined in the early part of this chapter are less easily recognised because of the exaggerated development of some, the suppression of others and the extensive distribution of sediment.

From the map in Fig. 114, nine natural divisions are evident on the reef surface. They include the outer shingle rampart which rises from sea level to a height of 2–4 ft. and then descends abruptly on the lee side to the reef flat. The inner shingle rampart is similar in size and shape to the outer rampart with which it tends to be parallel, but it consists of a more coherent mass of "coral fingers" embedded in sand and mud matrix. The boulder tract is the third zone and is strongly developed only on the western leeward margin. Within the shelter of the boulder tract lies the main sand cay which rises to a height of 16 ft. The remainder of the reef surface virtually corresponds to the reef flat, but five distinctive zones may be recognised within it. The mangrove swamp occupies the eastern quarter and is flanked on the west by a grassy, sandy mangrove park of equivalent size in which there are fewer, smaller trees. The western half of the reef surface contains the shallow sand flat and its southern neighbour the *Thalamita* flat which has numerous slabs and boulders strewn through the sand. Between the reef flat and the outer rampart there is a line of narrow pools, not more than 18 inches in depth, and these are referred to as moat. Superficially, there seems to be little resemblance be-

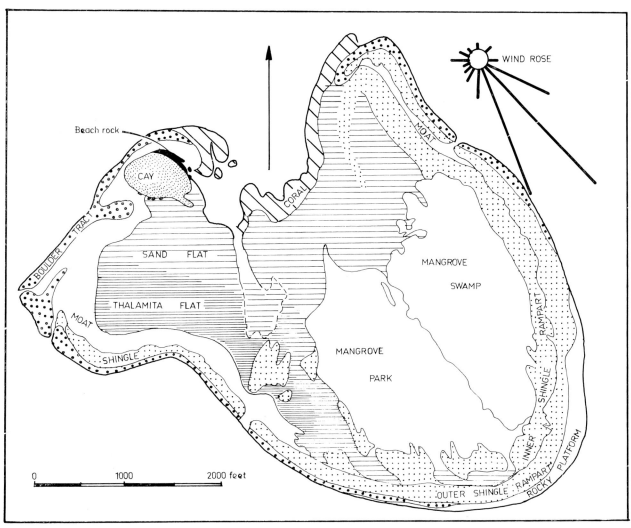

Fig. 114. Zonation of Low Isles Reef.

tween the surface zonation of the Inner Shelf platform reefs and their equivalents of the Marginal Shelf. However closer inspection of Low Isles Reef reveals a poorly developed algal rim which is covered for the most part by the outer rampart. Except on the northern margin, no living coral zone exists, nor do a recognisable dead coral zone and lagoon. Much of the reef flat is covered by boulders and slabs of honeycombed reef rock, presumably derived from an older reef surface during a phase of intensive erosion when the consolidated, older material was exposed. The material of the boulder tract contains fewer slabs of honeycombed rock and a higher proportion of large, broken coral heads and shingle. Its origin is probably similar to that of the rock slabs.

The total character of the Inner Shelf platform reefs is suggestive of incomplete erosion of an older reef surface and suppression of subsequent coral growth. The location of coarse rock slabs in the lee of the finer

shingle banks and the restriction of the main boulder tract to the western margin of the reef are not consistent with the pattern found on most other reefs, nor with the present forces that are operating in the area. The reasons for the anomalous features of these reefs are found in their protected location and in the extensive occurrence of plant life. It seems logical to assume that reef surfaces had reached the higher sea level prior to the 10-ft. drop that brought it to its present stand. Furthermore, it is very probable that in this phase of growth, the reefs did develop the main zones: algal rim, living coral and dead coral zones, and sand flat. The extremely mountainous nature of the adjacent mainland would have resulted in the same proximity of the reefs to the shoreline as prevails today, and the coastal vegetation, particularly mangroves would have had access to them. With lowering of sea level the surface organisms died through dessication. However erosion of the dead material apparently was

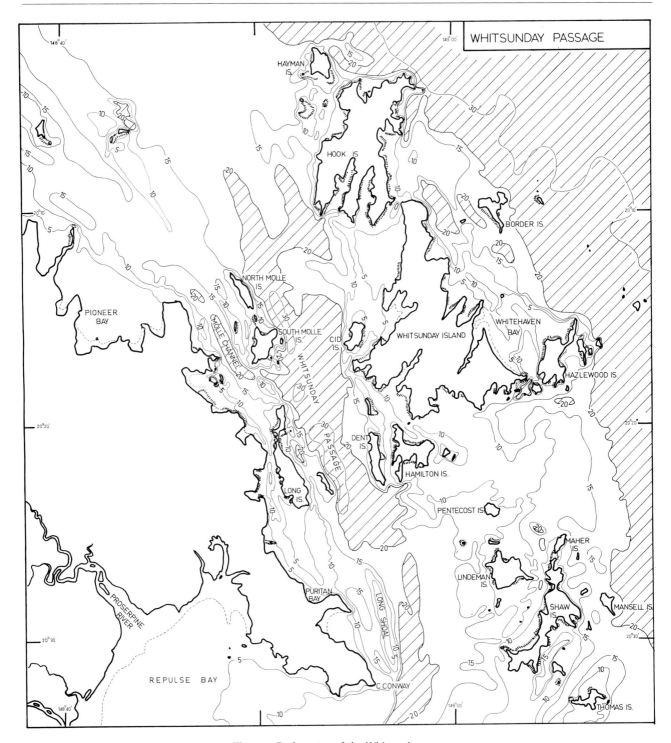

Fig. 115. Bathymetry of the Whitsunday area.

impeded by the surface vegetation and by the protection afforded by the mountainous mainland and the outer reefs. Such factors were not effective on the Marginal Shelf where the reefs were rapidly planed down and re-populated as the surface detritus was swept away by strong wave and current action. With the Inner Shelf platform reefs, wave attack was insufficient to destroy and remove much of the old reef surface, part of which had been lithified. Furthermore, the excessive sediment derived from the old surface spread across the reef and inhibited re-population by coral. Coarser detritus from the old surface contributed to the shingle banks, while larger residual masses formed the boulder tract.

As the ramparts formed, the reef flat was afforded even greater protection, and in turn, the mangrove vegetation expanded giving further protection to the flat. The inner rampart possibly represents the initial adjustment of this kind to the falling sea level. But with further regression, surrounding depths decreased and the reef was able to expand marginally. Increased surface erosion provided a greater shingle supply and so the second or outer rampart developed. The boulder tract in the west represents a residual deposit of this later erosion and its coarser size seems to have resulted from the greater abundance of compact, coral heads in the west.

In summary then, it may be observed that the Inner Shelf reefs are mainly platform types modified by the excessive sediment that has prevented re-population of the decayed reef surface and prolonged the exposure of reef rock which in other reefs has long since been covered by a faunal veneer. Another consequence of the surface protection and the mangrove–*Thalassia* invasion is the production of extensive areas of humic-carbonate mud, a material that is absent from the other reefs.

The Near Shore reefs include a wide variety that may be recognised as both fringing and barrier types in terms of their back reef character. They are extremely rare in the Southern Region where the great width of the shelf retards the influx of undepleted oceanic water. In the Central Region the Near Shore reef is more common. Numerous reefs border the islands of the Whitsunday–Cumberland Group and northward from this group, they become increasingly abundant (Fig. 117). Their distribution and density, as with other reefs, depend on the availability of suitable water and aeration, and we find their best development along shores where the shelf is less than 30 miles wide, and along shores which are bordered by deep channels, swept by strong tidal currents, exposed to heavy surf action or facing wide openings in the Marginal Shelf Zone of reefs. In the Whitsunday Group (Fig. 115, 118, 119) deep channels and strong tidal currents appear to be the controlling factors. The deep channels (Fig. 114) through which fast tidal currents flow, occur to the west of the group and reefs are more common on this leeward side than they are on the ocean side. Current activity which results from the large tidal range

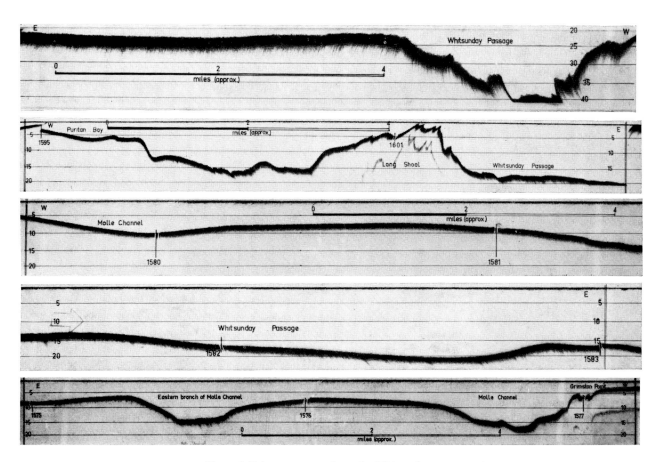

Fig. 116. Echogram traces from the Whitsunday area.

145

Fig. 117. Fringing reefs. A. Eastern side of Holbourne Island. B. Eastern side of Long Island.

in the area (15–20 ft.) is more effective than surf and wave action.

Many of the reefs of the Northern Region favour headlands, presumably because of greater exposure to wave attack. On the other hand, numerous reefs are found in the more protected bays and even along the edges of small river deltas. Whatever their location, one can generally account for reef growth in terms of channel proximity, current activity, exposure to wave attack, or effective penetration of oceanic water through the Marginal Shelf zone. There appear to be few restrictive influences that can be ascribed to the adjacent land mass. Influx of muddy sediment from rivers appears to have little or no effect on reef growth, as is

evidenced by the occurrence of comparatively large reefs at the mouth of the Mowbray River, shown in Fig. 62B. The only recorded destruction of Near Shore reefs is that of Stone Island Reef (HEDLEY, 1925) off Bowen, and in this case lowered salinity through excessive cyclonic rainfall (35.7 inches in 8 days at Bowen, 55 inches in 3 days at Mackay) was the cause. Re-population of the reef has since occurred. As with other reef zones, the reefs of the Near Shore Zone are dependent on adequate supplies of oceanic water, and it is proximity to the open ocean that determines the extent of their development.

The Near Shore reefs exist in a vigorous and changing environment. Wave action is augmented by ground swell, current rips develop where reefs and sand banks restrict the back flow of water from the surf zone, tidal and rip current patterns change as the wave fronts move in from new directions and as off-shore deposition is modified to accommodate the new wave attack. The dynamic barrier of stream discharge also varies seasonally, and in so doing, modifies the Near Shore water movement accordingly. In the mid-summer, the zone is subjected to the king tides as perigee and perihelion correspond, leading to abnormally deep immersion and long periods of excessive exposure and consequent dessication. The summer also witnesses the heavy monsoonal rains and cyclonic deluges of the Northern Region, resulting in reduced surface salinities. These factors all act unfavourably on reef growth and the Near Shore reefs reflect this influence in the irregular pattern of their development and in the unusual constitution of their faunas. Many of the reefs possess the normal zonation of the Marginal Shelf reefs, but others are characterised by extensive algal growth, both calcareous and non-calcareous, and by the prolific occurrence of molluscs and other organisms that normally contribute little to the main structure of reefs. Reef detritus is frequently more abundant on the surfaces of these reefs, and helps to inhibit organic growth.

### THE REEF PROVINCE AND ITS SUBDIVISION

#### *Subdivision*

The Darwinian influence is clearly reflected in all attempts at subdivision of the Great Barrier Reef Province. In their efforts to conform with Darwin's concept of reef ontogeny, and in particular of the barrier reef, authors have developed zonal subdivisions which are largely meridional in direction (JUKES, 1847; SPENDER, 1930; YONGE. 1930; STEERS, 1938; FAIRBRIDGE, 1950). The simplest schemes recognise the main "barrier" system (reefs of the Marginal Shelf), in the same sense as Darwin defined his barrier reef, and in so doing, recognition of a Great Barrier Reef "lagoon" (the Inner Shelf) was inevitable. The application of both terms—"lagoon" and "barrier"—to this vast province was unfortunate. In the first instance, individual reefs within the province have lagoons of the character and dimension of those which Darwin defined, lagoons formed by the enclosure of oceanic floor or island margins. Secondly the Inner Shelf which has been termed "lagoon" is largely non-carbonate, non-

Fig. 118. Fringing reefs bordering Long Island, Whitsunday Group.

reefal in character. Thirdly the size and depth of this enormous expanse are hardly consistent with the scale of lagoons of reefs. Usage of the term "barrier" is equally unfortunate, since the inner reefs of the Marginal Shelf actually face shoreward instead of seaward, and in the sense of Darwin's definition they are more truly barriers to the Shelf Edge reefs and vice versa. Later workers refined the early, simple zonation (SPENDER, 1930; STEERS, 1938; FAIRBRIDGE, 1950) and recognised three reef zones and two inter-reef belts: the fringing reefs, inner channel, inner reefs, outer channel and outer barrier, illustrated in Fig. 121.
While this zonation may be usefully applied to parts of the province, there are implicit in its structure two

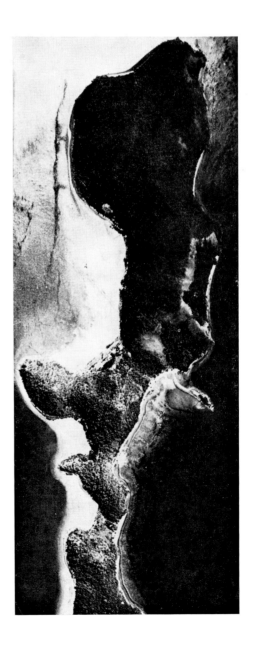

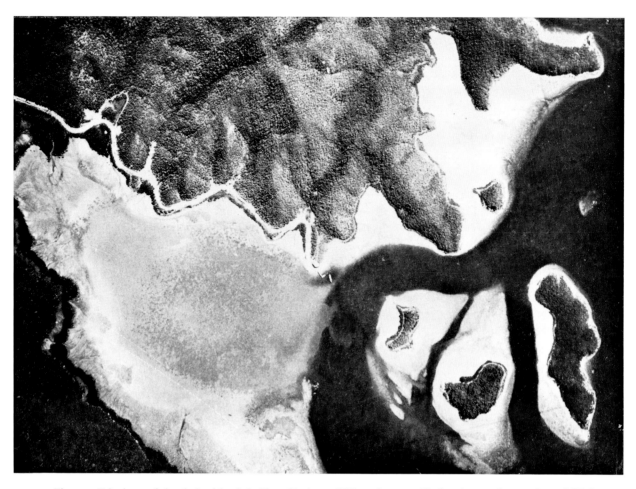

Fig. 119. Fringing reefs bordering islands in Shute Harbour, Whitsunday area. Shallow bay to the west is mud-filled.

features that may be challenged. The first perpetuates the assumption that the outer reefs are of true "barrier" type and the second implies that the inner reefs divide the shelf axially into two channels of comparable character, an implication which cannot be substantiated for the greater part of the shelf. The inner reefs of this zonation are, in fact, the inner reefs of the Marginal Shelf and the area between them and the Shelf Edge reefs varies greatly in width, depth and reef density. Where the Shelf Edge reefs are so close to each other as to restrict oceanic circulation of the back-reef area, which is the case in part of the Northern Region and in the Pompey Complex of the Southern Region, a comparatively wide, barren zone is found, and this may correspond to the outer channel. However, in the Central Region and the Swains Complex, Shelf Edge reefs are dispersed, oceanic circulation is not impeded, no barren zone forms and consequently no outer channel can be recognised.

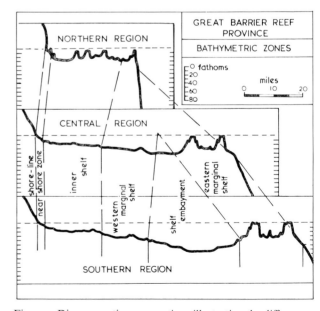

Fig. 120. Diagrammatic cross sections illustrating the differences in character of the three regions of the province.

148

Fig. 121. Map of the southern part of the Northern Region showing reef distribution in the "outer channel".

In the present work, the province has been divided into the three regions, defined in Chapter 4, viz: Northern—from latitude 10°S to 16°S; Central—froin 16°S to 21°S; Southern—from 21°S to 24°S. The regional division is based on the bathymetry (Fig. 120) which shows an overall increase in depth as one progresses southward, and on the patterns of reef distribution which are quite distinctive for each region. In addition, the shelf is zoned in a semi-meridional manner, according to the distribution of reef and non-reef areas. Six zones are recognised in each of the three regions, viz: Near-Shore and Inner Shelf reefs, Barren Inner Shelf, Inner Marginal reefs, Marginal dispersed reefs and Shelf Edge reefs.

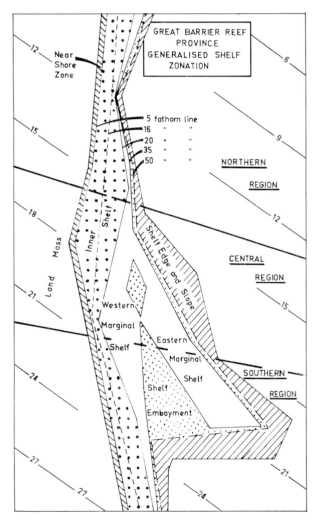

Fig. 122. Diagrammatic representation of the division and zonation of the Great Reef Province.

## Regions and zones

The mosaic of zones and regions illustrated in Fig. 122 provides a convenient basis for analysis of the province and for examination of the causes of different types of reef development and distribution. Throughout this work, it has been emphasized that the nature of individual reef development and the manner and density of reef distribution depend on the inter-relationship of several factors that are so different in their origin and in their influence. Such an observation is best substantiated by an examination of the regional and zonal differentiation of the province. The present topographic character of the continental shelf has developed in response to initial tectonic forces that warped, fractured and adjusted the crustal relief, to erosional and depositional processes that tended to subdue this relief, to the inherent differences in the composition of the crustal rocks, and to the varied organic reaction to the substrate, bathymetry and hydrology of the region. The variable width of the shelf is perhaps the most obvious feature that can be ascribed to tectonic factors, since neither erosional nor organic processes can account for the enormous depth changes that occur beyond the Shelf Edge. The restricted distribution of continental islands, the location of high coastal mountains, subsurface basement trends and the exposure of older metamorphic complexes on the adjacent mainland are further evidence of the tectonic influence. Because of its shape and its position relative to the rest of the South-West Pacific, the Queensland Shelf is subjected to hydrological influences that vary widely in their intensity along the length and breadth of this region. Furthermore, these influences are dependent on latitude, on tidal behaviour and on oceanic circulation patterns. The narrow part of the shelf faces the deep Coral Sea Basin across which moves the Trade Wind Drift. Divergence of the broad surface current occurs in the Coral Sea and one arm flows southward as the East Australian Current, the other flows westward towards Cape York Peninsula and then sweeps northward. This flow encounters the shelf near latitude 16°S, and it is north of this point that the near-continuous line of Shelf Edge reefs is developed. It might be inferred that the dense growth along the Northern Shelf results from the influx of carbonate-rich water that has risen from deeper layers of the Coral Sea in the zone of divergence of the Trade Wind Drift. This water would be warmed as it moved northward along the Shelf Edge and would attain carbonate saturations conducive to intensive lime secretion by organisms. Behind the outer reefs of the Northern Region, oceanic inflow is restricted and a barren zone extends leeward for 2–10 miles, a zone that is sparsely populated by small reefs and submerged reefal shoals. These grade westward into larger reef masses that face the Inner Shelf waters which flow southward under summer monsoonal influence and northward under the Trade Wind influence in winter and spring. Because of the narrow width of the shelf, the restrictive effect of the outer reefs on oceanic inflow is less than it is in part of the Southern Region where the shelf is ten times as wide. Beyond the western edge of the Marginal Shelf reefs, the Inner Shelf varies considerably in width, depth and reef population: there is an overall increase in depth and in reef abundance towards the north and a decrease in shelf width in the same direction. The Inner Shelf reefs are separated from the Near Shore reefs by a very narrow passage that is generally floored with terrigenous muds and intermixed carbonates. Thus the Northern Region has a strong line of outer reefs which tend to deplete the immediate back-reef area, but the inner Marginal Shelf, Inner Shelf and Near Shore Zones are so near the rich oceanic waters that reef populations of high density exist and almost overlap.

From latitude 16°S to 21°S, the reefs become progressively more dispersed until there are almost none along the Shelf Edge. In these latitudes three important changes occur. Firstly, the shelf is situated to the west of the large Coral Sea Platform, which supports an extensive reef province. Secondly, the main oceanic flow is southward near the shelf, after passing westward through the Coral Sea Platform reefs. Thirdly, the adjacent Queensland Trench is shallower and the continental slope has a gentler gradient. Thus, the carbonate-rich water from the Coral Sea Divergence travels much further than that of the northern branch, with the result that it has greater opportunity for mixing, and furthermore it passes through a reef province where it could well be depleted. The gentle gradient of the continental slope reduces the possibility of upflow of cooler water to the shelf reefs, and the southward direction of the East Australian Current permits less penetration of the shelf by oceanic waters. As a result, Shelf Edge reefs are sparsely developed, no restriction is imposed by them on the inflow of water into the back-reef area, no recognisable barren zone develops, and the inner reefs of the Marginal Shelf grow in all directions, tending to form lagoonal platform and ring reefs. One consequence of the increased shelf width is the disappearance of Inner Shelf reefs; this may also be related to the increasing depth as one moves southward. Near Shore reefs persist but in decreasing numbers. Thus, the Central Region has an undifferentiated Marginal Shelf zone of reefs, a widening Inner Shelf reefless zone and a declining Near Shore reef zone. It is an impoverished region that has resulted from poor oceanic supply due to unfavourable bathymetric conditions to the east, unfavourable current directions and excessive width.

Between latitudes 21°S and 24°S, the shelf widens to its maximum, the slope steepens and the East Australian Current sweeps over its eastern margin. In response to these better conditions, a strong system of Shelf Edge reefs develops for a large section of the region, back-reef depletion results in a wide barren zone (5–15 miles) and inner Marginal Shelf reefs become more abundant and face the wide expanse of the Inner Shelf and Shelf Embayment. No reefs grow on the Inner Shelf because of the great distance to the open ocean and also because of rapidly increasing depths to the south. Near Shore reefs are absent for the same reasons. Thus, the Southern Region is characterised for the most part by an outer reef zone, a barren zone, an inner Marginal Shelf reef zone and a wide, barren Inner Shelf and Near Shore zone. On the southern end of the Marginal Shelf, reefs are more dispersed and this seems to be related to the decreasing gradient of the adjacent continental slope. However, Shelf Edge reefs persist, but the barren zone of the Marginal Shelf disappears. In the very southern part of the Southern Region, the shelf narrows abruptly, and two reef groups are found: the Capricorn Group which extends in two westward lines and the Bunker Group which is a system of dispersed Shelf Edge reefs. An interesting aspect of these southern groups is the bottom ridge that appears to rise from the 32-fathom line and can be traced from Lady Elliot Island, northward through the Capricorn Group to latitude 21°S. The ridge is the site of the Bunker reefs and eastern Capricorn reefs. North of the Capricorn Group, large, submerged reefal shoals are found on the ridge and they become progressively smaller and are replaced by bryozoan accumulations and finally by quartzose sands as the ridge disappears near latitude 21°S. The ridge may represent an old shore-line feature or an ancient system of barrier islands which subsequently provided suitable locations for invasion by reef organisms. In the north where reefal shoals decline to bryozoan accumulations, the distance from open oceanic water is probably too great to permit survival of other reef organisms. The Capricorn reefs are similarly situated on ridges but their orientation is approximately east–west. Bathymetric analysis of the shelf suggests that the pre-Recent course of the Fitzroy River was through this area and the Capricorn ridges may well represent the relict levees of the ancient delta.

*151*

# Chapter 7 | Biological observations

A reef originates when a colonial organism invades an area, becomes attached to the sea floor and commences to secrete its carbonate skeleton, thereby ensuring its own survival against the physical forces of the aqueous environment and providing a protective structure for other organisms that are less well equipped to withstand these forces. In the present seas, the spawning and growth habits of corals result in their being the main group responsible for the initiation of reefs. Coral planulae are free swimming for periods ranging from several days to a few weeks, and in the event of their settling on clean, hard substrate, skeletal secretion begins and the coral colony may increase at the rate of 75% per annum. SAVILLE-KENT (1893) has emphasised that not all colonies develop into reefs and he suggested that a determining factor in reef formation is the accumulation and cementation of organic detritus within the colony thereby reinforcing the living organic structure and at the same time providing a stable foundation for continued organic expansion. Saville-Kent further suggested that consolidation of organic detritus could occur only in water of optimum salinity, carbonate saturation and temperature such as is found on the tropical shelves.

As the young reef colony develops it grows surfaceward, availing itself of better light penetration, warmer temperatures, and more effective oxygenation. Calcareous algae which also require these conditions, encrust the coral and reef detritus in the surface waters and contribute to the strength of the reef by forming a tough, resistant mantle that prevents destruction of the young colony as it rises into the zone of wave action. Molluscs, echinoderms, foraminifera, crustaceans and non-calcareous algae proliferate under the protection of the more resistant organisms. Because upward growth is limited by exposure at low tide level, further expansion of the organic community must be outwards and it is around the reef front, particularly in the spur-and-groove system, that most prolific coral growth occurs.

As the reef enlarges, it exerts an increasingly effective control on water circulation over and around itself, such that hydrologic zonation results in which specific zones favour particular assemblages of organisms. Broadly, the hydrologic zones are: (*1*) deep, off-reef water which circulates rapidly but not violently, under the influence of tidal flow and back-wash from the reef edge; (*2*) the surf zone at the reef front and algal rim, where warm, enriched oceanic water is vigorously aerated before sweeping across the flat or returning down the reef slope; (*3*) the shallow reef flat waters which fluctuate from depths of several inches at low tide to 10–20 ft. at high tide, and which are subject to varying degrees of wind ruffling and wave translation from the surf zone, and greater temperature variations; (*4*) lagoonal waters which are more protected, more static than those of the other zones.

Such diversity of water conditions is reflected in the marked differences between the various faunal groups that flourish in the particular zones. Coral and calcareous algae are the dominant components in reef faunas. Corals favour the reef front, immediately below the surf zone, and the area behind the algal rim which is swept by reduced surf. Calcareous algae inhabit two zones. The encrusting red algae, *Lithothamnion* and related genera, attain their maximum development in the surf zone. *Halimeda*, the most common green alga, thrives best in the reef front and on the outer reef flat. Whereas *Lithothamnion* prefers the unprotected surf zone, *Halimeda* and coral seek the benefits of surf water which has lost its energy on the algal rim and moves less violently across the reef flat or down the reef front. The manner of expansion of the reef depends then on the extent to which the main organic groups can develop.

## Corals

For coral growth, the main requirements are adequate food, oxygen for respiration, carbonate for skeletal secretion and temperatures conducive to normal physiological function. Corals are carnivorous organisms that feed on the minute animals ensnared in their tentacles, and they reject vegetable matter.

Oxygen is derived directly from the aerated surface waters, but in addition, the zooxanthellae contained in the polyps release oxygen in the course of photosynthesis and this is available to the coral. The association of these minute plants with the coral is an interesting one, and one which is mutually beneficial. The coral provides both protection and nutrient for the zooxanthellae, while the latter through their assimilation of carbon dioxide and release of oxygen, assist the respiratory process of coral. Furthermore, their assimilation of carbon dioxide prevents acidification of the immediate environment of the coral and this may well influence the manner and degree of secretion of skeletal carbonate.

The various coralline species have their own favoured zones within the reef complex, and in order to examine their distribution one might first consider the main forms in some convenient, systematic grouping. YONGE (1930, pp. 59–66) used shape as a basis for grouping the various species, and his method is adopted in the present analysis. Six main categories may be recognised, viz: (*1*) branching corals; (*2*) brain corals; (*3*)platy corals; (*4*) encrusting corals; (*5*) mushroom corals; (*6*) miscellaneous forms. The total number of genera and subgenera recorded from the Great Barrier Reef Province (WELLS, 1955) is 60 of which 57 are scleractinians and 3 are alcyonarian. Total species approach 350.

*Branching corals*

Branching corals (Fig. 123, 124, 125) are perhaps the most abundant species on the reef, reaching their maximum development in the living coral zone behind the algal rim and on the reef front. *Acropora* is the main genus. *A. hyacinthus*, the large dish-shaped form, is typical of the lower reef front and $2\frac{1}{2}$ fathom terrace. *A. palifera* is the encrusting, sheet-like form that is abundant on the outer reef flat as well as on the reef front. *A. pulchra* also occurs high on the reef front but is more common on the outer flat. It is characterised by the tufted, clump-like shape which it assumes and

Fig. 123. *Acropora* species on the south-western slope of Heron Reef at depths of 10–15 ft. (*A. hyacinthus*, *A. pulchra* and *Montipora*).

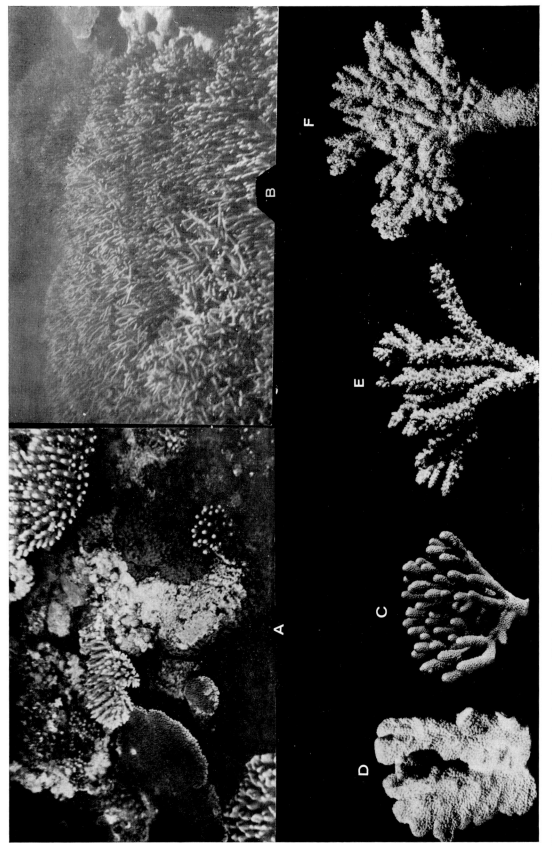

Fig. 124. *Acropora* species. A. Pickersgill Reef slope, with *A. hyacinthus, A. humilis* and soft coral. B. Heron Reef slope, 18–20 ft. – *A. pulchra* and *Montipora*. C. Close-up of *A. humilis*. D. *A. palifera*. E. *A. delicatula*. F. *A. decipiens.*

Fig. 125. A. *Pocillopora.* B. *Seriatopora.* C. Fauna on the edge of Stapleton Reef - mainly *Pocillopora, Goniastrea, Millepora tenera* and *Acropora.* D. Fauna adjacent to C - *Pocillopora, Millepora, Favia,* meandrine coral, and *Acropora.* E. *Platygyra* and *Tridacna crocea* on reef flat (coral zone) of Heron Reef.

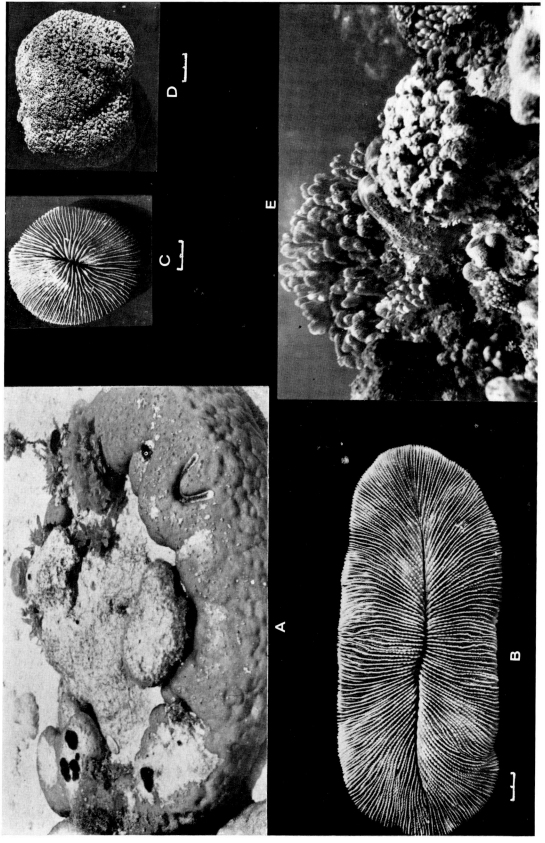

Fig. 126. A. *Porites* microatoll, sand flat, Heron Reef. B. Large fungiid coral, Stapleton Reef. C. *Fungia fungites* from reef front, Heron Reef. D. *Tubipora musica* from old beach rock surface, northern part of Swains Complex (Twin Cays Reef). E. *Millepora*-reef edge, Stapleton Reef.

by its slender buff-coloured branches with their pale blue tips. Typical of the reef flat are *A. squamosa* and *A. humilis* which are both cyathiform in shape and have short, stubby branches. *A. hebes* and *A. brueggemanni* are other inhabitants of the reef flat where they form microatolls. *A. decipiens* has strong, robust branches that spread closely along the reef surface, particularly on the top of the spurs. *A. delicatula* favours the side walls of the spurs and depressions in the reef front, where it develops as small bushy colonies consisting of thin, fragile branches.

The other members of this group are generally less robust in their structure and smaller in size. *Pocillopora* flourishes in the pools of the living coral zone behind the algal rim, but also occurs on the reef flat, reef front and the lagoonal margin. *P. bulbosa*, the main species, is a fragile, yellowish brown and pink, bushy-shaped form, with numerous, close fine branches. *Seriatopora* is an even more delicately constructed coral with numerous dichotomous branches that are generally brown. It occurs mainly on the reef slope and in the grooves, below the level of severe wave action. Another

branching coral that is more robust than the former two genera, but possibly less common is *Stylophora*. It, too, occurs mainly below the wave zone, on the reef slope. *Psammocora*, a small, brown coral of similar structure, flourishes both on the reef flat and on the reef slope. *Euphyllia* is perhaps the largest and strongest of this group of finer, branching corals and it also favours the reef slope.

*Brain corals*

Brain corals or meandrine corals (Fig. 125, 126, 127) are massive, rounded structures of great strength. Their lack of projecting branches makes them resistant to wave attack and one might expect to find them dominant in the surf zone of the reef front. This, in fact, is not the case. While some do occur on the reef front, they are subordinate to the main *Acropora* population. Their main area of growth is the middle and inner reef flat where they form rounded clusters or flat microatolls. *Favia* is a common type and consists of a rounded mass, the surface of which is pitted by small, uni-

Fig. 127. Reef slope fauna at depth of 25 ft., Heron Reef. *Coeloria, Sarcophytum, Acropora hyacinthus.*

Fig. 128. Terrace on reef slope at 30 ft., Heron Reef. *Sarcophytum* and *Acropora hyacinthus*.

form mouths which form a regular astraeoid mosaic. It ranges in diameter from a few inches to more than 2 ft. Closely related to *Favia* is the meandrine form *Platygyra* in which the mouths are elongated as ribbon-like depressions between the narrow skeletal walls. *Platygyra* attains dimensions similar to those of *Favia* and occurs in similar environments. *Lobophyllia* is another massive form in which the mouths are isolated, while in *Tridacophyllia* the isolated mouths are deeply depressed and separated by thin, fragile walls. *Tridacophyllia* is generally smaller and grows in the shelter of the larger brain corals and boulders of the outer reef flat.

Two genera of brain coral are responsible for the majority of microatolls that develop on the inner and middle parts of the reef flat. *Porites* is a brown, compact coral with numerous, small mouths. The upper, surface of the *Porites* microatoll is extremely flat and encrusted by calcareous algae (*Lithothamnion*), while microphytic algae and sediment cover the central part of the upper surface. Growth of the coral continues around the margins as the invading algae and sediment kill the central region, and colonies more than 20 ft.

in diameter may be developed. *Goniopora*, the other brain coral forming microatolls, varies in colour from light grey to blue.

*Platy corals*

The platy corals (Fig. 123, 129A) include a large number of genera and a wide range of shapes. They occur mainly on the lower reef front, but some genera such as *Montipora* also flourish in various parts of the reef flat. As a group, the platy corals are characterised by their thin, laminar skeleton which may be quite flat or folded to produce intricate, foliate patterns. *Montipora* is the most common of the group. It ranges in colour from green, yellow to brown, and it assumes many shapes: intricately folded laminae to flat platforms with ramose projections. Polyps of *Montipora* are extremely small and numerous. *Turbinaria* is a more robust form with larger polyps, but its skeleton is more delicately textured. *Merulina* combines the meandrine sculpture of the brain coral and the laminar structure of the platy coral. *Pachyseris* is similarly composite.

*159*

Fig. 129. Platy coral (? *Montipora*) with black crinoid (feather star) attached; depth 30 ft., Heron Reef slope.

*Encrusting corals*

The encrusting corals occur on the outer reef flat and on the reef front. They are characterised by their growth habit which permits them to encrust other organisms as well as reef detritus. In colour they vary from the brown and yellow of *Pavona* to the green and dark brown of *Cyphastrea* and *Galaxea*.

*Mushroom corals*

The mushroom corals (Fig. 126B, C) include *Fungia*, *Herpetolitha*, and *Polyphyllia*, which are unattached, single polyp forms with large central mouths. They occur mainly in the coral pools or moats of the outer reef flat and on the terraces of the reef slope. *Fungia* is the most common.

*Miscellaneous group*

The miscellaneous group (Fig. 125–128) includes the two important alcyonarians that develop skeletons, viz. the red organ-pipe coral *Tubipora* and the blue *Heliopora*. *Tubipora* occurs in most parts of the reef flat, whereas *Heliopora* favours the deeper reef front and reef slope.

In addition to these two, there are many soft alcyonarians: *Clavularia, Xenia, Sarcophyton, Lobophytum, Sinularia, Heteroxenia*, and the gorgonians *Juncella* and *Melitodes*.

Of the Hydrozoans, *Millepora*, the stinging or fire coral, is the most common. It occurs on the outer flat and reef front, and assumes many shapes and habits ranging from encrustations to massive foliate clusters to finely branched bushes.

*Algae*

The second dominant group of the reef consists of the calcareous algae (Fig. 130, 131). Their role in reef development was aptly described by YONGE (1930, p. 67) when he stated "The bricks are laid by the corals, but the cement which binds the bricks into a homogeneous rampart comes from a very different source. Among the lower plants or algae, are a group known as coralline algae, nullipores or *Lithothamnion*, which possess a smooth and solid skeleton of limestone and grow as an encrustation over rocks." The calcareous algae belong to two major groups. Chlorophyta or green algae and Rhodophyta or red algae.

Of the Rhodophyta, the main calcareous genera are *Lithothamnion, Lithophyllum, Porolithon, Amphiroa*, and *Amansia*. The calcareous Chlorophyta include *Halimeda, Penicillus*, and *Acetabularia*. The Rhodophytes *Lithothamnion, Lithophyllum*, and *Porolithon*, because of their closely textured skeletal structure and encrusting habit, are responsible for the survival of the reef mass against severe and continuous wave attack. They also contribute large amounts of detritus to the reef and off-reef sediment.

The Chlorophyta, such as *Halimeda*, play a minor role in the shielding of the reef against wave attack, but they are important in their contribution to sediment. *Lithothamnion* and related forms are most common on the algal rim and occur less abundantly on the middle and outer reef flat (zone of dead coral and living coral). *Porolithon* favours the zone of living coral. *Halimeda* flourishes in almost every part of the reef: middle and outer reef flat, algal rim, reef front, reef slope and lagoon. *Acetabularia* is restricted to the reef flat and *Penicillus* occurs only on the inner reef flat.

*Further members of the reef community*

The other important members of the reef faunas include molluscs (gastropods, lamellibranchs, scaphopods, cephalopods), foraminifera, echinoderms, ascidians, crustaceans, and polychaete worms. While many species of these groups are largely destructive in that they penetrate and break up coral and algal structures, they contribute large quantities of detritus to the reef mass and in so doing play an important role in its growth.

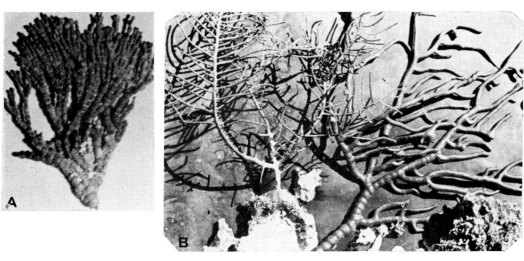

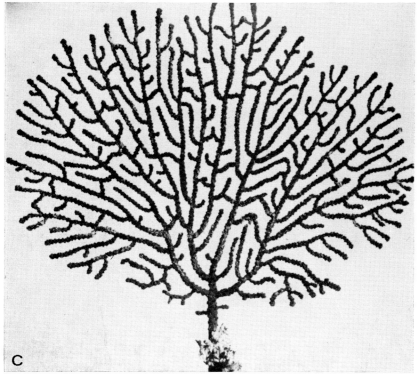

Fig. 130. A. *Halimeda monile* from Heron Reef. B. Alcyonarian *Mopsella* and related genus from the Southern Shelf Embayment, at 35 fathoms. C. Gorgonid from the off-reef floor, Pompey Complex.

*Gastropoda*

The molluscan fauna is possibly the most varied of all the groups.

One of the widely distributed families of the Class Gastropoda is the Trochidae or top shells (Fig. 131D), represented by three abundant species: *Trochus niloticus* (Button Shell) which reaches the greatest size (5 inch diameter) and is white with red bands, *Trochus fenestratus*, a smaller, green-ridged form seldom more than $1\frac{1}{2}$ inches high, and *Trochus maculatus*, a purplish red form of similar size with a beaded sculpture. All three favour the surf zone of the algal rim, where they browse on algae and in so doing remove particles of reef material.

A related family that is less common is the Haliotidae (ear shells or abalone) (Fig. 131E) which feed similarly in somewhat more protected waters. *Teinotis asinina* (Ass's Ear) and *Ovinotis ovina* (Sheep Ear) are two typical species with very nacrous, iridescent, ear-shaped shells distinctively marked by a row of holes along one side.

The Turbinidae (turban shells) (Fig. 131F) are well represented on the reefs, particularly on the algal rim and on shingle banks. *Turbo marmoratus* is the very large, dark-green form (10 inches high) found in the Torres Strait reefs. *Turbo petholatis* (Green Cat's Eye Turban), *Turbo chrysostomus* (yellow-mouthed, ridged shell) and *Turbo argyrostoma* (Silver-Mouthed Turban) are smaller forms ($2$–$2\frac{1}{2}$ inches high) that occur throughout the province.

Small, strikingly coloured shells of the Neritidae (Fig. 131G) are found in great abundance on the beach rock and on shingle banks of most reefs. These are the "bleeding tooth shells", so named because of the blood-coloured teeth that are developed on the columellar deck at the mouth of the very large body whorl. They rarely exceed $1\frac{1}{2}$ inches in dimension, and the shell is generally dark, relieved by vivid flecks. Many species are represented in the reef faunas: *Nerita polita*, *N. chamaeleon*, *N. albicilla*, *N. plicata*, *N. costata*, and *N. lineata*. *Melanerita melanotragus* is the common black form known as "the Crow".

*Melaraphe*, the common periwinkle of the Littorinidae, occurs in the same environments favoured by Neritidae. Its species are small (less than $\frac{1}{2}$ inch high) and varied.

In the northern, Inner Shelf and Near Shore reefs, whelks or horn shells (Fig. 131H, I) of the family Telescopiidae are common where mangrove swamps have formed. Related species of *Pyrazus* and *Cerithium* of the family Cerithiidae are also found on the other reefs. These are narrow, high-spired forms (2–4 inches) with many whorls and generally ribbed or beaded sculpture.

One of the most noticeable and attractive groups of reef gastropods is the Strombidae or wing shells (Fig. 131K, L). They are striking both in their varied shapes and in their delicate coloration. Their main habitat is the sand flat where they feed on vegetation and decaying animal matter. They are also found behind the boulder tract. All are characterised by their expanded outer lip which in some cases is extended into prongs (e.g., *Lambis* or Spider Shell). They have strong, robust shells, highly polished on the inside and ribbed or nodular on the outside. Many species of this family are represented in the reef faunas. Notable among these are *Labiostromus epidromus* (Sail Stromb), *Strombus lentiginosus* (Freckled Stromb), *Conomurex luhuanus* (Red-Mouthed Stromb), *Lambis bryonia* (Giant Spider Shell), *L. chiraga* (Gouty Spider Shell), *L. lambis* (Smooth Spider Shell), and *L. scorpio* (Scorpion Shell). The tritons or family Cymatidae form another spectacular group of varied abundance on the reefs. The shells are generally large and beautifully coloured, the best known being the Trumpet Shell or *Charonia tritonis* (up to 18 inches in length).

Helmet shells (family Cassidae) include several large species (Fig. 131N), the most common being the Giant Helmet, *Cassis cornuta*, which grows up to 14 inches in length. The shell is robust, angular, with rows of tubercles. Its outer surface is dull white, but the inside is a lustrous orange colour.

A similar group is the family Tonnidae (Fig. 131O), represented on the Great Barrier Reef by *Cadus rufus*, the Partridge Tun. It is a barrel-shaped form with large body whorl, marked by alternating brown and white bands.

The family Naticidae (the sand snails or moon shells) includes small, robust, sub-spherical shells (Fig. 131P) with distinctive colour patterns of alternating lines, bands or flecks. The many species favour the sand flat, where they burrow just under the surface, in search of small lamellibranchs which they pierce in the umbonal region prior to drawing out the soft parts.

Cowrie shells of the family Cypraeidae (Fig. 131Q–S) are abundant on the algal rim and outer reef flat. They are most conspicuous because of their well-rounded shape, narrow toothed aperture, very high lustre and unusual colour patterns. There are numerous species in the family, the most common being *Cypraea tigris* (Tiger Cowry), a large form reaching 5 inches in length, generally dark brown in colour with darker spots. *Arestorides argus* (Eyed Cowry), *Ravitrona caputser-*

Fig. 131. A. *Lithothamnion* encrusting base of brain coral; B. *Aviscutum olungius* (Near-Shore Zone, Southern Region); C. Fissunellid (same occurrence); D. *Trochus niloticus* (Corbett Reef edge); E. *Teinotis asinina*; F. *Turbo pulcher* (Corbett Reef rim); G. *Nerita polita* (Howick Reef flat); H. *Contumax modulosus* (Tydeman Reef-beach of sand cay); I. *Turritella cingulifera* (Near-Shore Zone, Southern Region); J. *Telescopium* (Howick Reef-beach); K. *Lambis lambis* (Turtle Group-reef flat); L. *Canarium canarium*; M. *Biplex pulchella* (Near-Shore Zone, Southern Region); N. *Cassis* cf. *cornuta*; O. *Cadus rufus* (Cairns Reef flat); P. *Uber pyriformis* (Corbett Reef, sand flat); Q. *Ornamentaria annulus* (Corbett Reef); R. *Lyncina lyax* (Opal Reef flat); S. *Cypraea tigris*; T. *Chicoreus*; U. *Menathais pica* (Corbett Reef flat); V. *Mancinella mancinella* (Corbett Reef flat); W. *Reticunassa paupera*; X. *Aulica rutila* (Tydeman Reef-sand flat); Y. *Oliva erythrostoma* (Corbett Reef-sand flat); Z. *Oliva episcopalis* (Lizard Island-beach). Magniflcations indicated by scales which all correspond to 2 cm.

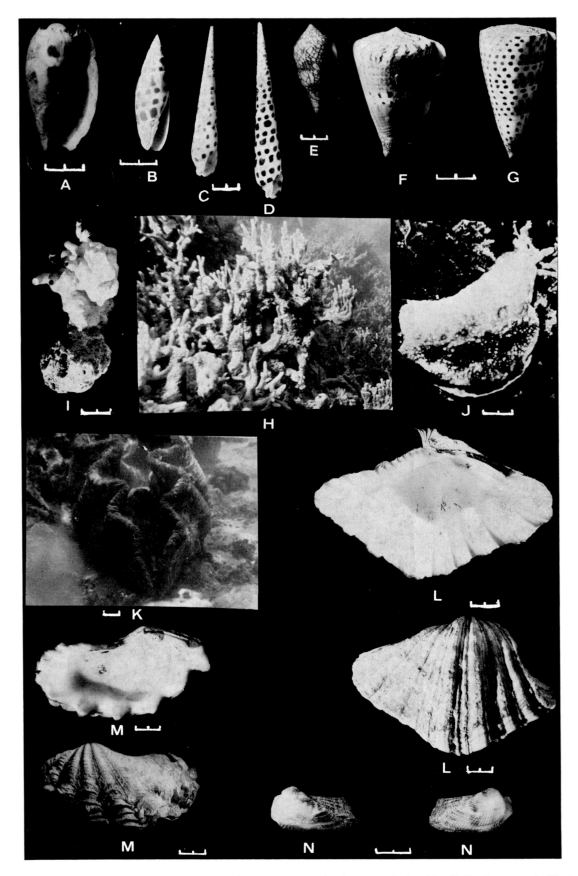

Fig. 132. A. *Cymbium amphorus* (Corbett Reef); B. *Mitra mitra* (Tydeman Reef - beach);  C. *Terebra muscaria* (Corbett Reef flat); D. *Terebra subulata* (same locality); E. *Darioconus textile*; F. *Rhizoconus capitaneus* (Cairns Reef flat). G. *Conus litteralus* (Corbett Reef flat); H. *Vermetus maximus* in the lagoon of a small reef of the Southern Pompey Complex; I. *Vermetus maximus*; J. *Aplysia angasi* (Heron Island - coral zone); K. *Tridacna crocea*, 35 inches in length (edge of coral zone, Tydeman Reef). L. *Hippopus hippopus* (Turtle Reef - inner flat); M. *Tridacna fossor* (Stapleton Reef); N. *Arca alladin* (Near-Shore Zone, Southern Region).

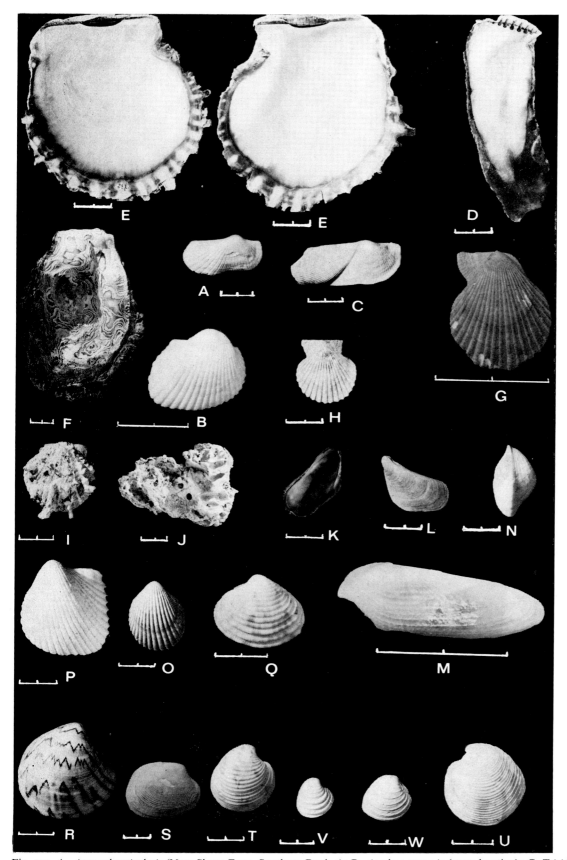

Fig. 133. A. *Arca subnavicularis* (Near-Shore Zone, Southern Region); B. *Anadara trapezia* (same location); C. *Trisidos yongei* (same location); D. *Isognomen isognomen* (Cairns Reef); E. *Pinctada margaritifera* (Grubb Reef); F. *Saxostrea,* cf. *gradiva* (Grubb Reef); G. *Nimachlamys curtisiana* (Southern Region, Near-Zone Shore); H. *Annachlamys leopardis* (same location); I. *Spondylus,* cf. *ducalis* (Corbett Reef); J. Borings of *Lithophaga* in coral; K. *Modiolus auriculatus*; L. *Trichomya hirsuta*; M. *Pholas obturamentum*; N. *Hemicardium subretusum*; O. *Regozara flava*; P. *Fragum unedo* (Pickersgill Reef); Q. *Anomalocardia subnodulosa*; R. *Lioconcha castrensis* (Corbett Reef); S. *Tapes turgida*; T. *Venus embrithes*; U. *Tigammona chemnitzi*; V. *Placamen foliacea*; W. *Placamen calophila*.

165

Fig. 134. A. *Tellina inflata*; B. *Asaphis deflorata*; C. *Cardita incrassata*; D. *Atactodea striata*; E. *Nautilus pompilus*; F. *Linckia laevigata* (Opal Reef); G. *Archaster typicus* (Grubb Reef-sand flat); H. *Patriella* (Nymph Reef); I. *Echinometra mathaei* (Nymph Reef-boulder zone); J. *Tripneustes gratilla* (Nymph Reef-sand flat); K, L, M. Echinoids from the Northern Region; N. *Ophiocoma erinaceus* (Nymph Reef); O. *Macrophiothrix longipeda* (Nymph Reef); P. Holothuria (Low Isles).

166

*pentis* (Serpent's Head), *Nivigena melwardi* (Melward's Cowry), *Ornamentaria annulus* (Ringed Money Cowry), and *Amphiperas ovum* (Egg Cowry) are other common reef species.

Murex shells, members of the family Muricidae (Fig. 131T) are found in the reef faunas and also on the off-reef floor. They are characterised by their elaborately sculptured shells, with flanges, spines and nodules giving added strength to their robust structure. Like the Naticidae, they pierce the shells of oysters and other molluscs from which they consume the soft parts. *Chicoreus* (Giant Murex), *Acupurpura tenuispina* (Spiny Woodcock), and *Marchia clavus* (Rudder Murex) are the main forms found on the reefs.

Closely related to the previous group is the family Thaididae (Fig. 131U, V), which contains comparatively small, short-spired, robust shells with heavily developed nodules and ridges. Members of this family are abundant reef dwellers and are known as purples because of the dye released by them. *Menathais pica* (Magpie Purple), *Mancinella kieneri* (Kiener's Purple) and *M. mancinella* (Pimpled Purple) are the main species found in the boulder tracts and beach rock.

Somewhat similar to this family is the family Nassariidae (dog whelks) which includes many species of small, rounded, robust shells ornamented with ridges and nodules (Fig. 131W). They are carnivorous like the Naticidae and Muricidae, and cause extensive destruction amongst the lamellibranch faunas. *Nassarius papillosus* (Papillose Dog Whelk) reaches lengths of 2 inches and is probably the largest form. *N. coronatis* is a smaller, slender form. Both species are common on the sand flat and the off-reef floor.

The family Volutidae (Fig. 131X, 132A) includes some of the largest and most colourful species found on the reef flat and the off-reef floor. They are all sand-burrowing, carnivorous animals, feeding mainly on other molluscs. *Cymbium amphorus* (Baler Shell) and *C. umbilicatus* (Umbilicate Baler Shell) are the two large forms (more than 12 inches in length) found on the Great Barrier Reef. Their shells are characterised by the wide body whorl and the spines which extend from its upper margin. *C. amphorus* is pink to orange in colour and *C. umbilicatus* tends to be golden brown. The smaller *Cymbiola rutila* (Blood-Red Volute) which rarely exceeds 3 inches in length, is also a common reef species and is characterised by its broad-banded, blotchy colour pattern which is dominated by red. *Cymbiolacca pulchra* (Beautiful Volute) is also a small form, but it is characterised by its shouldered whorls and spines. Similar to the Volutidae in form and habit are the members of the family Olividae (Fig.

131Y, Z). They have long, robust shells that exhibit a high lustre on their smooth, colourful external surface. A small spire projects dorsally from the main body. The olive shells are medium sized, rarely exceeding 5 inches in length. They burrow in sand and feed on other molluscs. *Oliva erythrostoma* (Red-Mouthed Olive) is a yellow form banded with green and purple shades and flecked with dark brown; *Oliva maura* (Black or Moor Olive) is a slightly smaller black form; *Oliva cruente* (Lilac Spotted Olive) is even smaller, and has a creamy colour with large flecks of lilac; *Oliva ispidula* (Varicoloured Olive) is the smallest member of the four species, and its colour ranges from tan to dark green, with various flecks, bands and lines of other colours. All four species are abundant on the sand flat.

The family Mitridae (Fig. 132B) includes numerous species found in the sand and gravels of the reef surface. The mitre shells are long, turreted, robust forms ranging in size from 1 to 6 inches, and showing a wide variety of surface sculpture and colour pattern. The most common is possibly *Mitra mitra* (Giant Mitre) which has a very distinctive orange spotted pattern on an otherwise white surface, and the smaller *Mitra pontificalis* which is similarly coloured but has dorsal whorl spines. At least ten other members of the family are represented in the reef faunas.

The auger shells belong to another family Terebridae (Fig. 132C, D), and are also elongate, robust, many-whorled forms, characterised by their rather graceful shape. Like the mitres and volutes they inhabit the sandy areas as well as the deeper off-reef floor. More than ten species occur in the Great Barrier Reef. *Terebra dimidiata* (Divided Auger) and *T. maculata* (Spotted Auger), both long forms (4–8 inches) are among the more common members of the group.

Near relatives of the Terebridae are the poisonous cone shells: family Conidae (Fig. 132E–G). The cones include a large number of species, all characterised by their conical shape, short-spired, solid structure and brilliant colouring. They are abundant on the algal rim and outer reef flat where they live in depressions and crevices, feeding on other molluscs. Most of them are from 4 to 6 inches in length. *Coronaxis marmoreus* (Marble Cone) is the common black form with large, white, triangular markings; *Darioconus textile* (Cloth-of-Gold Cone) is equally common and is brilliantly coloured with reticulate, orange-brown lines on a lustrous white surface; *Conus generalis* (General Cone) is somewhat smaller and is marked by brown and white bands on a black base.

An interesting and not uncommon gastropod family is that of the Vermetidae or worm shells (Fig. 132H).

Their shape is similar to that of worm tubes and their attachment, in colonies, to coral and reef debris is unusual. *Vermetus maximus* (Great Coral Worm Shell) occurs on the algal rim and spurs of the outer reefs, and develops tubes that may attain lengths of 6 inches and diameters of 1 inch. It feeds on phytoplankton.

The family Aplysiidae (Fig. 132I) is an unusual gastropod group represented in the reef fauna by the Angas' Sea Hare (*Aplysia angasi*). This sea hare is a large animal (12 inches long), with a very small yellow shell enclosed by the extensive, flabby mantle, the edges of which are tentacular and generally folded upwards as the animal browses on reef vegetation. The soft mantle varies in colour from green to red with black bands and spots irregularly distributed.

## Lamellibranchiata

The species of the second class of molluscs, the Class Lamellibranchiata, are possibly as varied as, and certainly more numerous than, the gastropods.

Perhaps the most conspicuous lamellibranch of the reef flat is the clam (Fig. 132J, K, L), represented by the species *Tridacna deresa*, the Giant Clam, which attains dimensions of more than 4 ft., *Hippopus hippopus*, the Horse-Shoe Clam which is generally less than 1 ft. in length, and the smaller *Tridacna crocea*, *T. elongata* and *T. maxima* var. *fossa*. All are characterised by their brilliantly coloured mantles, the colour being due to minute plant cells contained in the mantle. The Giant Clam (*T. deresa*) is not fastened to the substrate. The other species are attached firmly by their byssus and they bore into the reef surface by a rocking motion which enables their shoulders to grind away the underlying reef material. In this manner they produce substantial quantities of fine sediment.

The small Dog Cockle (*Tucetona amboinensis*) of the family Glycymeridae is fairly numerous in the sandy off-reef floor of the northern region. It has a solid, sub-circular shell, $1\frac{1}{2}$–2 inches in diameter, with approximately 20 broad ribs and a banded red to purple colour pattern.

*Ennucula superba* of the Nuculidae is also found at similar depths. It is approximately 1 inch in diameter and is characterised by numerous teeth (30), its solid, smooth white shell and its asymmetric, rounded outline.

The Cowl Shell (*Ustularca renuta*; originally called *Arca fusca*) of the family Arcidae (Fig. 132M, 133A–C), is common on the sand flat and also occurs on the off-reef floor. It has a sub-quadrangular shape with an extremely wide hingeline, numerous fine teeth and fine radial ribs. In colour it is purplish-brown with white umbones.

The White Hammer Oyster (*Malleus malleus*) of the family Vulsellidae (Fig. 133D), is an elongate form (2–8 inches) with an extended, toothless hinge, found below low tide mark on and around reefs. A similar species is the Toothed Pearl Shell (*Melina nucleus*) which is rounded rather than elongate but which has the flaky shell structure of the preceding form.

The family Pteriidae (Fig. 133E) includes the main species of pearl shell. The Broad-Winged Pearl Shell (*Austropteria lata*), the Black-Banded Winged Pearl Shell (*Electroma zebra*) occur in off-reef floor sands and Near Shore areas up to depths of 9 fathoms. They are spectacular shells, obliquely extended, sometimes to a degree where the hinge projects as a spine or rod, and they have a very lustrous, deeply coloured nacre. The larger species average 6–8 inches in maximum dimension. There are more than six species of the true pearl shell found in the reef province. *Pinctada margaritifera* (Black Lip Pearl Shell) averages about 6 inches in diameter; *Pinctada maxima* (Golden Lip) is generally larger (10 inches) and heavier and has a lustrous cream to silver nacre. They occur on the reef surface but more commonly on the off-reef floor, down to depths of 40 fathoms.

The oysters, family Ostreidae (Fig. 133F), have many representatives in the Great Barrier Reef. *Saxastrea amasa* is the Coral Rock Oyster, an elongate, evenly plicate, purplish coloured form which grows to 4 inches and is abundant among the boulders, near the reef edge. *Lopha cristigalli* or Coxcomb Oyster is a reddish, thinner, more rounded, plicate form that generally lives below low tide level. *Lopha hyotis* or Hyotoid Oyster is a very large, brown to blue form, up to 8 inches in diameter, that occurs mainly below low tide level in the Near Shore reefs. *Ostrea procles* (Flattened Oyster) is a flat, sub-circular yellowish form approximately 2 inches in diameter, found under boulders on the Inner Shelf reefs.

The thorny oysters (family Spondylidae) include the solid, ribbed, spiny shells such as *Spondylus ducalis* (Fig. 133I) which is the pinkish form, 2–3 inches in diameter, that is fairly abundant among the boulders of the outer reef flat and algal rim.

Several species of the family Mytilidae (Fig. 133J–L) are important members of the reef community. The genus *Lithophaga*, or date mussels, includes the species that bore into coral and other reef material, causing widespread weakening and destruction in the reef mass. *Lithophaga* bores by a chemical process in which acid is secreted to dissolve the host material. The Golden Date Mussel (*L. obesa*) is the largest (more than 3 inches long) and possibly the most common species, and is found mainly in the boulder tract at and below low tide mark. Its shell is elongate, oval in shape, and has a smooth, light-brown surface. *L. teres* is a large dark-brown to black, shiny form. The Winged Mussel (*Modiolus auriculatus*) belongs to the group of horse mussels, and is characterised by its rather inflated, rounded, hairy shell with flattened margins and golden colour. *Botulopa silicula* is a Boring Horse Mussel, rather small (1 inch long). Both species occur in the boulder tract.

The family Gastrochaenidae includes another group of boring mussels. They burrow into sediment, rock, shells, coral, etc., forming a tube of debris cemented together. *Gastrochaena frondosa* is a small, elongate, yellowish-white shell with fine concentric lines and gaping ventral margin. These mussels cause extensive structural damage to the reef.

Two important groups of boring lamellibranchs are the Pholadidae (angel's wing borers) and the Teredinidae (cobra or shipworms). The pholads (Fig. 133M) are small, white, wing-shaped shells with fine radial and concentric ornament. *Parapholas incei* is the Coral Borer, 1–2 inches long. The shipworms have long soft bodies which have small white valves at the anterior end. They bore in timber and have little effect on the main reef mass.

Heart cockles of the family Cardiidae (Fig. 133N–X) are abundant on the reefs. They are typically heart-shaped with high beaks and prominent ribs that result in interlocking margins. Each valve carries four large teeth. *Fragum unedo* (Strawberry Cockle) is the most common species, reaching a size of 2½ inches. It is white with rows of transverse, red lamellae. *Fragum fragum* is a smaller, white form. *Regozara oxygonum* is a more rounded, finer-ribbed form, yellow in colour. All inhabit the sand flat.

The family Tellenidae (Fig. 134A) includes several species that are abundant in vegetated sand and sandy-mud areas. All burrow in the sediment, and the flat, elongate shell is well adapted for this mode of life. *Tellinella virgata* (Striped Sunset Shell) is approximately 2½ inches long and has a very distinctive colour pattern of radial pink bands on a white surface that becomes yellow in the umbonal region. *Quidnipagus palatum* is sub-circular in outline and has a wrinkled surface that is white in colour and yellow towards the umbo. *Acropagia remies* is a very large, circular form (up to 3½ inches diameter) with coarse concentric wrinkles.

*Scaphopoda*

An interesting molluscan group is the Class Scaphopoda, sometimes known as the tooth shells. They range from microscopic to a length of 5 inches, and are curved, tapering tubes that are found on muddy and sandy floors in the deeper off-reef areas, where they consume foraminifera and other microorganisms. The small tubular skeletons are readily transported and are commonly found in reef top sands as well as in the deeper sediments which they normally inhabit.

*Dentalium* is the main genus found in the reef province. The amphineurans or chitons are another widespread group that is particularly abundant in the inter-tidal zone. They are unique in that they are multi-valved molluscs, consisting of eight overlapping plates surrounded by a tough, muscular band. The two common species in the Great Barrier Reef are *Acanthopleura spinosa* (Spiny Chiton) and *Acanthozostera gemmata* (Giant Chiton). Both are abundant on beach rock and in the boulder tract. They feed on algae which they rasp from the rock surface and, in so doing, they gradually form depressions in the surface.

*Cephalopoda*

The Class Cephalopoda includes the nautiloids, cuttle-fish and squids. While the coiled shells of *Nautilus pompilius* (Pearly Nautilus) (Fig. 134E) and *N. macromphalus*, the smaller internal skeleton of the squid *Spirula* and the cuttle bones of *Sepioteuthis* and *Metasepia* are noticeable components of beach debris, they are not abundant by comparison with other molluscan groups.

*Echinodermata*

The Phylum Echinodermata is well represented in the reef faunas by members of the Asteroidea, Echinoidea, Ophiuroidea, and Holothuroidea. However, the Crinoidea are poorly developed, being represented mainly by the Feather Star (*Comanthus parvicina*).

The Asteroidea (sea stars) (Fig. 134F–H), characterised by their hollow star-like arms and colourful exterior, include many reef species, most of which live on the reef flat and in the boulder tract. *Linckia laevigata* (Fig. 134F) is the common, bright-blue form, *L. guildingii* the similar fawn-coloured species, both of which are common on the outer reef flat and algal rim. Other species include *Archaster typicus*, a straw coloured sea star that burrows in the sandy areas, *Patriella exigua* which hides in pools among the boulder tract, *Culcita novaeguineae* or Pin Cushion Sea Star with its stunted arms, *Asterope carcinifera*, *Echinaster luzonicus*, *Fromia elegans*, and *Nardoa pauciforis*. The sea stars are carnivorous, feeding mainly on lamellibranchs and causing extensive destruction of the molluscan faunas. The Crown of Thorns (*Acanthaster planci*) is a spectacular, spiny form which grows to more than 2 ft. in diameter. It feeds on coral polyps and in some areas where it reaches plague proportions, the species results in serious damage to the coral, e.g., Green Island 1966.

The Echinoidea (Fig. 134I–M) include a few species which are abundant on the reef. Most of them are vegetable feeders. *Diadema setosa* is the black, long-spined sea urchin which lives in groups in the coral pools of the outer reef flat. *Echinometra mathaei* is the boring species with short, strong, sharp spines that is common on the algal rim where it grinds out spherical hollows in which it lives. *Heterocentrotus mamillatus* (Slate-Pencil Urchin) has thick, blunt pencil-like spines and is less abundant than the other two species. *Tripneustes gratilla* is another member of the reef fauna. It has short white spines, tipped with orange, projecting from a large, brown to purple test. *Salmacis sphaeroides* is a dark, densely and finely spinose form, less common than the other species.

The Ophiuroidea or brittle stars (Fig. 134N, O) are abundant on the reef surface as well as in deeper waters beyond the reefs. Characteristic of the group are the long, extremely flexible, snake-like arms which the animal breaks off when escaping from predators. The main test of the animal is generally small, and unlike the sea stars, they are sediment filterers, digesting decaying organic matter from the sediment as it is carried into the mouth. As a group, the ophiuroids are quite beautiful in their colours, shapes and spinose covering. The more common species include *Ophiarachnella infernalis*, *O. gorgonia*, *Ophiarachna incrassata*, *Ophiocoma erinaceus*, *O. insularia*, *Ophioarthrum pictum*, and *Macropheothrix longipeda*.

Holothuroidea (sea cucumbers or beche-de-mer) (Fig. 134P) is distinguished from other echinoderm groups by its leathery, armoured body wall reinforced by innumerable, multi-shaped calcareous ossicles which correspond to the true skeleton of echinoids, ophiuroids and asteroids. Most common is the black, soft-skinned *Holothuria leucospilota* which is numerous on the sand flat where it filters the bottom sediment in its quest for contained organic matter and produces small conical mounds of faecal pellets ½–1 inch long. *Stichopus variegatus* is the larger, spotted brown, rough-skinned species common in the coral pools and around lagoonal margins. *Synapta maculata* is the extremely long, worm-like species which has a ring of tentacles at its mouth.

The Echinodermata exert an extremely important influence in the reef community. Asteroids are capable of tremendous damage to corals and molluscs, echinoids are less destructive but do bore into the reef surface, ophiuroids and holothurians continually rework the reef sediment, possibly sorting and reducing grain size in the process.

*Crustacea*

The Phylum Crustacea (Fig. 135A, B) is represented abundantly by crabs (Brachyura and Anomura), prawns and shrimps (Natantia), crayfish (Palinura), barnacles (Cirrepedia) and sand hoppers (Amphipoda). All play important roles in the destruction and preservation of the reef mass, in the production of detritus from skeletal organisms and in their own contribution to reef sediment.

Of the Cirrepedia, the common forms are *Tetraclita squamosa* (Acorn Barnacle) and *Lithotrya* (Boring Barnacle) both of which inhabit the boulders on the algal rim and beach rock in the intertidal zone of sand cays.

Amphipods are also common in the crevices and hollows beneath the boulders and shingle.

The main species of prawn include *Aspheus strenuus* (Pistol Prawn), *Hymenocera elegans* (Coral Prawn), *Stenopus hispidus* (Banded Shrimp), *Goniodactylus chiragra* (Mantis Shrimp), and the Yabby or Ghost Nipper (*Callianassa australiensis*).

Crayfish are represented by several gaudily-coloured species of the large *Panulirus*, the most common being *P. longipes* (Painted Crayfish) and *P. versicolor*.

There is an abundant, diverse population of crabs throughout all reefs. Hermit crabs (Fig. 135B) of the species *Clibanarius striolatus*, *C. virescens*, *Dardanus megistos*, *D. fabimanus*, and *D. deformis*, inhabit the dead shells of gastropods and are found in almost every zone of the reef. Related to this group is the small Scuttle Crab (*Petrolisthes lamarcki*) which inhabits the shingle banks and boulder tract.

Of the true crabs (Brachyura) there are innumerable species. *Atergatis ocyroe* and *A. floridus* (Shawl Crab) flourish throughout the reef flat and algal rim, and especially in the coral pools. *Calappa hepatica* (Box Crab) favours the more protected parts of the reef flat and is a common inhabitant of the less dense mangrove areas. *Eriphia sebana* and *E. laevimana* (Red-Eyed Crab) are found mainly in the coral pools of the outer flat. *Grapsus strigosus* is the agile, long-limbed, Green Crab that is common in the boulder tract and shingle banks. *Ocypoda cerathophthalma* and *O. cordimana* are the fast moving, nocturnal creatures known as Sand or Ghost Crabs, that burrow in the beaches of the sand cay. *Thalamita crenata*, the heavy Blue-Green Swimming Crab, lives in the mangrove areas and rarely ventures on to the open reef flat. *T. admete* and *T. stimpsonii* are the swimming forms typical of the open flat. *Trapezia cymodoce*, a small purplish crab and *Haplocarcinus marsupialis*, shelter in the more delicate branching corals (*Pocillopora, Seriatopora*) the latter actually living within the coral skeleton. Forms of similar habit are *Cryptochirus* which prefers the more massive brain corals such as *Favia*, and *Caphyra laevis* which lives in the coral *Xenia*.

*Polychaeta and other worms*

Polychaete worms (constituting an order of the Class Chaetopoda) form a very significant, though small element in the reef community. They are characterised by their segmented bodies, crown of tentacles, and in most forms, segmental bristles or setae. Some species are free swimming, others are sedentary and develop tubes either by lime secretion or by the agglutination of sand grains and shell debris.

The free swimming forms are carnivorous and include the colourful, bristly *Eurythoe complanata*: a bristly, salmon-coloured worm found on the reef flat. *Phyllodoce* is a smaller (3 inches long) green worm with paddle-like cirri on its sides.

In the tube-forming polychaetes, the animal has neither jaws nor teeth and feeds on organic debris in the water. *Terebella*, found under rocks, has a fragile tube of debris, and bright creamy tentacles. *Sabellastarte* has a papery tube, and a bright, flower-like head that has resulted in it being called the Feather-Duster Worm. Serpulid species, possibly belonging to *Galeolaria*, form encrustations of fine calcareous tubes on boulders and shells.

The gephyrean worms of the Class Supunculida are quite different from the polychaetes in that they are unsegmented, and they do not have setae or bristles. *Phascolosoma*, the main representative of this group, known as the Peanut Worm, occurs under boulders and shingle on the reef top and also in the deeper off-reef water. It is unique in its manner of locomotion: the anterior end is extended and thinned and then the rest of the worm is drawn over the anterior end by introversion. The animal burrows in mud and sand,

ingesting the sediment and extracting contained organic material.

*Ascidiacea*

Ascidians or sea squirts are comparatively abundant over the entire reef surface, and have also been recovered from deeper waters. They are of particular interest to the sedimentologist because of their minute, elaborately designed spicules which are found in great abundance in the reef, inter-reef and terrigenous sediments. Their primitive shapeless appearance belies their high level in the evolutionary tree, belonging as they do to the Phylum Chordata. The main species of the reef province are compound forms such as the bright blue or green *Diplosoma virens*, the white *Didemnum candidum*, *Chorizocarpa sydneyensis*, and *Botrythis magnicoecus*, all of which thrive near the reef margins.

*Polyzoa*

Polyzoans (or bryozoans) are not well represented in the fauna on the reef surface. However, they may be extremely prolific on the reef slopes, particularly on the windward sides of reefs. They appear to favour the zone below that of violent surf activity, where the reduced surf and unrestricted oceanic circulation combine to provide a nutrient-rich, aerated environment. In the fore-reef regions, polyzoans contribute large quantities of detritus to the sediment. It is also interesting to observe that polyzoans are abundant on the reefal shoals more remote from the open oceanic waters presumably because they have a greater tolerance than corals for depleted waters. While the polyzoan fauna is not well known, preliminary examination of reef samples reveals a surprisingly wide diversity of species. The more common ones include the encrusting *Membranipora membranacea*, the irregularly chambered *Cellepora* which resembles coral, and *Retepora graeffei*, the Lace Coral, with its intricately folded, finely meshed zooarium.

*Foraminifera*

The Foraminifera (Fig. 135C–O) are a major component of the reef fauna and are the dominant group in the inter-reef areas and on the Inner Shelf. They appear to be extremely sensitive to environmental influences and provide a valuable key to facies interpretation. The fauna of the reef surface is perhaps the least varied in terms of species, whereas that of the Inner Shelf where the carbonate fraction of the sediment

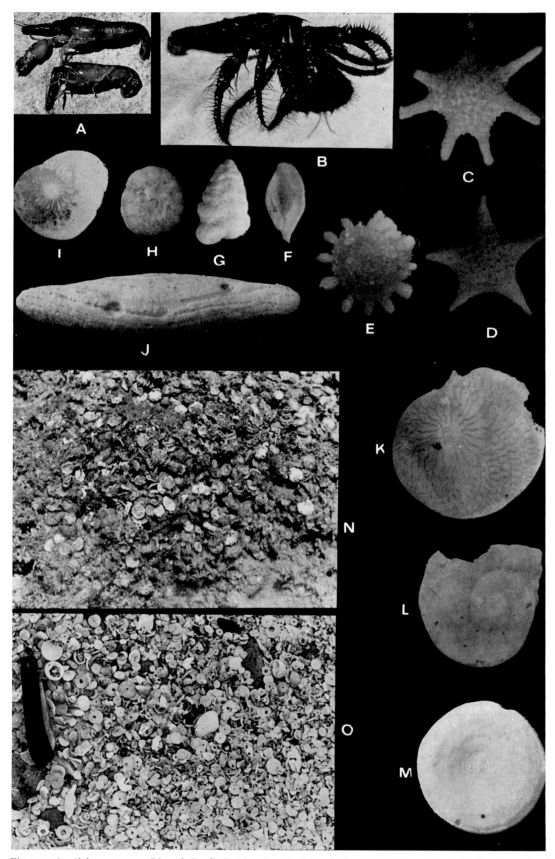

Fig. 135. A. *Alpheus strenuus* (Nymph Reef); B. Hermit crab (Lizard Island - fringing reef); C, D. *Baculogypsina* (×10); E. *Calcarina* (×10); F. ? *Spiroloculina* (×15); G. *Textularia* (×20); H. *Amphistigina* (×15); I. *Heterostegina* (×5); J. *Alveolinella* (×4); K. *Heterostigina* (×5); L. ? *Operculina* (×1); M. *Marginopora* (×2); N. Live *Marginopora* in algal pool in the lee of the boulder zone, Nymph Reef; O. *Marginopora* beach, Puritan Bay, Whitsunday area.

TABLE II

FORAMINEFERAL SPECIES OF GREAT BARRIER REEF (after COLLINS, 1958)

| | Trinity Opening | Off-reef Shelf | Reef Flat | Mangrove |
|---|---|---|---|---|
| **ASTRORHIZIDEA** | | | | |
| Astrorhizidae | | | | |
| *Astrorhiza* cf. *arenaria* | x | | | |
| *Marsipella cylindrica* | a | | | |
| *Hyperammina friabilis* | x | | | |
| *H. mestayeri* | x | | | |
| *Botellina tasmanica* | | a(liz.) | | |
| *Discobotellina biperforata* | | x (16–37f) | | |
| *Sagenina frondescens* | | x | x | x |
| *S. divaricans* | | x | | |
| Saccamminidae | | | | |
| *Psammosphaera parva* | a | | | |
| *P. fusca testacea* | x | | | |
| *Saccammina consociata* | x | | | |
| *Proteonina difflugiformis* | x | | | |
| *P. cushmani* | a | | | |
| *P. micacea* | x | | | |
| *Thurammina albicans* | x | | | |
| *Technitella legumen* | x | | | |
| *Webbinella hemisphaerica* | x | | | |
| *Diffusilina humilis* | | x(liz.) | | |
| Involutinidae | | | | |
| *Involutina* sp. | x | | | |
| *Glomospira charoides* | x | | | |
| *G. elongata* | a | x | | |
| *Lituotuba minuta* | | x | | |
| *Tolypammina vagans* | x | | | |
| *Ammolagena clavata* | x | | | |
| **LITUOLIDEA** | | | | |
| Reophacidae | | | | |
| *Reophax micaceus* | x | | | |
| *R. dentaliniformis* | x | | | |
| *R. scotti* | | x | x | x |
| *R.* cf. *catenatus* | | x(low) | | |
| *R. guttifer* | x | | | |
| *R.* aff. *aduncus* | a | | | |
| *R. spiculifer* | x | | | |
| *R. scorpiurus testaceus* | a | | | |
| *R. agglutinatus* | | x | | |
| Lituolidae | | | | |
| *Haplophragmoides canariensis* | x | | | |
| *Cribrostomoides* aff. *wiesneri* | x | | | |
| *Ammobaculites reophaciformis* | x | | | |
| *A. agglutinans* | x | x(low) | | |
| *A. americanus* | a | | | |
| *Ammomarginulina ensis* | a | | | |
| *A. australiensis* | | a | a | a |
| *Placopsilina bradyi* | | a | | |
| *Nouria polymorphinoides* | | a | | |
| *N. tenuis* | | x(low) | | |
| *N. textulariformis* | | x | | |
| *Haddonia minor* | | x | | |
| Textulariidae | | | | |
| *Textularia fistulosa* | a | | | |
| *T. candeiana* | | x | | |
| *T. vola* | x | | | |
| *T. orbica* | | a | a | a |

| | Trinity Opening | Off-reef Shelf | Reef Flat | Mangrove |
|---|---|---|---|---|
| Textulariidae (continued) | | | | |
| *T. kerimbaensis* | | a | a | a |
| *T. foliacea* | | a | a | a |
| *T. porrecta* | | x | x | x |
| *T. conica* | | x | x | x |
| *T. vertebralis* | | a(low) | | |
| Trochamminidae | | | | |
| *Trochammina globigeriniformis* | a | | | |
| *T. rotaliformis* | | a | x | x |
| *Remaneica* aff. *plicata* | a | | | |
| *Carterina spiculotesta* | x | x | | |
| *Ammosphaeroidina sphaeroidini-*<br>*formis* | | x | | |
| Verneuilinidae | | | | |
| *Siphogaudryina rugulosa* | | a | | |
| *S.* cf. *wrightiana* | | x | | |
| *S. siphonifera* | | x | | |
| *Pseudogaudryina concava* | x | | | |
| *Pseudoclavulina juncea* | x | | | |
| *P. scabra* | x | | | |
| *Eggerella australis* | | a(low) | | |
| *E. polita* | a | | | |
| *Dorothia arenata* | a | | | |
| *D. inepta* | | a | | |
| *Karreriella apicularis* | a | | | |
| *K. attenuata* | x | | | |
| *Valvulina conica* | a | | | |
| *Clavulina multicamerata* | | a | a | a |
| *C. pacifica* | | x | x | x |
| **MILIOLIDEA** | | | | |
| Miliolidae | | | | |
| *Quinqueloculina anguina arenata* | | a | | |
| *Q. berthelotiana* | | x | x | x |
| *Q. bicarinata* | | x | x | x |
| *Q. bidentata* | | x | x | x |
| *Q. crassicarinata* | | a | a | a |
| *Q. crenulata* | | x | x | x |
| *Q. cuvieriana queenslandica* | | x | x | x |
| *Q. quinquecarinata* | | a | a | a |
| *Q. lamarckiana* | | x | x | x |
| *Q. milletti* | | a | a | aa |
| *Q. neostriatula* | | a | a | a |
| *Q. polygona* | | a | a | a |
| *Q. pseudoreticulata* | | a | a | a |
| *Q. samoaensis* | | x (turtle) | | |
| *Q. semireticulosa* | | x | | |
| *Q. sulcata* | | a | a | a |
| *Q. tropicalis* | | x | | |
| *Q. rugosa* | | x | | |
| *Massilina subrugosa* | | a | a | |
| *M. secans tropicalis* | | | x | |
| *M. corrugata* | | a | a | a |
| *M. minuta* | a | x | | |
| *Pseudomassilina australis* | | x | | |
| *Spiroloculina angulata* | | a | a | a |
| *S. aperta* | | a | a | |
| *S. communis* | | a | a | a |
| *S. disparilis* | x | x | | |

TABLE II (continued)

| Miliolidae (continued) | Trinity Opening | Off-reef Shelf | Reef Flat | Mangrove |
|---|---|---|---|---|
| S. foveolata | | a | a | a |
| S. lucida | | | | x |
| S. rugosa curvatura | | x | | |
| S. scita | | a | a | a |
| Sigmoilina schlumbergeri | x | | | |
| S. australis | x | | | |
| Spirosigmoilina bradyi | | a | | |
| S. parri | x | x | | |
| Articulina pacifica | | x | x | |
| A. tricarinata | x | | | |
| A. sagra | x | a | | |
| A. queenslandica | x | | | |
| Tubinella funalis | | a | | |
| T. inornata | x | | | |
| Nubeculina divaricata advena | | a | | |
| Hauerina diversa | | x | | |
| H. pacifica rugosa | | x | | |
| H. fragilissima | | a | | |
| H. involuta | | a | a | a |
| H. bradyi | | a | | |
| Schlumbergerina alveoliniformis | | a | | |
| Ammomassilina alveoliniformis | | a | | |
| Triloculina bertheliniana | | a | a | a |
| T. bicarinata | | a | a | a |
| T. littoralis | | a | a | aa |
| T. oblonga | | a | a | a |
| T. quadrata | | a | a | a |
| T. sublineata | | a | a | a |
| T. subrotunda | | | a | a |
| T. terquemiana | | a | a | a |
| T. transversistriata | | x | x | x |
| T. tricarinata | | a | a | a |
| Edentostomina cultrata | | x | | |
| E. durrandii | | a | | |
| E. rupertiana | | a | | |
| E. milletti | | x | | |
| Pyrgo striolata | a | x | x | x |
| P. denticulata | | x | x | x |
| P. subglobulus | x | | | |
| P. depressa | | a | a | a |
| **Ophthalminidae** | | | | |
| Cornuspira involvens | | a | a | a |
| Cornuspirella diffusa | | x(low) | | |
| Nodophthalmidium simplex | x | | | |
| N. gracilis | a | x | | |
| Nodobaculariella rustica | | | x | |
| Vertebralina striata | | a | | |
| Ophthalmidium inconstans | x | | | |
| O. circularis tropicalis | a | | | |
| Polysegmentina circinata | | a | | |
| Planispirinella exigua | a | a | | |
| P. involuta | x | | | |
| Weisnerella auriculata | | a | a | a |
| Nubecularia decorata | | | x | |
| Nubeculopsis queenslandica | | x | | |
| Parrina bradyi | | a | a | a |
| **Peneroplidae** | | | | |
| Peneroplis planatus | | a | a | a |
| P. pertusus | | a | a | a |
| P. arietinus | | a | | |
| Spirolina cylindraceus | | a | x | x |

| Peneroplidae (continued) | Trinity Opening | Off-reef Shelf | Reef Flat | Mangrove |
|---|---|---|---|---|
| Monalysidium politum | | x | x | x |
| Sorites marginalis | x | x | | |
| Amphisorus duplex | | x | x | x |
| Marginopora vertebralis | | aa | aa | a |
| **Alveolinidae** | | | | |
| Alveolinella quoyi | | aa | | |
| **Fischerinidae** | | | | |
| Fischerina pellucida | x | | | |
| **LAGENIDEA** | | | | |
| **Lagenidae** | | | | |
| Lagena ampulla-distoma | | x | | |
| L. auriculata | | x | | |
| L. chasteri | | x | | |
| L. elongata | | a | a | a |
| L. gracillima | | a | a | a |
| L. laevis | | x | | |
| L. pacifica | x | | | |
| L. perlucida | | a | a | a |
| L. spiralis | | x | | |
| L. striato-punctata | x | | | |
| L. striata | | aa | aa | aa |
| L. sulcata | a | a | a | a |
| Oolina hexagona | x | | | |
| O. pseudocatenulata | a | | | |
| O. squamosa | x | | | |
| Fissurina contusa | | x | | |
| F. clathrata | x | | | |
| F. formosa brevis | x | | | |
| F. lacunata | x | x | | |
| F. lagenoides | | x | | |
| F. sublagenoides | x | x | | |
| F. lucida | | a | a | a |
| F. marginato-perforata | a | a | a | a |
| F. orbignyana | a | a | a | a |
| F. walleriana | x | | | |
| F. radiato-marginata | x | | | |
| F. semistriata | x | | | |
| F. staphyllearia | x | | | |
| F. wrightiana | | x | | |
| F. varioperforata | x | | | |
| Parafissurina unguis | x | | | |
| Nodosaria calomorpha | a | | | |
| N. proxima | x | x | | |
| N. pyrula | a | | | |
| Dentalina antarctica | x | | | |
| D. californica | x | | | |
| D. inflexa | x | | | |
| Vaginulina bassensis | x | | | |
| Marginulina glabra | x | | | |
| Amphicoryne scalaris | a | | | |
| A. hirsuta | x | | | |
| Planularia aff. tricarinella | x | | | |
| Lenticulina iota | a | | | |
| L. peregrina | x | | | |
| Robulus altifrons | a | | | |
| R. cf. cultratus | a | | | |
| R. formosus | x | | | |
| R. vortex | | x | | |

TABLE II (continued)

| | Trinity Opening | Off-reef Shelf | Reef Flat | Mangrove |
|---|:-:|:-:|:-:|:-:|
| **Polymorphinidae** | | | | |
| Guttulina regina | x | | | |
| Globulotuba entosoleniformis | x | | | |
| Pyrulina extensa | x | | | |
| Glandulina laevigata | | a | | |
| G. semistriata | | x | | |
| G. echinata | x | x | | |
| Sigmomorphina terqueminaa | x | | | |
| Laryngosigma williamsini | x | | | |
| **BULIMINIDEA** | | | | |
| **Buliminidae** | | | | |
| Buliminella cf. parallela | | x | x | x |
| B. latissima | x | | | |
| B. milletti | | x | x | x |
| B. spicata | a | a | | |
| Buliminoides williamsonianus | | x | x | x |
| Ungulatella pacifica | | x | | |
| Bulimina barbata | a | | | |
| B. marginata | a | x | | |
| B. rostrata | | x | | |
| B. oblonga | x | | | |
| Globobulimina australiensis | a | | | |
| Virgulina complanata | x | x | x | x |
| V. pauciloculata | a | a | | |
| Delosina complexa | | x | | |
| Reussella spinulosa | a | a | a | a |
| R. spinosissima | | x | x | x |
| Chrysalidinella dimorpha | | a | a | a |
| Mimosina affinis | | a | | |
| M. rimosa | | a | | |
| M. echinata | a | a | | |
| Trimosina milletti multispinata | | x | | |
| Uvigerina proboscidea | | x | x | x |
| U. porrecta | a | x | | |
| Siphouvigerina fimbriata | x | x | | |
| Siphogenerina striata curta | | x | x | x |
| S. virgula | a | a | a | a |
| Trifarina bradyi | x | | | |
| Gumbelitria vivans | a | a | | |
| Bolivinella elegans | a | | | |
| Bolivina abbreviata | | x | x | x |
| B. alata fimbriata | x | | | |
| B. compacta | | x | x | x |
| B. hantkeniana | x | | | |
| B. quadrilatera | x | | | |
| B. rhomboidalis | | x | x | x |
| B. subtenuis | x | | | |
| B. tortuosa | x | | | |
| B. zanzibarica | | x | | |
| Loxostomum convallarium | | a | a | |
| L. strigosum | x | | | |
| L. mayori | x | x | | |
| L. limbatum | a | a | a | a |
| Bifarina elongata | x | x | | |
| B. queenslandica | | x | x | x |
| Rectobolivina bifrons | x | | | |
| **Cassidulinidae** | | | | |
| Cassidulina elongata | | x | | |
| C. laevigata | | x | | |
| Orthoplecta clavata | | x | | |

| | Trinity Opening | Off-reef Shelf | Reef Flat | Mangrove |
|---|:-:|:-:|:-:|:-:|
| **Chilostomellidae** | | | | |
| Chilostomella oolina | x | | | |
| Seabrookia pellucida | a | x | | |
| Pullenia quinqueloba | x | | | |
| Sphaeroidina bulloides | a | | | |
| Nonionella pulchella | | x | | |
| Nonion subturgidus | | a | | |
| N. cf. depressulus | | x | x | x |
| N. scapha | | | | x |
| **ROTALIDEA** | | | | |
| **Spirillinidae** | | | | |
| Spirillina vivipara | a | a | a | a |
| S. limbata | | x | | |
| S. decorata | x | | | |
| S. inaequalis | | x | | |
| Planispirillina denticulata | | x | | |
| Mychostomina revertens | x | x | x | x |
| Patellina corrugata | x | x | x | x |
| P. altiformis | | x | | |
| **Rotalidae** | | | | |
| Discorbis rugosus | | x | | |
| D. subvesicularis | | x | x | x |
| Discopulvinulina bertheloti | | x | | |
| D. mira | | a | a | a |
| D. lobatula | x | | | |
| D. subcomplanata | | | | x |
| Rosalina orbicularis | a | | | |
| R. orientalis | | a | a | a |
| R. frustata | | x | | |
| Mississippina pacifica | x | | | |
| Conorbella patelliformis | | x | x | x |
| C. pulvinata | | x | | |
| C. pyramidalis | x | x | | |
| C. tabernacularis | a | a | a | a |
| C. corrugata | | x | | |
| C. opercularis | x | | | |
| C. earlandi | x | | | |
| Discorinopsis tropica | | | | x |
| Bronnimannia haliotis | x | x | | |
| Poroeponides lateralis | x | a | x | x |
| Patellinella jugosa | x | | | |
| P. nitida | x | | | |
| P. carinata | x | | | |
| Globorotalia tumida | x | | | |
| G. canariensis | a | | | |
| G. menardii | x | | | |
| Cancris auriculus | | a | a | a |
| Eponides repandus | | | | x |
| E. tubuliferus | | x | | |
| Gyroidinoides soldanii | x | | | |
| Truncorotalia truncatulinoides | x | | | |
| Höglundina elegans | a | | | |
| Rolshausenia inflata | | a | a | a |
| Torresina haddoni | x | | | |
| Pseudoparrella pulchra | | a | a | a |
| Epistomaroides polystomelloides | | a | a | a |
| Epistomariella milletti | | x | | |
| Anomalinella rostrata | | x | | |
| Siphonina tubulosa | | x | x | x |
| Siphoninoides glabrus | | a | a | a |

TABLE II (continued)

| | *Trinity Opening* | *Off-reef Shelf* | *Reef Flat* | *Mangrove* | | *Trinity Opening* | *Off-reef Shelf* | *Reef Flat* | *Mangrove* |
|---|---|---|---|---|---|---|---|---|---|
| ROTALIDEA (continued) | | | | | ROTALIDEA (continued) | | | | |
| S. echinatus | | x | x | x | E. craticulatum (large reef species) | | a | a | a |
| Rotalia erinacea | | x | x | x | E. crispum (large) | | a | a | a |
| R. murrayi | | x | x | x | E. hispidulum | | a | a | a |
| Streblus papillosus | | a | | | E. aff. josephinum | | | | x |
| S. convexus | | x | x | x | E. limbatum | | a | a | a |
| S. tepidus | | x | x | x | E. oceanicum | | x | x | x |
| | | | | | E. pacificum | x | | | |
| Ceratobuliminidae | | | | | | | | | |
| Geminospira bradyi | x | | | | Globigerinidae | | | | |
| Cushmanella primitiva | x | x | | | Globigerina bulloides | x | x | x | x |
| Lamarckina scabra | | x | | | G. cf. dubia | x | | | |
| Robertina tasmanica | x | | | | Globigerinella aequilateralis | x | | | |
| R. australis | a | | | | Globigerinoides sacculiferus | a | | | |
| Robertinoides oceanicus | x | | | | G. conglobatus | x | x | x | x |
| R. subcylindricus | x | | | | Pulleniatina obliquiloculata | x | | | |
| | | | | | Sphaeroidinella dehiscens | x | | | |
| Anomalinidae | | | | | | | | | |
| Anomalina tasmanica | a | | | | Pegidiidae | | | | |
| A. colligera | a | | | | Physalidia reniformis | | x | | |
| Cibicides praecinctus | | a | | | Pegidia dubia | | x | | |
| C. subhaidingeri | a | | | | | | | | |
| C. lobatulus | | x | x | x | Planorbulinidae | | | | |
| | | | | | Planorbulina rubra (encrusting) | | a | a | |
| Amphisteginidae | | | | | P. acervalis | | x | x | x |
| Amphistegina radiata | | a | a | a | Acervulina inhaerens | | x | x | x |
| | | | | | Gypsina vesicularis | | a | a | a |
| Calcarinidae | | | | | G. fimbriata | | x | | |
| Calcarina calcar | | a | a | a | Sphaerogypsina globulus | | a | a | a |
| C. venusta | | a | | | Planogypsina squamiformis | | x | | |
| Tinoporus baculatus | | a | a | a | Carpenteria monticularis | | x | | |
| T. hispidus | | a | a | a | Homotrema rubrum | | x | x | x |
| Baculogypsina sphaerulata | | | a | | Miniacina miniacea | | x | x | x |
| | | | | | | | | | |
| Cymbaloporidae | | | | | Nummulitidae | | | | |
| Cymbaloporetta bradyi | a | a | a | a | Operculina ammonoides | | a | a | a |
| C. squammosa | a | a | a | a | O. bartschi | | a | | |
| Cymbaloporella tabellaeformis | x | x | x | x | Operculinella venosa | | a | | |
| Tretomphalus milletti (littoral) | x | a | x | x | Heterostegina suborbicularis | | a | | |
| T. planus | x | x | x | x | H. operculinoides | x | | | |
| T. clarus | | x | | | Cycloclypeus carpenteri | x | | | |
| | | | | | | | | | |
| Elphidiidae | | | | | | | | | |
| Elphidium advenum | | a | a | a | | | | | |

x = present; a = abundant; aa = very abundant

declines is perhaps the most diverse. In the inter-reef areas, foraminifera are responsible for a large part of the bottom sediment. The only detailed study of the Great Barrier Reef faunas has been carried out by COLLINS (1958) and he identified the species collected from the Northern Region, during the 1928 expedition. Table II lists these species and indicates the broad zones where they occur as well as their abundance.

*Vertebrata*

In addition to the large invertebrate fauna of the reefs and surrounding seas, two smaller groups inhabit the region and exert an influence on the sand cays and islands.

The first of these two groups includes the birds (Fig. 136, 137) which nest on the numerous small islands, certain species being restricted to particular islands. Possibly the most common, most widely distributed species is *Larus novaehollandiae*, the Silver Gull which is found throughout the reef province. Next in abundance is the group of terns: *Anous minutus* (Noddy Tern) which nests in *Pisonia* trees, *Sterna anaethata* (Bridled Tern), *S. bergii* (Crested Tern), *S. sumatrana*

Fig. 136. A. *Chelonia mydas* in coral zone of Heron Reef; length of shell approximately 30 inches; B. *Chelonia mydas* in open water between Stapleton and Howick Reefs; C. Tree nesting terns - *Anous minutus* (Heron Island); D. Ground-nesting terns - *Sterna fuscata*, (Tydeman Reef cay); E. Tern's nest, Tydeman Cay.

(Black-Naped Tern), *S. dougalli* (Roseate Tern), and *S. fuscata* (Sooty Tern) which are all ground nesters. The large gannets *Sula leucogaster* and *S. dactylatra*, and the Frigate Bird (*Fregata minor*) inhabit the less vegetated sand cays, particularly those near the shelf-edge reefs in the Swains Complex and in the Northern Region. *Puffinus pacificus*, the Mutton Bird, is also a ground nester but it has very distinctive habits in that it burrows in the same manner as rabbits. Two striking though less common species are the Reef Heron (*Demigretta sacra*), and the White Breasted Eagle (*Haliaetus leucogaster*).

The main results of the dense bird population on the various cays and islands is the continual formation of guano which is mixed in with the humus and sand, sometimes producing a hard surface crust. The burrowing activity of *Puffinis pacificus* is also important in that sand to depths of 2 ft. is reworked and brought to the surface.

The second group of animals that frequent the sand cays includes three species of turtle: *Chelonia mydas* (Fig. 136A, B), the common Large Green Turtle, *Caretta caretta*, the Loggerhead Turtle, and *Eretmochelys imbricata*, the Hawkbill Turtle. All invade the

sand cays for nesting, and in the process they dig to depths of 3 ft., scattering sand over an area of several square yards. On some cays, the entire zone above high water mark consists of the mounds and depressions formed by turtles which, like *Puffinis pacificus*, are responsible for continual reworking of the sands on the cays.

BIOLOGICAL ZONATION

*Regional zonation*

The broad biological zonation of the Great Barrier Reef Province conforms closely with the bathymetric–physiographic pattern.

In the Near Shore Zone, muddy inter-tidal regions are dominated by the mangrove flora: *Rhizophora mucronata* and *Avicennia officinalis*, with which are associated the molluscs *Nerita*, *Pyrazus* and *Telescopium*, the giant swimming crab *Scylla serrata* and the worms *Thalassina* and *Clibinarius*. The sandy and rocky inter-tidal areas are markedly different (ENDEAN et al., 1956) in that their upper part is dominated by the oyster

Fig. 137. A. Fledgling tern (*Sterna fuscata*) on Tydeman Cay; B. Tern population, Tydeman Cay; C. Nesting gannets and fledglings - *Sula leucogaster* (Gannet Cay, Swains Complex); D, E. Bridled terns, *Sterna anaethata*, Tydeman Cay.

*Crassostrea amasa*, the gastropods *Nodolittorina*, *Melaraphe* and *Planaxis*, and the barnacle *Chthamalus*. The lower part is characterised by the barnacle *Tetraclita*, the chiton *Acanthozostera gemmata*, and algae. Below the inter-tidal levels, the Near Shore fauna varies with the nature of the substrate, whether muddy or sandy, but in both types foraminifera and pelecypods are dominant. *Elphidium*, *Textularia*, *Lagena*, *Quinqueloculina*, and *Triloculina* are the common foraminiferal genera, while scaphopods (*Dentalium*) and the pelecypods *Notovola fumata* (King Scallop), *Mimachlamys gloriosus*, *Decatopecten strangei*, *Chlamys radula*, *Gloripallium pallium* (Painted Scallop), *Malleus albus* (White Hammer Oyster), *Austropteria lata* (Broad-Winged Pearl Shell), *Pinna deltodes* (Razor Shell), *Spondylus wrightianus*, *Trichomya hirsuta*, *Cardita incrassata*, *Fragum fragum* (White Strawberry Cockle), and *Circe sugillata* (Tapestry Shell) are the main molluscan representatives.

The Inner Shelf faunas beyond the main reef zones are comparatively sparse. Foraminifera are again significant, the more common genera including *Elphidium*, *Textularia*, *Marginopora*, *Alveolinella*, *Quinqueloculina*, *Triloculina*, and *Lagena*. Molluscs are less abundant and less varied than those of the Near Shore Zone, although most members of that zone are represented. Echinoids are found, particularly in the sandy muds, the common species being *Amblypneustes ovum* and *Tripneustes gratilla*. Brittle stars also occur on the more sandy bottoms. Calcareous algae, particularly *Halimeda*, occur over most parts of the Inner Shelf, but never reach the abundance of the reef floras.

On the Marginal Shelf, two major faunal zones are found; that of the reef masses and that of the deeper, inter-reef areas. The inter-reef floor is generally covered with fine carbonate sand and silt on which a large foraminiferal population is dominant. *Textularia*, *Siphogaudryina*, *Quinqueloculina*, *Massilina*, *Spiroloculina*, *Hauerina*, *Triloculina*, *Pyrgo*, *Peneroplis*, *Marginopora*, *Alveolinella*, *Lagena*, *Cibicides*, *Amphistegina*, *Elphidium*, *Operculina*, and *Heterostigina* are well represented. The alga *Halimeda* and various molluscan species thrive in more restricted, more suitable parts of the area. The fauna and flora of the reef mass are the most prolific and most varied of the entire province.

### Reef zonation

The biological zonations of Low Isles and Yonge Reefs in the Northern and Central Regions have been described by MANTON and STEPHENSON (1935) and the al-

gal zonation of Heron Reef has been described by CRIBB (1966). No other reefs of the province have been analysed to the same degree.

The Low Isles Reef zonation is best illustrated graphically as in FIG. 165 (based on MANTON and STEPHENSON, 1935, plates 2–4). Algae occur mainly in the shallow pools of the reef top and are virtually absent from the reef slope and the drier parts of the reef flat. Brown algae are fewer than the green and red algae, and all decrease in abundance below depths of $1\frac{1}{2}$ fathoms. Below 35 fathoms, the green algae are dominant. Coral is dominant in the pools near the reef edge and on the slope below depths of 2 ft. The many species of *Acropora* reach their maximum abundance on the seaward slope, where they are less exposed to silting and temperature fluctuation. They are less numerous in the coral pools behind the reef crest. Massive corals—*Porites*, *Favia*, *Goniastrea*—occur on the slope, in the coral pools and on the outer flat. Because they are more resistant to silting and heating, they have a wider, though sparser distribution than the species of *Acropora*. The dominant corals of the pools are *Montipora ramosa*, *Pocillopora bulbosa*, *Favia*, *Goniastrea*, and *Leptastrea*. Towards the muddier areas, *Fungia*, *Galaxea*, *Symphyllia*, and *Goniastrea* are more common. These large polyped forms are better able to remove mud. In the deep muddy areas beyond the slope, only *Stylopora*, *Lobophyllia*, *Astreopora*, and *Favites* can survive.

On the reef flat and mangrove park, coral and algae are subordinate to other groups. Typical of the sandy areas are *Salmacus*, the burrowing echinoid; *Natica*, *Terebra*, and *Oliva*, burrowing gastropods; *Pterocera* (Spider Shell), *Meloamphora* (Bailer Shell), and *Cassis cornuta* (Helmet Shell), large gastropods; and the starfish *Astropecten* which works its way down into the sand. Many of these forms also occur in the dead coral zone. In addition, one finds *Stoichactis* (a giant anemone), *Hippopus hippopus* and *Tridacna crocea* (clams), *Pinna* (Razor Shell), *Ostrea crista galli*, *Cyprea* (a cowrie), *Haliotis assininus*, *Centrechinus setosus* (a black echinoid) and *Linkia* (a blue starfish). The weeds *Sargassum* and *Thalassia* are most abundant in and around the mangrove park. Also in this area are found the echinoid *Tripneustes*, the swimming crab *Scylla serrata*, and the gastropod *Pyrazus palustris*.

On the Heron Reef (CRIBB, 1966) a broad three-fold zonation of the algae has been recognised corresponding to the beach, reef flat and seaward margin, each of which is subdivided into "bands". The algal composition of these zones and bands has been summarised in Table III.

## TABLE III

DISTRIBUTION OF ALGAL SPECIES ON HERON REEF (after CRIBB, 1966)

(* = dominant species)

| Beach zone | Reef flat | Algal rim and reef front |
|---|---|---|
| **Sandy beach** | **Inshore gutter or moat** | **Boulder zone** |
| *Entophysalis deusta* | *\*Enteromorpha clathrata* | *Entophysalis deusta* |
| *\*Enteromorpha clathrata* | *Penicillus sibogae* | *Halimeda discoidea* |
| *Ostreobium reineckei* | *Padina gymnospora* | *Halimeda opuntia* |
| *Coralline algae* | *\*Gelidillea bornetii* | *Caulerpa racemosa* |
| | *Champia parvula* | *Chlorodesmis comosa* |
| **Beach rock** | *Jania adhaerens* | *Turbinaria ornata* |
| *Entophysalis deusta* band | | *Sargassum* |
| *\*Entophysalis deusta* | **Sand flat and dead coral zone** | *Ralfsia* |
| *\*Calothrix crustacea* | | *Peyssonelia* sp. |
| *Calothrix pilosa* | *Hormothamnion enteromorphoides* | *Lithothamnion* sp. |
| *Phormidium tenue* | *Oscillatoria margaritifera* | *Liagora cenomyce* |
| *Lyngbya semiplena* | *Lyngbya majuscula* | |
| *Rivularia atra* | *Lyngbya semiplena* | **Laurencia–Palythoa band** |
| *Kyrtuthrix maculans* | *Calothrix crustacea* | *Dictyosphaeria intermedia* |
| *Enteromorpha clathrata* | *Fremyella grisea* | *Boodlea composita* |
| *Monostroma* sp. | *Valonia ventricosa* | *Halimeda discoidea* |
| *Pseudendoclonium submarinum* | *Microdictyon obscurum* | *Halimeda opuntia* |
| *Cladophora* sp. | *Acetabularia moebii* | *Chlorodesmis comosa* |
| *Pilinia* | *Acetabularia clavata* | *Caulerpa racemosa* |
| | *Udotea javanensis* | *Turbinaria ornata* |
| *Kyrtuthrix maculans* band | *Rhipidodesmis caespitosa* | *Sargassum* sp. |
| *\*Kyrtuthrix maculans* | *Cladophora crystallina* | *\*Laurencia pannosa* |
| *\*Entophysalis deusta* | *Enteromorpha clathrata* | *\*Laurencia obtusa* |
| *\*Entophysalis conferta* | *Boodlea composita* | *Gelidiella acerosa* |
| *\*Microcoleus tenerrimus* | *Dictyosphaeria versluysii* | *Laurencia flexilis* |
| *\*Lyngbya rivularianum* | *\*Chlorodesmis comosa* | *Laurencia papillosa* |
| *\*Calothrix crustacea* | *\*Halimeda opuntia* | *Jania adhaerens* |
| *\*Spirulina tenerrima* | *\*Halimeda discoidea* | *Hypnea* sp. |
| *\*Mastigocoleus testarum* | *\*Halimeda cylindracea* | *Tolypiocladia glomerata* |
| *\*Oscillatoria chalybea* | *\*Halimeda macroloba* | *Peyssonelia* |
| *Enteromorpha clathrata* | *\*Caulerpa racemosa* | *Lithothamnion* |
| *Cladophora crystallina* | *\*Padina gymnospora* | *Crouania* |
| *Gelidiella bornetii* | *\*Dictyota bartayresii* | *Amphiroa foliacea* |
| *Erythrotrichia carnea* | *\*Chnoospora implexa* | |
| | *\*Hydroclathrus clathratus* | **Reef front** |
| *Gelidiella bornetii* band | *\*Pocockiella variegata* | *Chlorodesmis comosa* |
| *Calothrix crustacea* | *\*Sargassum polycystum* | *Caulerpa racemosa* |
| *Coccochloris elabens* | *\*Sargassum crassifolium* | *Dictyosphaeria versluysii* |
| *Lyngbya nordgardhii* | *Turbinaria ornata* | *Halimeda discoidea* |
| *\*Enteromorpha clathrata* | *Ectocarpus mitchellae* | *Halimeda opuntia* |
| *\*Cladophora crystallina* | *Ectocarpus indicus* | *Turbinaria ornata* |
| *Sphacelaria* sp. | *Ectocarpus irregularis* | *Gelidiella adnata* |
| *Ectocarpus* sp. | *Sphacelaria furcigera* | *Laurencia* sp. |
| *\*Gelidiella bornetii* | *Sphacelaria tribuloides* | *Lithothamnion* |
| *Erythrotrichia carnea* | *Sphacelaria novae-hollandiae* | *Peyssonelia* |
| *Goniotrichum alsidii* | *Ralfsia* | *Lithophyllum moluccense* |
| *Asterocytis ornata* | *Gelidiella acerosa* | |
| *Lophosiphonia scopulorum* | *Gelidiella bornetii* | |
| *Laurencia* sp. | *Herposiphonia tenella* | |
| | *Jania adhaerens* | |
| | *Gelidiopsis intricata* | |
| | *Ceramium gracillimum* | |
| | *Centroceras clavulatum* | |
| | *Centroceras clavulatum* | |
| | *Lophosiphonia scopulorum* | |
| | *Tolypiocladia glomerata* | |
| | *Peyssonelia hariotii* | |
| | *Lithothamnion simulans* | |
| | *Amansia glomerata* | |
| | *Hypoglossum* | |

TABLE III (continued)

| Beach zone | Reef flat | Algal rim and reef front |
|---|---|---|
| | Living coral zone and pools | |
| | *Mastigocoleus testarum* | |
| | *Pilinia* | |
| | *Pseudopringsheimia* | |
| | *Ostreobium reineckei* | |
| | *Acetabularia moebii* | |
| | *Caulerpa racemosa* | |
| | *Halimeda discoidea* | |
| | *Halimeda opuntia* | |
| | *Halimeda incrassata* | |
| | *Codium spongiosum* | |
| | *Cladophoropsis vaucheriaeformis* | |
| | *\*Porolithon* | |
| | *Peyssonelia hariotii* | |
| | *Laurencia* sp. | |
| | *\*Lithophyllum moluccense* | |
| | *Amphiroa foliacea* | |
| | *Amphiroa crassa* | |
| | *Hypnea nidulans* | |

# Chapter 8 | Sediments

In view of the enormous areal extent of the Great Barrier Reef Province, of its range of bathymetric and hydrologic conditions and of the geological diversity of the shelf and adjacent land mass, it is not surprising to find wide variation in its sedimentary cover. The Near Shore Zone includes fine sandy, quartzose beaches, coarse sandy and gravelly quartzose–feldspathic beaches, pebble and boulder beaches, large intertidal mud flats and extensive sand flats. Muds and muddy sands with localised carbonate concentrations typify the Inner Shelf while in places its eastern borders have comparatively mud-free sands. The Marginal Shelf where maximum reef growth occurs is covered by fine, muddy carbonate sands. On the reef surfaces, carbonate gravels and coarse sands are dominant over the reef flat. Finer sands and silts are typical of the lagoons, while boulder accumulations of widely varying magnitude and shingle banks occur on the reef crests or rims. The bases of the reef masses are fringed with narrow zones of carbonate gravels and coarse sands. In addition to its diversity of sediment type, the province is characterised by the general abruptness of transition from one type to another. Furthermore, the sediments are predominantly detrital terrigenous and bioclastic in origin. The contribution of inorganically precipitated material, particularly carbonate, is negligible.

Composition—both mineralogical and biological—also shows extreme variation. The terrigenous sands of the Near Shore and Inner Shelf are predominantly quartzose, and they carry the imprint of aeolian, fluviatile and marine processes, having been derived from the large dune systems of the present coastal region, from the granitic and sandstone hinterlands drained by the eastern rivers and from the pre-Recent dunes and beaches which were submerged by the later transgressions of the Quaternary. The non-carbonate muds of these two zones are comparatively constant in composition. Kaolinite averages 20%, montmorillonite 60% and illite 20%, and there is no marked progressive change in their proportions with distance from shore, distance along the province or with depth. The composition of reef-surface sediment changes rapidly in response to the main faunal changes across the reef, and there are significant differences in sediments from different reefs largely because of variations in their faunal constitution. The major components of the surface sediments are lithothamnioid algae (17–40%), *Halimeda* (10–30%), coral (20–40%), foraminifera (8–20%), mollusc (4–15%), and echinoid, bryozoan and crustacean detritus (which together make up less than 5%). In the inter-reef areas the relative proportions change markedly, viz. lithothamnioid algae (0–15%), *Halimeda* (5–65%), coral (5–10%), foraminifera (15–40%), mollusc (20–35%), and bryozoans (5–30%).

In addition to the detritus from the present reef faunas, a large proportion is derived through the erosion of old, dead reef surfaces which have been subjected to subaerial attack since the last fall of sea level. This material, although altered and largely recrystallised, can still be identified in terms of its biological origin, and it represents an important and distinct component in the sediment, particularly that of the inter-reef areas in the Southern and Central Regions and of all zones in the Northern Regions. Another alteration in sediment of the Inner Shelf has given rise to the very distinctive "speckled sands". These form when a relatively high percentage of foraminiferal tests, particularly those of *Marginopora* and *Alveolinella*, are present. Reducing conditions within the bottom sediment result in the reduction of iron to the sulphide with consequent black staining of the test. In other zones where the tests have been exposed to oxidising conditions, the iron oxide so formed gives them a rust colour and the "rusty sand" facies can be recognised, although its areal limits are less sharply defined than those of the speckled sands. In the more terrigenous facies of the Inner Shelf and Near Shore Zones, reaction involving iron results in the formation of glauconite inside foraminiferal tests.

The variation in the sedimentary character of the province, the abruptness of facies change and the factors responsible for these changes are best examined with the aid of distribution maps and charts. In the following pages several distribution patterns are developed and assessed.

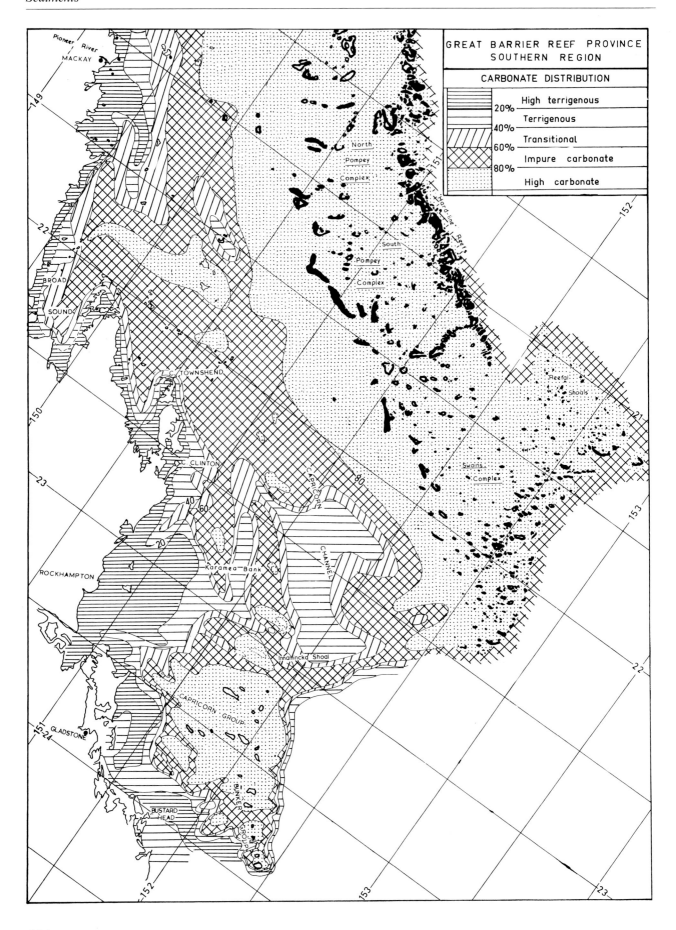

## DISTRIBUTION PATTERNS IN SEDIMENTS

### Carbonate distribution

Although reefs occupy a significant portion of the continental shelf north from latitude 24°S, and although they exert a controlling influence on the sedimentary processes, carbonate sediments are predominant in less than two-thirds of the entire province.

In Fig. 138A–D, the carbonate content of the sediments has been determined by measurement of the amounts of acid-soluble material, and these values have been plotted on a 20% interval. Sediment with more than 80% soluble material forms the high-carbonate facies; 60–80%, the impure-carbonate facies; 40–60%, the transitional facies and less than 40% the terrigenous facies. It has also been useful to recognise a high-terrigenous subfacies with less than 20% soluble fraction, but this is not well-represented throughout the entire length of the province. Examination of each facies in terms of areal and depth relationships reveals progressive changes from south to north.

### Terrigenous facies

The terrigenous facies (Fig. 139) shows a general decrease in width as one moves northward. In the Gladstone–Bustard Head area of the Southern Region it averages 15–20 miles whereas in the Northern Region beyond Princess Charlotte Bay it is approximately 1 mile. Exceptions to this progressive narrowing are found near the mouths of major streams. Near the Fitzroy River, the facies reaches a maximum width of 29 miles, near the Pioneer–Proserpine Rivers it is 19 miles, near the Burdekin–Haughton it is 18 miles and near the Herbert River it is 18 miles. Expansion of the facies also tends to occur where there are large areas of coastal dunes, high tidal range and strong tidal currents, e.g., Curtis Island, Shoalhaven Bay, Princess Charlotte Bay. The average width of the facies is 17 miles in the Southern Region, 14 miles in the Central and 4½ miles in the Northern Region.

The northward reduction in the width of the facies is due largely to wedging out of the high-terrigenous subfacies (Fig. 140) which disappears near Townsville (latitude 19°15′S). This non-calcareous sediment, consisting of quartzose sands and muddy sands, is restricted to the Southern and south Central Regions and owes its development to several related factors. In the first case, near the northern limit of the subfacies the shelf narrows considerably and the reefs of the Marginal Shelf Zone are nearer to the shore line than those to the south. The closer reefs supply some carbonate detritus to the terrigenous facies. Secondly, the narrow shelf allows the ready penetration of oceanic water which brings with it pelagic faunas that contribute to the Near Shore sediment. The third factor, related to the narrowing of the shelf and the penetration of oceanic water, is the development of Near Shore reefs. They become increasingly abundant north of Townsville and contribute significant quantities of carbonate to the terrigenous facies: between 20% and 40%. The additional sources of carbonate all serve to dilute the high-terrigenous subfacies until it loses its identity in the main facies.

Fig. 139. Sediment from the terrigenous facies (Sample 24) (×3.2).

Fig. 140. Sediment from the high-terrigenous subfacies (Sample 309 - Fitzroy mouth). (×3.2).

*189*

Depth range of the terrigenous facies changes from south to north. It varies from 0 to 20 fathoms in the Southern Region, 0 to 12 fathoms in the Central Region and 0 to 6 fathoms in the Northern Region. This progressive decrease in maximum depth is consistent with the regional bathymetric trend of the shelf. It is also possible that the closer proximity of reefs as one moves northward may prevent eastward expansion of the facies with deeper water.

A seemingly anomalous, but nevertheless large occurrence of the terrigenous facies is found in the Southern Shelf Embayment where it is surrounded by the transitional and impure-carbonate facies and separated from the land mass by the Capricorn–Bunker Reef Complex. It covers an area of more than 900 square miles, at depths of 40–70 fathoms. Although it is a low-carbonate sediment, it differs from the material of the terrigenous facies fringing the land mass in that it consists almost entirely of mud. Its occurrence is a reflection of the low energy conditions that prevail at depths below 10 fathoms on the shelf and embayment. The inability to move coarse reef detritus for even moderate distances at these depths accounts for the small contribution from the Capricorn–Bunker Complex and the Swains Complex. Furthermore, it will be shown later that carbonate material finer than silt is not abundant in the reef sediments and presumably is not produced in significant quantity. The only sediment then that can be transported into the embayment is the fine terrigenous suspension that survives flocculation in the Near Shore Zone and is carried seaward where it can settle slowly in this deep area, remote from sources of terrigenous and carbonate sand.

*Transitional facies*

The transitional facies (Fig. 141) with 40–60% carbonate content, is generally narrower than any of the others. In the Southern Region, its width is from 1½ to 2 miles, in the Central Region from 6 to 11 miles and in the Northern Region from 3 to 4 miles.

On the regional scale the narrow strip of transitional or mixed carbonate–terrigenous sediment is conspicuous because of the contrasting pattern produced by the other, wider facies. One might reasonably infer that its restricted extent reflects very limited migration of material from the reef and terrigenous zones or possibly the encroachment of one facies on to the other. In either case, the area of intermixing is small and this may be regarded as evidence of low-energy conditions and consequently of low transport capacity of shelf waters. If this were not so, then the area of intermixing should be more extensive. When detailed analysis of the sediments is carried out, it is found that the change from terrigenous to impure-carbonate sediments is even more abrupt than is suggested by the regional pattern. In the area adjacent to Gladstone in the Southern Region and the Cairns offshore area in the north Central Region, carbonate values rise from 25% to 75% over distances of less than one mile.

The transitional facies varies in its bathymetric range. In the Southern Region it occurs mainly at the 16-fathom level, but extends in some areas to 20 fathoms, and on the northern and eastern borders of the Capricorn Reefs, where the floor descends into the Southern Shelf Embayment, transitional sediments form a nar-

Fig. 141. Sediment from the transitional facies (Sample 3303) between terrigenous and carbonate zones, south of Mackay (×1.4). Note strong bryozoan component.

Fig. 142. Impure-carbonate facies (Sample 219) north of Capricorn Group (×3.2).

row zone between 24 and 28 fathoms. However, these deeper occurrences are exceptional and related to the unusual bathymetry of the Southern Region. Furthermore, the deeper transitional sediments are mainly muds.

The transitional facies in the Central Region appears to be restricted to the interval between 14 and 22 fathoms. Because of its greater width in this region (6–11 miles) and its larger bathymetric range, more effective processes of sediment dispersion may be suspected. Two features of the Central Region are its very high tidal range which results in strong tidal currents, and the absence of an effective Shelf Edge reef system that could diminish the intensity of waves sweeping in from the open ocean across this section of the shelf. The increased activity of both waves and currents could provide the energy level necessary for dispersion, a level that does not appear to have been reached on the Inner Shelf of the Northern and Southern Regions. A third, though possibly less significant, feature of the Central Region is that three of the four large river systems of eastern Queensland empty their loads along its western margin: Pioneer–Proserpine, Burdekin–Haughton, and Herbert. The supply of terrigenous material would appear to be greater than that afforded to the other regions and would enhance the possibility of its wider dispersion into zones that would normally be more calcareous.

The depth range of the transitional facies in the Northern Region is from 9 to 12 fathoms, which is not consistent with its range further south. The shallower occurrence is, in part, a reflection of the regional trend towards decreasing shelf depths in the north, and a reflection of the influence of the numerous Near Shore and Inner Shelf reefs as well as the closer proximity of the Marginal Shelf reefs. In this case, the greater supply of reef detritus and the comparatively small influx of terrigenous material permit the westward expansion of a strong carbonate fraction into the sediments of the shallow, Inner Shelf. Only in the large, wide Princess Charlotte Bay is there expansion of the facies and this is caused by the influx of terrigenous sediment from the Normanby River system on the south and the extensive reef development on the north and east.

Although there is a variable range of depth and width for the transitional facies, in the Southern and Central Regions it appears to be located mainly at the 16-fathom level. The level has already been recognised in the bathymetric analysis of the shelf and evidence has been presented to support the view that the 16-fathom plain and gradient change were developed at a time of lower sea level. Detailed sampling at this level in the

Southern and north Central Regions has revealed that a considerable part of the transitional facies consists of molluscan debris that has affinities with the present inter-tidal faunas. This lends further support to the possibility of a 16-fathom strandline and may also provide an explanation for the sharp increase in carbonate content in the transitional sediments. The poor definition of the 16-fathom feature in parts of the Central Region and the expansion of the transitional facies in such areas may well result from the same cause, viz. erosion and dispersal under stronger-energy conditions. It has been noted already that the tidal range of this region is comparatively large and that the sparse Shelf Edge reefs provide little protection against oceanic swell. The higher level of energy then would allow wider dispersal of sedimentary material and also tend to obscure bathymetric features by sediment infilling and possibly by mild erosion. In the Northern Region, the 16-fathom terrace has provided a foundation for much of the reef development and the transitional facies has been shifted shorewards. Its occurrence in this region does not have the same significance, but the existence of a later strand line at the 10 fathom level may have helped to localise the facies in the 9–12 fathoms interval. Because of the prolific growth of reefs in the immediate vicinity, it is difficult to differentiate reefal and old inter-tidal bioclastic material, and so the influence of the 10-fathom strandline on the present position of the transitional facies has been obscured.

*Impure-carbonate facies*

The impure-carbonate facies (Fig. 142) with 60–80% carbonate, forms an extremely irregular belt that branches in the Southern Region around the large area of terrigenous sediment in the Southern Shelf Embayment. Its eastern margin is quite sinuous and reflects the somewhat random distribution of the inner reefs of the Marginal Shelf and of the deeper passages through these reefs. The areal pattern is most complex in the Southern Region. Around the Capricorn–Bunker Complex, the facies occupies a zone 2–6 miles wide, but further east beyond the terrigenous sediments of the Shelf Embayment, it ranges from 7 to 15 miles. Further north, in the lee of the Pompey Complex, the facies reaches a maximum width of 35 miles, and is separated from a western development 7–15 miles in width, by a narrow belt of high carbonate sediment. The Central Region has a less varied zone of impure carbonates, averaging 2–6 miles. Local expansion of the facies to 25 miles occurs off the Bowen and Townsville areas.

A relatively constant width of 2–5 miles is typical of the Northern Region. Depth variation is also extreme in the Southern Region, becoming less marked further north. The south-western branch of the facies belt ranges from 18 to 40 fathoms, while that along the eastern side of the Southern Shelf Embayment occurs between 32 and 50 fathoms. In the Central Region its depth range is more restricted: 16–22 fathoms, except in the Bowen–Townsville sector where it extends to 34 fathoms. It is even more restricted in the Northern Region, occurring mainly between 10 and 16 fathoms, although isolated developments around Near Shore reefs are found between 2 and 6 fathoms.

Factors controlling the distribution of the transitional and impure-carbonate facies are the same but their relative influences are different. Because of the greater depths, energy levels are lower and the degree of transportation less. Increased distance from the land area and consequently from the terrigenous source, and closer proximity to the main reef developments favour higher carbonate fractions. Furthermore, because of distance and depth, the terrigenous and carbonate fractions contributing to the facies are generally more finely grained than those of the terrigenous, transitional (except in the Southern Shelf Embayment) and high-carbonate facies. Some of the carbonate material may be derived from old strandline accumulations (particularly at the 20-, 32- and 36-fathom levels) and indigenous benthonic foraminifera and molluscs as well as from the finer grades of reef detritus, and the carbonate mode tends to be coarser than that of the intermixed terrigenous material. The sinuous eastern margin of the facies, particularly in the Northern and Central Regions is indicative of the very limited degree of transportation of reef detritus. Except for the inter-reef passages where tidal scour is most effective, and the extensive belt west of the Swains and Pompey Complexes in the Southern Region, the impure-carbonate facies closely borders the zone of main reef development of the Marginal Shelf. Its projection into the passages is caused by tidal-current transport. Its remoteness from the Southern Region reefs is a reflection of the massive source of carbonate detritus in this area (the widest area of reef development), of the strong tidal-current activity and of the effective wave action from south-east swell which sweeps along the southern, leeward side of the Marginal Shelf reefs. It is also probable that reef development on the Southern Marginal Shelf has a longer history than that of any other part of the province and consequently, the accumulation of carbonate sediment has been greater.

*High-carbonate facies*

The high-carbonate facies (Fig. 143) with more than 80% carbonate, is restricted to the areas of reef growth except in the Southern Region where a discontinuous belt extends northward from the Capricorn reefs for more than 70 miles. This belt rises from depths of 32 and 36 fathoms to levels as shallow as 6 fathoms. At its southern end it contains abundant reef faunas which form "reefal shoals" or submerged reefs. These become progressively deeper to the north and are finally replaced by isolated accumulations of skeletal carbonate, largely of bryozoan origin and in the extreme north by molluscan detritus. The facies appears to have been formed by the accumulation of shell detritus from ancient inter-tidal faunas that existed at the 32- and 36-fathom shorelines, and by contributions from later reefal organisms that colonised the old strandline features as sea level rose. Further north on the same trend as the southern belt but unrelated to it, are more large isolated developments of high-carbonate sediment. These occurrences are mainly in the 16–20 fathom interval, and the carbonate is derived from molluscan debris. It is possible that they represent old shoreline accumulations formed during low stands of sea level at 16 and 20 fathoms.

The high-carbonate facies of the reef areas in the Northern and north Central Region does not extend for more than 1 mile beyond the reef margins. In the southern Capricorn–Bunker complex, it spreads for 5–10 miles, except in the north-west where its boundary

Fig. 143. High-carbonate facies (Sample 3047) from Swains Complex (×1.4). *Halimeda* and foraminifera dominant.

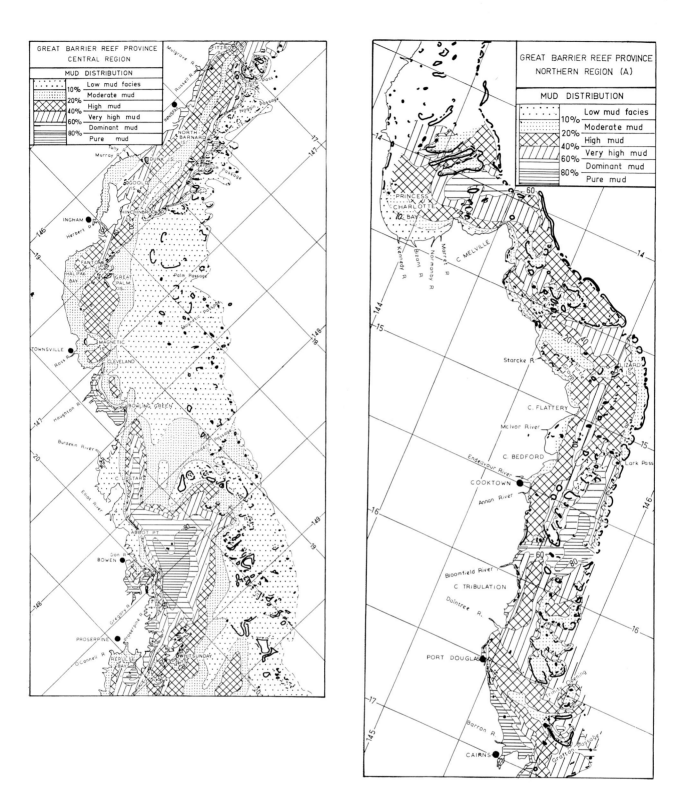

Fig. 144A–D. Mud-sand distribution, Great Barrier Reef Province. (For Fig. 144D see reverse side.)

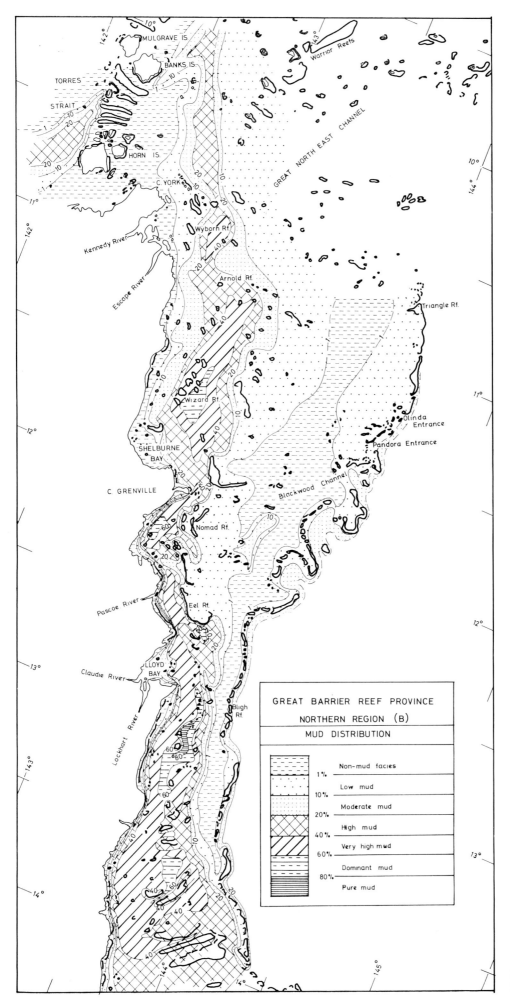

Fig. 144D.
Legend see reverse side.

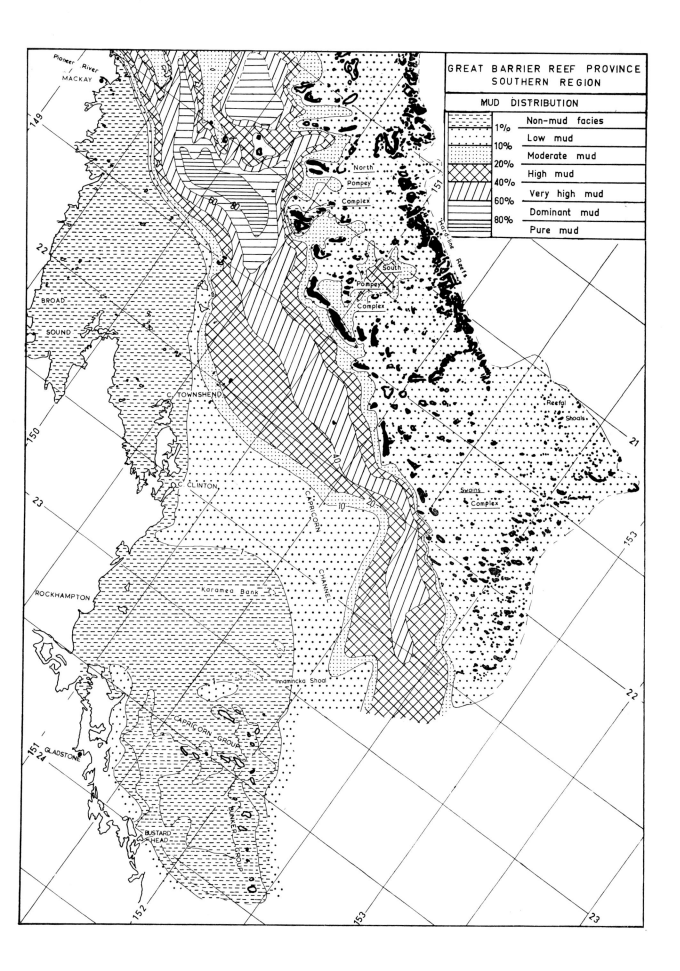

is more than 15 miles from the reefs. By contrast, the facies south from latitude 20°S (east of the Whitsunday Group) to the Swains Complex at latitude 22°S is characterised by its great expansion beyond the western limits of the reef area. Opposite the Pompey and North Swains Complexes, the facies extends westward for 15–25 miles, while further north it reaches a maximum of 40 miles.

The marked expansion of the facies is related to factors already discussed in connection with the impure-carbonate facies, viz. the massive source of carbonate detritus from the widest reefal area of the shelf, the strong tidal-current activity in the sector of highest tidal range and dense reef growth, and the possibly greater age of the Marginal Shelf reefs south of latitude 20°. Furthermore, the progressive northward decrease in shelf depth favours higher energy levels and more effective transportation. In the Northern Region, this factor is counterbalanced by a reduction in the size of the reef area and consequently of detrital carbonate supply, and by closer proximity of the land mass. Thus the greater energy in the shallower Northern Region is expended both on a smaller carbonate source and on an adjacent terrigenous facies which helps to contain the carbonate facies.

## Mud distribution

The mud of the Queensland Continental Shelf is predominantly terrigenous in origin. Very little fine carbonate is contributed by the reefs and in this respect the Great Barrier Reef Province differs markedly from others such as the Bahamas and Florida. Except in the reefs of the Southern Marginal Shelf which is more than 100 miles from land, a terrigenous-mud fraction is present throughout most of the reef area and it is quite significant in the Northern Region. The mud pattern has developed in response to several factors, the relative influences of which change as one progresses northward through the province or seawards from the shoreline. Most important are wave and tidal forces, bathymetric character, shelf width, density and proximity of reefs, proximity of land, stream discharge, lithological character of drainage basins, climatic variation and coastal vegetation. The influences of all can be recognised when the mud–sand facies pattern is examined. In Fig. 144A–D, this pattern is based on six sedimentary types, viz. sand facies (less than 1% mud), slightly muddy sand facies (1–10% mud), muddy sand facies (10–20% mud), very muddy sand facies (20–40% mud), sandy mud facies (40–80% mud), and mud facies (more than 80% mud). The first two types—sand and

slightly muddy sand facies—are the most extensive and together occupy more than half the total area of the province.

## Sand facies

The sand facies (less than 1% mud) is virtually restricted to the Southern Region where it covers the western quarter of the shelf and to the reef surfaces which, collectively for the entire province, comprise an area of comparable size. Terrigenous, carbonate and mixed sands (Fig. 145) occur in the western part of the Southern Region whereas those of the reef surfaces are purely carbonate.

The distribution pattern of the western facies is conspicuous in that it consists of two widely expanded areas connected by an extremely narrow band. The southernmost area extends seaward for 35–75 miles from the coastline between Bustard Head and Waterpark, a distance of 90 miles. The second area flanks the land between Broad Sound and Mackay (120 miles) and reaches a maximum width of 42 miles. Connecting the two is the narrow band, less than 5 miles in width, that borders the Port Clinton–Cape Townshend sector. Depth ranges in which the facies occurs vary from 0–10 fathoms near Mackay, to 0–40 fathoms off the Fitzroy River mouth.

The occurrence of the facies in the Broad Sound and Bustard Head–Waterpark areas is suggestive of a relationship with the Fitzroy River since both areas belong to the older drainage systems of the Fitzroy. Furthermore, the facies is virtually unique to the Southern Region. It is either absent or poorly developed off the other major streams to the north—Proserpine, Burdekin, Herbert, Normanby—and in seeking causal factors, one might profitably consider the aspects of the Fitzroy system and the Southern Region that distinguish them from the other parts of the province. In the first instance, the Fitzroy discharges on the southern margin of the province where exposure to the open ocean and south-east swell as well as the tidal flow favour long-shore movement of sediment in a northerly direction. Immediately to the south is the large Maryborough Basin with its extensive Mesozoic sandstone formations that have been dissected by major streams such as the Mary, Burnett and Kolan Rivers. Their submarine courses are directed north-eastward, and it is conceivable that they supplied large quantities of sand to the shelf, particularly during times of lower sea level, and it is this material that has been moved and is still being moved by the northward, long-shore flow. The movement and accumulation of comparatively clean sand during low stands of sea level was intensified by wind action leading to large-scale dune formation, relics of which are well preserved along the present coastline. Subsequent transgression brought much of the dune material into the higher energy environment of the Near Shore Zone where wave and tidal scour effectively dispersed it across the Inner Shelf. In addition to this southern source of sand, the ancient Fitzroy Basin may also have provided a substantial contribution to the Inner Shelf. Although the present basin is now largely denuded of friable sandstone and granitic material, the existence of extensive sandy alluvium in its valleys is evidence of their previous contribution to the Fitzroy load which, at lower sea level, was deposited on the present Inner Shelf. Thus the Fitzroy and the southern rivers of the Maryborough Basin appear to have supplied the sediment for this facies. However, hydrodynamic factors are responsible for the concentration of these relatively mud-free deposits. The unprotected shelf is exposed to vigorous wave action generated by the prevailing South-East Trades, and mud deposition is effectively prevented. In addition, high tidal range results in strong current movement which assists in the seaward dispersal of sand and the further removal of mud. Furthermore, as one moves northward, the Inner Shelf comes under the protection of the Marginal Shelf reefs, wave activity is reduced and long-shore drift declines. In the Mackay–Broad Sound area the tidal directions change from north-flooding to south-flooding, with consequent convergence of tidal streams near Broad Sound and opposition to further long-shore drift north of here. There is no reason to doubt that similar patterns of water movement existed during phases of lower sea level. The net effect of the change in tidal direction and of the reduction in wave intensity northward from Broad Sound is reflected in the wedging of the facies which finally disappears near Mackay. With negligible northward drift and opposing tidal movement, migration of southern sand ceases. The absence of a substantial source north of Mackay and the lower energy level of the Near Shore Zone prevent a comparable sand movement in the Central and Northern Regions. The great expansion of the facies in the Bustard Head–Waterpark area is due to additional supply of carbonate sand from the Capricorn–Bunker reef complex, situated near the Shelf Edge. Because of the dual supply of sediment from both land and reef, the sand facies occupies the entire shelf in this area.

Except in the southern area where both carbonate and terrigenous materials contribute, the eastern limit of the sand facies approximates the eastern border of the transitional facies defined on carbonate content. The relationship between the transitional facies and the 16-fathom level has already led to the suggestion of ancient strandline control on its formaton, in as much as inter-tidal faunal development and later reef growth were localised by strandline features. A similar influence appears to have been exerted on sand accumulation. Since the main sand movement occurs in the surf zone, it is to be expected that during the phase of the 16-fathom sea level, sand accumulation would have occurred in the adjacent Near Shore Zone as well as in the dunes bordering the old shoreline. In the northern area of the sand facies—Broad Sound to Mackay—the eastern limit rarely reaches depths of 20 fathoms.

*Slightly muddy sand facies*

The slightly muddy sand facies (1–10% mud) includes the predominantly terrigenous sediments of the Inner Shelf of the Southern Region and the carbonate sediments of the inter-reef areas of the Marginal Shelf throughout the entire province.

The terrigenous sediments (Fig. 146) reach their maximum development in the re-entrant between the Broad Sound and Capricorn–Bunker areas of the sand facies. This expansion, 30–40 miles wide, possibly reflects the neutral zone between the old and newer drainage systems of the Fitzroy. The zone is too remote from either to have received sand at a rate sufficient to lower the mud–sand ratio to the level of the sand facies, but the rate was sufficient to enable it to expand seawards into areas where muddy sediments would normally have formed. North from this area, the facies narrows abruptly and continues towards Mackay as a narrow band less than 3 miles wide. In the Central Region it is largely absent while in the Northern Region it is represented by narrow intermittent bands, 1–4 miles wide, north of Cape Flattery. Its poor development beyond the Southern Region is due to the same factors that have restricted the sand facies. The lack of sand source, decreasing tidal range and reduced water movement have inhibited sand migration in parts of the Central Region particularly. Furthermore, the big influx of mud from coastal streams such as the Proserpine, Burdekin, Herbert, Tully, Russell, Barron and Daintree which drain the well-vegetated, high rainfall belt of Queensland, effectively dilutes the sand fraction. Extensive mangrove growth also contributes to the accumulation of mud in-shore and this provides source material for seaward transportation. The narrowing and shoaling of the shelf as one moves northward results in compression of the facies zones as well as

Figure 145. Sand facies (Sample 3291), Near Shore, south of Mackay (×1.4).

Fig. 147. Slightly muddy carbonate sand of the Marginal Shelf (Sample 3192), Southern Pompey Complex (×1.4).

greater intermixing of sands and muds.

The slightly muddy sand facies of the Marginal Shelf (Fig. 147) extends almost continuously for the entire length of the province. It occupies the inter-reef areas and consists of detritus swept from the reefs, detritus derived from inter-reef benthos, particularly foraminifera, molluscs, *Halimeda*, and bryozoans, and terrigenous mud that has been carried seaward from the coastal region. In the Southern Region a maximum width of 70 miles is reached in the Swains Complex, north of which the average width is 35 miles. Expansion of the facies to 53 miles occurs north-east of Townsville followed by an abrupt reduction to 3–10 miles, a width that persists for the remainder of the province

to the north. In the Southern and Central Regions, the facies occurs mainly at depths of 26–36 fathoms. North of Cooktown, its depth range decreases to 5–10 fathoms.

*Muddy sand facies*

The muddy sand facies (10–20% mud) (Fig. 148) forms the narrow, gradational zone between the sandier facies of the Inner Shelf and Marginal Shelf and the muds of the deeper, axial part of the shelf.

In the Central and Northern Regions where significant accumulation of mud occurs in the Near Shore Zone, the muddy sand facies displaces the main sand facies.

Fig. 146. Slightly muddy sand (Sample 3002), Inner Shelf, east of Cape Clinton (×1.4).

Fig. 148. Muddy sand (Sample 3112) west of Lakatoi Reef, Southern Pompey Complex (×1.4).

*199*

Width of the facies varies from 2 to 5 miles throughout the entire province, with local expansion to 8 miles in the Townsville area and 7–10 miles east of Hinchinbrook Island. The facies occurs at depths of 40–50 fathoms along the margins of the Southern Shelf Embayment, but northward on the Central and Southern Inner Shelf it shoals to 8–14 fathoms. Along the Marginal Shelf it averages 30–36 fathoms. In the Northern Region it rarely occurs at depths exceeding 10 fathoms. In the Whitsunday area powerful currents generated by high tidal variation and controlled by the festoons of large mountainous islands and deep channels, sweep southward scouring the muds, sands and gravels that are brought down by the fast-flowing streams in this mountainous, high-rainfall belt. The intensity of current movement is such that in many of the channels only gravel survives, large sand ridges aligned with the islands are formed and extensive mud flats are developed in the shallow, protected bays. The muddy sand facies forms the axial zone extending southward from the Whitsunday Passage, and it is flanked by sediment of higher mud content, which ultimately surrounds it further south near Mackay where the more open bathymetry dissipates the current. North of Ingham, the inshore muddy sand facies disappears. This is due in part to the higher rate of mud accumulation caused by the higher rainfall, dense tropical vegetation, mountainous coastal belt, numerous streams and the predominance on the adjacent land of Palaeozoic metamorphic rocks of pelitic character and Tertiary basalts. Prolific mangrove growth also favours mud deposition. North of Cooktown, the facies re-appears—extensive coastal dunes and Mesozoic sandstone formations as well as lower rainfall enable the sand fraction to increase and the narrower shelf and stronger tidal currents result in more effective removal of mud from the Near Shore Zone.

*Very muddy sand facies*

The very muddy sand facies (20–40% mud) is more extensive than the previous facies which it flanks. Except for its occurrence in the Near Shore Zone of protected bays, the facies (Fig. 149) develops between 30 and 70 fathoms in the Southern Region, but in the Northern and Central Region it ranges from 5 to 20 fathoms. Its width is quite variable, but it averages 10–20 miles. In the Southern Region it flanks the axial belt of muds and sandy muds of the central shelf, which widens northward and then bifurcates as it approaches the Central Region at latitude 21°S. The eastern branch terminates between Whitsunday Island and Tideway

Reef near latitude 20°30′S. The western branch extends along the edge of the Whitsunday Group and a small arm projects further westward into Repulse Bay. The main western branch continues northward beyond the Whitsunday area where the central shelf muds are more extensive and the very muddy sand facies forms narrow flanking zones. North of the Burdekin River mouth, the two zones converge and continue with interruptions to Hinchinbrook Island, beyond which the facies moves shoreward. In the northern part of the Central Region, the mud content of the shelf sediment decreases seaward until an axial zone of muddy sand is reached and beyond this zone mud again increases towards the reefs. North of Cairns, the coarse zone is represented by the very muddy sand facies, which has an irregular distribution, as at Cairns where it forms a "shadow" behind Arlington Reef, obliquely transecting the main shelf trends. In the Northern Region it is the major facies of the shelf.

*Sandy mud and mud facies*

The sandy mud (40–80% mud) and mud facies (more than 80% mud) are restricted to the central part of the Southern Region where the belt expands from an average of 7 miles near the Swains Reefs to more than 45 miles in the northern part of the region. It is 5–8 miles from the reef margin. Between the Southern and Central Regions, a western displacement of the facies occurs. This shift may be related to the reversal in shelf gradient from south to north, a reversal that also separates the ancient southern Fitzroy drainage system from that of the Burdekin. Bifurcation of the facies

Fig. 149. Very muddy sand (20–40% mud), between Bell Cay and Cape Townshend. (Sample 3264) (×1.4).

occurs in the same manner as the previous facies, and north of the Whitsunday Group there is a significant expansion of the mud over the greater part of the Inner Shelf. The facies is interrupted by the muddy sands of Flinders Passage and re-appears north of Townsville where it is virtually restricted to the Near Shore Zone. In the Northern Region it is less extensive and forms mainly in the deeper re-entrants of the reef zone and occasionally in the Near Shore Zone.

The proportion and distribution of mud in the shelf sediments depend on two basic factors, viz. the quantity supplied and the energy conditions of the shelf. Whether or not the suspended mud load settles is determined by the intensity and type of wave movement over the shelf as well as tidal current activity. Since the settling velocity of clay sized material (finer than 0.005 mm) is less than 0.002 cm/sec, then for settling to occur, the orbital velocity of water particles within a wave at depth must be less than 0.002 cm/sec. For silt the limiting velocity is 0.3 cm/sec, for fine sand 2.5 cm/sec and for medium sand 7 cm/sec. When the equations for orbital velocity in Airy waves (INMAN, 1963) are applied to wave measurements on the shelf, it is evident that mud deposition is not favoured in the Southern Region at depths less than 16 fathoms, particularly on the broad, open shelf area at the southern end of the province. Here, wave dimensions exceeding 8 ft. height, 700 ft. length and 12 sec period are rare. Orbital velocities for such waves at depths of 100 ft. are of the order of 2.7 cm/sec, which is well above the critical velocity for mud and near that for fine sand. Smaller waves of 4 ft. height, 90 ft. length and 4 sec period are more common throughout the province and at depths of 50 ft. their orbital velocities are of the order of 0.3 cm/sec, which is near the critical velocity for silt. At depths greater than 70 ft. orbital velocity for waves of this magnitude is negligible. Thus as one moves northward and the protection of the Marginal Shelf reefs improves, wave effects should decrease and mud deposition should occur at smaller depths and this generally means a shoreward migration of the mud facies. In parts of the Central Region where the Marginal Shelf reefs are more sparsely distributed, wave movement is not impeded and high orbital velocities may develop across the shelf floor. Clear evidence of this is found in the contraction of the mud and sandy mud facies between latitudes 19°30′S and 18°S and the considerable expansion of the slightly muddy sand facies.

Beyond latitude 18°S the shelf narrows abruptly and reef density increases. While the narrower shelf favours more intensive wave activity, this effect is counter-balanced by the increasing protection afforded by the progressively denser reef development as one moves northward.

The second basic factor controlling the mud pattern is the quantity supplied by the land mass. It is obvious from the facies map that a greater proportion of mud is present in the Near Shore Zone of the Northern and north Central Regions. The sector of the shelf where this occurs corresponds to the high rainfall belt of Queensland, and the adjacent land area is characterised by dense tropical vegetation, mountainous topography and numerous fast-flowing coastal streams. The reduced wave intensity as well as the protection afforded by near-shore islands and reefs allow low energy environments to develop and it is in these that mud is deposited.

If the broad pattern of shelf facies is examined one finds that in the Southern Region there is an eastward progression from the shoreline to more muddy sediments on the deeper, axial zone of the shelf. In the Central Region this progressive change is more obscure, and in the north Central and south Northern Regions, the progression appears to be reversed, with the axial shelf zone having lower mud values than the Near Shore Zone. This apparent reversal is due to the heavy supply of land-derived mud which is deposited in the Near Shore Zone and encroaches over the normal progression of sand and muddy sand. Its limit of encroachment is near the axial zone, which in effect is a relict facies. Beyond the axial zone, normal mud deposition occurs. North of Cooktown, where somewhat more arid conditions prevail, the axial zone of low mud values disappears and the normal eastward progression is resumed. It is interesting to note that the inner reefs of the Marginal Shelf in this northern region are aligned with the axial zone to the south, possibly indicating that this relatively mud-poor zone has provided a suitable substrate for reef colonisation.

*Distribution of organic and mineral components*

The major components of the shelf sediments include quartz and the skeletal material of coral, molluscs, bryozoans, foraminifera, *Halimeda*, and lithothamnioid algae. Echinoid, crustacean and clay-mineral fractions are generally subordinate. Their distribution patterns in the Southern Region are illustrated in Fig. 150–157. Data from the Central and Northern Regions have not yet been analysed, and while it is anticipated that the broad trends will be the same for them as for the Southern Region, the reduction in shelf width as well as the differences in reef distribution may well cause significant modifications. As with the carbonate- and mud-facies patterns, the distribution maps for the individual components reflect the relative influences of the same controlling factors, viz. hydrodynamic forces, bathymetric character, shelf width, reef density and proximity, stream discharge, lithological character of the drainage basins, climatic variation and coastal vegetation. In addition, the location and size of the various faunas, both present and pre-Recent, as well as the mobility of particular skeletal types exert a significant influence on the facies patterns. The relationship between pre-Recent strandlines and ancient faunas is evident in the distribution of almost every component. The strandline influence that is most clearly reflected by the individual components is that at 32 fathoms. In the analysis of the mud and carbonate distribution, the influence of the 16-fathom strandline was more conspicuous.

*Quartz distribution*

The distribution of quartz in the Southern Region is illustrated in Fig. 150 where intervals of 1%, 10%, 20%, 40%, 60% and 80% have been used. The main quartz facies, with more than 60% of quartz, is restricted in its distribution, and rarely extends to depths beyond 16 fathoms.

In the very south, the main quartz facies occurs on the Inner Shelf, separating the main carbonate facies of the Capricorn–Bunker Reef Complex to the east from the less quartzose Near Shore sediments of the Bustard Head–Gladstone Harbour sector to the west. Within the area are sand ridges of strong relief, aligned parallel with Curtis Island and rising from depths of 10 fathoms. Sands of these ridges are extremely well-sorted and comparatively fine grained and they probably represent the old bars formed in the Port Curtis estuary through the erosion and re-deposition of coastal dune material at a time of lower sea level, possibly the 10-fathom level. Quartzose sand banks off the southern tip of Facing Island, at the entrance of Gladstone Harbour, are exposed at low tide. They are of more recent origin, having been derived from coastal dunes as well as from material carried shorewards from the older deposits. CONAGHAN (1964) has described the hydrodynamic situation under which they form, and from his work it is evident that the high velocity of tidal currents, accentuated by constricted channels, is the dominating influence.

The second main area of quartzose sediment occurs off the Waterpark sector of the coast, just north of the Fitzroy mouth, and extends to approximately the 16-fathom line. The comparatively low values of quartz in the Fitzroy area (except for the shallow sand ridges) are due to dilution by carbonate material derived from an abundant molluscan benthos and from the nearby reefs of the Capricorn Group. Off Waterpark, the quartz facies is more distant from reef influence, and the original sands deposited by the ancient Fitzroy which flowed through Waterpark have survived in a comparatively pure form. In the Broad Sound area, quartz-rich sediments are restricted to the long, shallow ridges that are so numerous. On the deeper floor, the sediments contain a high molluscan fraction which depresses the quartz content.

The third main area of the main quartz facies occurs off the mouth of the Pioneer River and extends southeastward almost to the 16-fathom line. Lack of molluscan benthos and remoteness of reefs, as well as the considerable supply of sand from the Pioneer River have enabled the most quartzose sediments of the Southern Region to form in this comparatively small area. East of the Pioneer River, near the central part of the shelf, a small, narrow belt of very quartzose sediment occurs between 28 and 32 fathoms. This occurrence is related to the main belt of moderate quartz values which will be considered subsequently.

Non-quartzose sediments (less than 1%) are restricted to the Marginal Shelf reef zones and to the adjacent slope. Their maximum development is found in the Swains Complex and the Southern Pompey Complex which are more than 80 miles from the land mass and which are separated from it by the Southern Shelf Embayment, 35–70 fathoms in depth. As the shelf narrows northward, the low-quartz facies (1–10%) encroaches the reef zone of the Marginal Shelf and due east from Mackay, these weakly quartzose sediments extend to the Shelf Edge. In the Capricorn–Bunker Complex of the Western Marginal Shelf, the low-quartzose facies encroaches to approximately the 16-fathom line, beyond which values greater than 1% rarely occur. North of latitude 21°S, at the northern limit of the Southern Region, the non-quartzose facies extends shorewards from the Marginal Shelf reefs to the 20-fathom line, which is less than 30 miles from the land. This expansion of the facies coincides approximately with the stream divide between the ancient Fitzroy and Burdekin drainage systems and possibly owes its existence to the lack of fluviatile deposition in this neutral zone during the period when the Fitzroy and Burdekin systems carried large sand loads into the adjacent areas of the shelf.

The low-quartz facies (1–10%) has its maximum de-

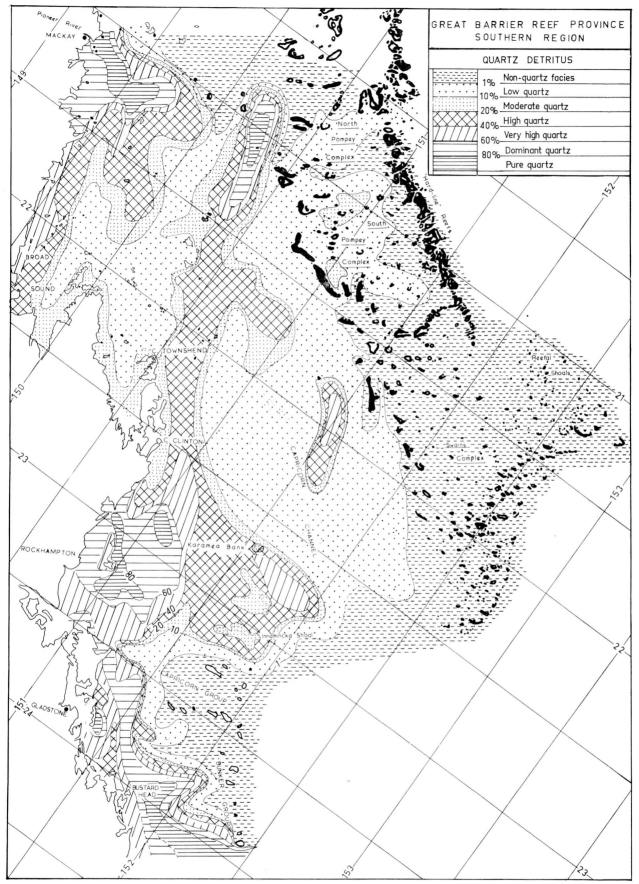

Fig. 150. Distribution pattern of quartz.

velopment in the Southern Shelf Embayment and on the northern Inner and Marginal Shelves. Its occurrence in the Embayment and northern Marginal Shelf is at depths greater than 30 fathoms, and the values of quartz are in part a reflection of the low transport capacity of shelf waters beyond this depth.

On the northern Marginal Shelf, the existence of the low-quartz facies as well as smaller occurrences of the moderate-quartz facies (10–20%) within the Pompey Complex is difficult to explain in terms of the transport capacity of shelf waters at the present time. The distance from the land source exceeds 60 miles and depths greater than 30 fathoms separate the complex from the coastline. It is very probable that the quartz in this area represents a relict facies, formed at the time of the 32-fathom sea level when the shelf to the west would have been exposed and no bathymetric barrier prevented the influx of terrigenous sediment. Its survival in the reef complex has been possible because of the very low rate of carbonate sedimentation in this particular part of the complex. Because of the dense growth of the Shelf Edge reefs and their resultant effect on water circulation in the back-reef zone, few reefs have developed here and the supply of reef detritus is correspondingly small. Thus, the original quartzose facies has not been greatly contaminated with later carbonate. Furthermore, the narrow passages through the Shelf Edge reef wall result in strong tidal currents and tidal overfall that tend to remove reef detritus from the area. The two factors—low production of detritus and effective removal by current action—have prevented the masking of the relict-quartzose facies. These factors become even more significant in the Northern and Central Regions.

North of Broad Sound, the low-quartz facies occupies a considerable area of the Inner Shelf, in depths ranging from 8 to 20 fathoms. The main components in this area are molluscan fragments, lateritic material and aggregations of calcareous and terrigenous grains. Depression of the quartz values is due to the abundance of these other components. Higher quartz values occur in the numerous shallow sand ridges on the western side of the area.

Possibly the most significant facies is that with high-quartz values ranging from 20 to 60%. In the south, it forms a very narrow band (less than 3 miles) separating the carbonate sediments of the Capricorn–Bunker Reef Complex from the main quartz facies to the west. North of the Capricorn Reefs it expands considerably and encloses the reefal shoals: Innamincka, Douglas, Haberfield, Goodwin, Edgell, Moresby, and Karamea. Further north it narrows to 15–20 miles

and continues as far as latitude 21°S where it is truncated by the non-quartzose facies that crosses the shelf from the vicinity of Mackay to the Shelf Edge. A smaller development of the facies occurs in the Southern Shelf Embayment and another occurs along the Near Shore Zone and western Inner Shelf between Broad Sound and Mackay. Its existence in the Pompey Complex has been discussed already.

The main occurrence of the highly quartzose facies, extending from the Capricorn Reefs to the northern non-quartzose facies, is a comparatively narrow belt, the eastern margin of which corresponds approximately with the 32-fathom line. On either side it is flanked by low-quartzose sediments, and at its northern end it grades into an axial zone of strongly quartzose material. Along its eastern side in the south, it carries reefal shoals and northward beyond latitude 22°30′S accumulations of bryozoan detritus displace these, and in turn are displaced by increasingly quartzose sand. The obvious relationship between the facies and the 32-fathom level provides further evidence of the control exerted by this old strandline on the present character, both reefal and sedimentary, of the province. In this instance, the facies would appear to represent a relict sediment formed under the higher energy conditions of the ancient Near Shore Zone and contaminated subsequently by the organic detritus derived from faunas, particularly colonial groups, that invaded the mud-free substrate as the sea transgressed westward. In the south, the limit of coral invasion appears to have been near latitude 22°30′S. Northward, the increasing protection of the Marginal Shelf reefs and the abrupt widening of the shelf adversely affected the hydrological conditions normally favoured by coral, and bryozoan communities became dominant. Beyond latitude 21°30′S, even bryozoans declined. Today, few living bryozoans exist in the zone, but the large accumulations of bryozoan detritus provide evidence of their previous abundance. Their main concentration shifts slightly eastward from the highly quartzose facies as one moves southward, and in general the bryozoan detritus is more widely distributed, a feature that will be examined further when the bryozoan facies is considered.

The extreme narrowing of the highly quartzose facies west of the Capricorn–Bunker Complex, and its occurrence at shallower depths (16–20 fathoms) are not consistent with its character further north, but both anomalies are related to the westward expansion of the carbonate sediments of the reef complex. In the first instance, the narrow band represents the western margin of the normal highly quartzose facies and in the sec-

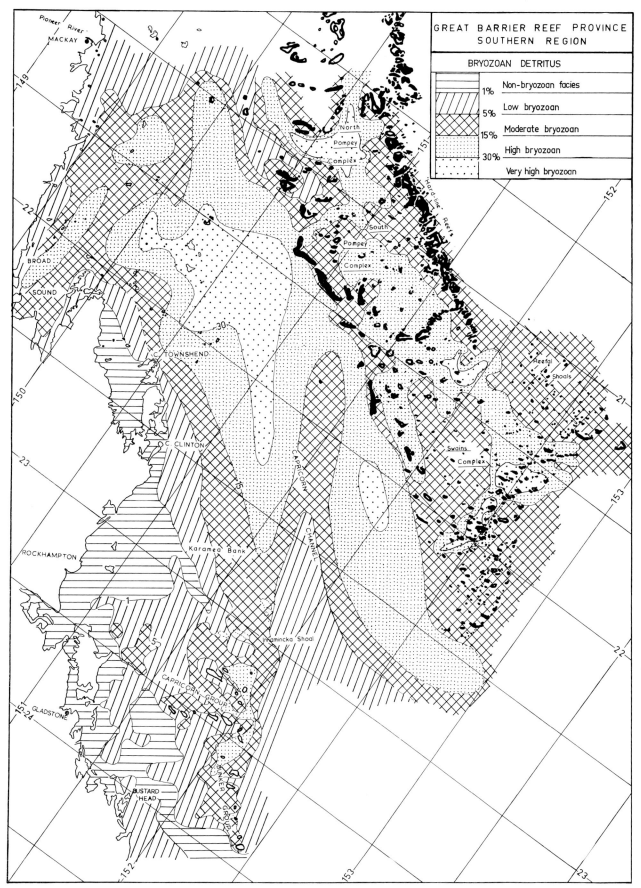

Fig. 151. Distribution pattern of bryozoan detritus.

205

ond instance the facies has been encroached from the east by the reef carbonate. Furthermore, if no reefs had developed, the eastern margin of the main northern facies would probably have extended southward on a line coinciding with the eastern margin of the present reefs.

The small development of the facies in the deeper Shelf Embayment near latitude 22°S is difficult to explain. It occurs within a depth range of 42–48 fathoms, and it is located near the junction of two well-defined depressions which appear to be the main course and a major branch of the pre-Recent Fitzroy system. Marked gradient changes at the 48-fathom level have been recognised and their implications considered in the earlier bathymetric analysis. It is conceivable that the junction of two major streams and the subsequent rise of sea level to the 48-fathom line resulted in the localised concentration of quartzose material in this vicinity. Its absence to north and south may be due to the fact that no other major branch joins the old Fitzroy course from the west and thus conditions favouring sand deposition were not developed. It is interesting to note that a strong bryozoan accumulation occurs less than 4 miles to the east, and this association may possibly have the same significance as the one recognised in the main facies belt at the 32-fathom level.

The moderately quartzose facies between Broad Sound and Mackay occupies the Near Shore Zone and the western edge of the Inner Shelf. It is largely a stage in the normal gradation from highly quartzose sediments of the beach and intertidal region to the muddy, more calcareous facies further off-shore. The gradation into less-quartzose sand is controlled by the abundant molluscan benthos which contributes a very large fraction of skeletal material to the sediment. The southeastward expansion of the mainly quartzose sands from the Pioneer River causes a similar displacement of the highly quartzose facies.

*Bryozoan component*

The distribution pattern for the bryozoan component is illustrated in Fig. 151, where five intervals have been used, viz: less than 1%, 5%, 15%, 30% and more than 30%. Bryozoan detritus is difficult to identify, particularly when thin sections of the sediment are used. Its microstructure is not distinctive and because of the delicate nature of its skeleton, large recognisable fragments are rarely encountered in the section. Identification is less difficult when the unconsolidated sample is examined under a binocular microscope, but in this

case the problem of reliable measurement is then encountered. Because of these difficulties, analyses of bryozoan content are less accurate than those of the other components and unless both methods are used, analytical results are suspect. In the distribution pattern presented in Fig. 151, relatively wide intervals have been used in order to offset the inaccuracies that are inevitable in the analysis. In spite of this, significant trends are recognisable and, as with the other components, bryozoan trends reflect something of the influence of the various factors controlling sedimentation in the province.

The non-bryozoan facies (less than 1%) is restricted to the southern Near Shore Zone and Inner Shelf of the Southern Region, where very quartzose sediment is dominant, viz. opposite Waterpark and the entrance to Gladstone Harbour. Lack of bryozoan material is possibly related to the unsuitable substrate in this area. In addition, if the bulk of material found in the province is relict, and there is evidence to support this view, then the shallow Near Shore area would have been exposed at the time when the main faunas flourished in the deeper northern zones.

The low-bryozoan facies (1–5%) is also restricted to the western side of the province as well as to the southern deeper part of the Shelf Embayment. North of the Capricorn Reefs, it forms a band less than 10 miles wide, flanking the shoreline. West of the Capricorn Reefs it expands considerably in the direction of the Fitzroy River mouth and southward in the direction of the entrance to Gladstone Harbour. This expansion appears to result from the westward transportation of material derived from the area of reefs, where one would expect to find the main source of bryozoan detritus, both modern and ancient. It has been suggested already that the 32-fathom strandline which was clearly effective in its control of the moderately quartzose facies as well as the northern bryozoan accumulations, was also a controlling factor in the localisation of the Bunker Reefs and, presumably, of associated bryozoan faunas in the pre-Recent. It is from this zone that the detritus has been moved shoreward as the sea transgressed. The limit of its migration has been determined by the increasing distance of the source and the decreasing energy level with transgression. Because of its fragile and generally intricate structure, bryozoan material has greater buoyancy and greater potential for transportation than most other organic detritus. This possibly accounts for the wider spread of its various facies relative to that found for other components. However, there is no evidence to suggest that this dispersal is still occurring. On the contrary, it wonld seem that little movement of skeletal material is being effected at the present time in any but the Near Shore Zone.

The moderate-bryozoan facies (5–15%) is essentially a transitional zone flanking the main areas of bryozoan accumulation. It is always wider on the leeward side of these areas. In the Capricorn–Bunker Complex it is not strongly developed. North from here the facies bifurcates, the wider arm extending parallel with the shoreline, the narrow eastern arm extending along the western edge of the Southern Shelf Embayment and then reversing southward. On the Eastern Marginal Shelf it is most extensive in the Swains Complex where it occupies more than half the entire area. In the Pompey Complex further north, bryozoan material is more abundant and this facies is virtually restricted to two bands flanking the main reef zone. Living bryozoans are more prolific on the Eastern Marginal Shelf than elsewhere in the province, and they appear to favour reef fronts below depths of 3 fathoms. The somewhat depressed values of the bryozoan component in the western half of the Swains Complex has been caused by the excessive deposition of *Halimeda* detritus which reaches maximum concentrations in this complex.

The high-bryozoan facies (15–30%) is the one of greatest significance in the Southern Region. It is represented by several small occurrences in the Capricorn–Bunker Complex, Broad Sound and the Southern Shelf Embayment and by two major developments, viz. the long, widening tongue that extends northward from the Capricorn–Bunker complex, along the eastern Inner Shelf to the latitude of Mackay (a distance of more than 100 miles), and the large central areas of the Pompey Complex and Northern Swains Complex on the Marginal Shelf. It is represented in the Capricorn–Bunker complex as a narrow fringe around the individual reefs and is probably derived largely from the present fauna of the reef slopes. A proportion may be relict material from earlier accumulations on the 32-fathom strandline. In the Broad Sound area, the high-bryozoan facies forms two narrow zones parallel with the coastline, in a depth range of 6–16 fathoms. Such an occurrence is unusual for the Southern Region. The material has possibly been derived from the small reef developments around many of the numerous islands that occur in this area or it may have been transported by strong tidal currents from the main belt of bryozoan sediment 10–15 miles further east. On the other hand, there may be existing fauna in the area which has not yet been discovered. In the Southern Shelf Embayment, its occurrence is probably related to the greater mobility of bryozoan-skeletal material which has been moved further from the adjacent Swains Complex than other components.

The main tongue of the Inner Shelf, extending over a length of more than 100 miles, ranges in depth from 16 to 40 fathoms, with its axial zone approximating the 36-fathom line. Between latitudes 21°30'S and 22°S, the tongue expands to a width of 70 miles and north of here it contracts abruptly to less than 20 miles. The area of expansion coincides with the area where tidal directions change from north to south, and where tidal range approaches a maximum. The location of the main part of the facies immediately to the east of the 32-fathom strandline and of the highly quartzose facies is suggestive of an ancient fauna in the Near Shore Zone of the 32-fathom sea. Accumulation of bryozoan detritus would have occurred in this zone. Because of its structural character the detritus was readily dispersed, both landward and seaward, as the sea transgressed and, in the southern part where the shelf is more exposed to the open ocean, this dispersal would have been more effective. As a result, the facies gradually narrows and is assimilated into sediment dominated by other components. Where the tongue widens, the shelf is protected by the Marginal Shelf reefs and dispersal through wave action is reduced. On the other hand, the convergence of tidal directions from north and south and the resulting currents provide a situation favourable to the movement of material into this area, and the concentration of such material. The deflection of tidal currents westward into the Broad Sound area favours a westward extension of the facies. Thus, the hydrodynamic as well as the eustatic factors appear to be responsible for the localisation of the high-bryozoan facies. As the shelf shoals northward beyond latitude 21°S, the 32-fathom line disappears into the Marginal Shelf reef zone and muds from the Central Region replace the bryozoan sediment.

On the Marginal Shelf, the facies is developed in three areas which are separated by zones of lower bryozoan values. Its distribution is related to hydrodynamic factors as well as to the present and ancient faunas of the shelf. The average depth of the shelf in the Swains and Pompey Complexes is 32 fathoms with occasional depressions of 36 and 40 fathoms. In the immediate back-reef areas of the Shelf Edge reefs, the floor is free of sediment and it is reasonable to assume that no significant deposition has occurred on the rest of the floor since the lower 32-fathom sea level. The main modification to the Marginal Shelf has been in the renewed growth of reefs on the old surface, and it would seem that the bulk of sediment derived from the reefs has been deposited in and around them, or carried into the Southern Embayment and down the continental slope. Comparatively prolific bryozoan faunas occur on the reef slopes today, below the main level of surf action. Presumably the situation was similar during the time of lower sea level. The hydrodynamic factor is largely concerned with tidal-current activity. Because of the abrupt eastward expansion of the southern part of the province for 50 miles beyond the line of the northern Shelf Edge reefs a large re-entrant exists between the Swains and Pompey Complexes. The northern margin of the re-entrant is formed by the dense wall of "hard-line" reefs of the Pompey Complex while the southern margin is poorly defined by the enormous expanse of dispersed reefs and reefal shoals that characterise the northern part of the Swains Complex. It is into this re-entrant that the main tidal flood is funnelled south-westward through the Swains Complex and into the Southern Shelf Embayment. A similar situation on a smaller scale develops in the Pompey Complex where there are sufficiently large passages through the Shelf Edge reef wall. The areas directly affected by this strong current activity have comparatively low values of bryozoan detritus. However, bordering these areas are the main accumulations of the high-bryozoan facies. In the northern part of the Swains, the facies occupies a triangle formed by the Shelf Edge reefs on the south-east, the reefal shoals on the north and the current swept zone on the west. In the Southern Pompey Complex it occupies the greater part of the inter-reef zone between the Shelf Edge and inner Marginal Shelf reefs, with maximum concentrations occurring along the southern border with the current swept areas. In the Northern Pompey Complex the same distribution is evident, with maximum concentrations flanking the passage through the Shelf Edge reefs.

The facies pattern and its relationship with tidal-current activity can but lead to the conclusion that either the bryozoan detritus cannot survive in the area of strong currents or other components have been brought in by the currents thereby diluting the bryozoan fraction. In the case of the Swains Complex, dilution has occurred. The area of reefal shoals on the north contains the highest concentration of *Halimeda* detritus of the entire province (over 65%), while the inter-reef area to the west has values of up to 50%. This material is swept into the current zone, thereby depressing the bryozoan values. In the Southern and Northern Pompey Complex, the low-bryozoan values appear to result from removal of material by the faster, though less extensive, currents that flow through the narrower reef passages. There is no build-up of *Hali-*

*meda* comparable with that in the Swains Complex. The less disturbed zones adjacent to the current flow allow the transported detritus to settle, thereby increasing the normal concentration.

*Molluscan component*

Four intervals have been selected to illustrate the distribution of molluscan material in Fig. 152. They are the non-molluscan facies (less than 10%), the low-molluscan facies (10–20%), the moderate-molluscan facies (20–30%) and the high-molluscan facies (greater than 30%). The Inner Shelf and the central part of the Marginal Shelf are the main areas of molluscan concentration.

The non-molluscan facies (less than 1%) occupies the axial part of the Southern Shelf Embayment, the eastern part of the Marginal Shelf and restricted parts of the southern Inner Shelf as well as the greater part of the Inner Shelf at the junction of the Southern and Central Regions. In the south, minimum values occur off-shore from the Gladstone Harbour entrance and the Fitzroy–Waterpark sector. Both areas belong to the high-quartzose facies, related to the Fitzroy drainage system. Low molluscan values may be due to the unfavourable substrate limiting benthic faunas or to the continuing influx of quartzose sand from coastal dunes and shelf ridges. In the Southern Shelf Embayment, such values result from the sparse benthos and from dilution by bryozoan material. On the southern Marginal Shelf, the non-molluscan facies co-incides with the high *Halimeda* area.

The low-molluscan facies (1–10%) occurs mainly in the Near Shore Zone and shallow part of the Inner Shelf, as well as throughout the greater part of the Marginal Shelf. It also forms a narrow transitional zone along the western margin of the Southern Shelf Embayment, between the non-molluscan facies in the embayment and the moderate-molluscan facies to the west.

The moderate-molluscan facies (20–30%) extends over a very wide zone that occupies the greater part of the Inner Shelf and over large inter-reef areas of the Marginal Shelf, particularly in the south. On the Inner Shelf of the Capricorn–Bunker area, the facies forms a fringe on the lee of the reefs and also projects westward as three arms that almost reach the Near Shore Zone. These arms are located in the vicinity of the old courses of the Fitzroy and may well be related to the bathymetric and sedimentary features that resulted from earlier fluvial processes. In comparing the molluscan and quartz distribution patterns it is evident that the molluscan facies favours areas where quartz

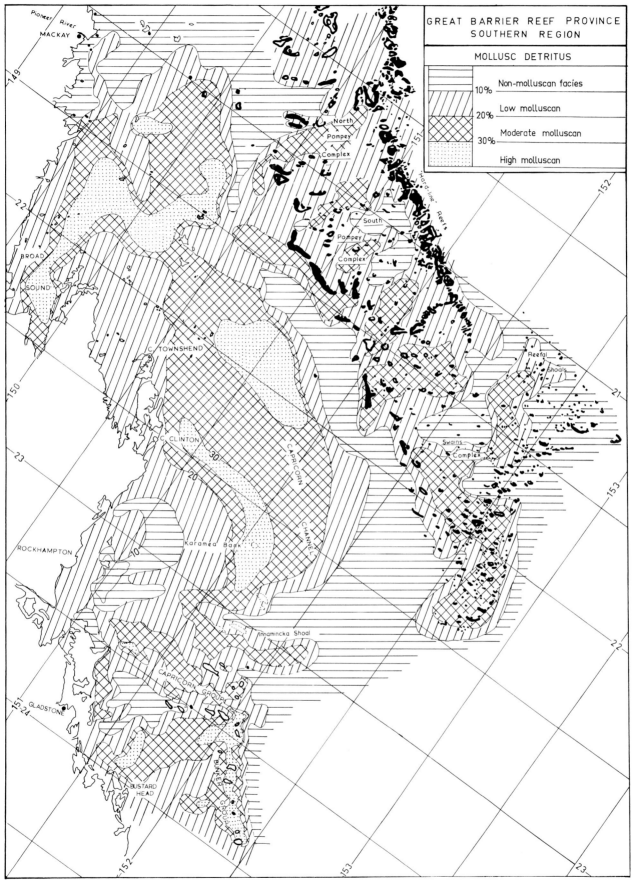

Fig. 152. Distribution pattern of molluscan detritus.

values are reduced and where there is a moderate mud fraction. It is possible then, that in the Capricorn–Bunker area, reef colonisation favoured the older, higher levees of the Fitzroy distributaries while the deeper stream beds provided the sites for subsequent deposition of quartz-poor sediment favoured by molluscan faunas. North of the Capricorn reefs, the facies expands to a maximum width of 55 miles and continues to the northern margin of the Southern Region. It ranges in depth from 10 to 48 fathoms. The main development of the facies is generally on the seaward or off-shore side of the high-quartzose facies. In the Broad Sound area where depths are less, this relationship with quartzose sediment is maintained. The facies in Broad Sound owes its origin to the present molluscan benthos which inhabits the slightly muddy sediments beyond the main sand deposits. It is possible that the larger facies development on the eastern side of the Inner Shelf has resulted from the accumulation of detritus from both the present deeper-water faunas and the ancient Near Shore faunas of the 32-fathoms sea. On the Marginal Shelf, the moderate-molluscan facies is quite extensive on the inter-reef floor of the Swains Complex, where it is divided into two areas separated by the barren zone over which tidal currents sweep south-westward from the marginal re-entrant between the Swains and Pompey Complexes. In the Pompey Complex, there are several large, isolated occurrences, mainly along the axial zone. Another narrow belt is found on the western side of the two large inner reefs of the shelf, viz. Denton and Eton.

The high-molluscan facies (greater than 30%) occurs only on the Inner Shelf, in three main developments. The most southerly one encloses the Capricorn and Bunker Reefs, while the northerly one extends northward from Broad Sound and is connected with the main molluscan zone of the Inner Shelf. This zone has three areas of high molluscan content, all situated between the 26- and 34-fathom levels.

*Halimeda component*

The *Halimeda* component is most important in the Marginal Shelf where it reaches extremely high concentrations (more than 65%). It is also an important criterion throughout the rest of the province, even when its values are small, because it provides a useful index for demarcation of the main reef and reef-influenced areas from those that are almost totally terrigenous. The division between the two can be drawn at the 1% level of *Halimeda*. Since this skeletal type is readily recognised both in thin section and on external features,

its proportion in sediment can be measured with an accuracy greater than that for most other components. In Fig. 153 the distribution pattern of the *Halimeda* component has been developed on five intervals, drawn at 1%, 10%, 20% and 30%. The most noticeable aspect of the pattern is the sharp separation of the extreme types of facies. The high (20–30%) and the very high (greater than 30%) *Halimeda* facies are virtually restricted to the southern third of the Marginal Shelf (i.e., the Swains Complex). The non-*Halimeda* facies (less than 1%) is restricted to the Southern Shelf Embayment, the Near Shore Zone and the greater part of the Inner Shelf north of Broad Sound. The moderate facies (10–20%) is dominant on the central third of the Marginal Shelf (i.e., the Southern Pompey Complex) and in the Capricorn–Bunker Complex. To the north of both areas, the low-*Halimeda* facies (1–10%) is dominant. In addition to the sharp separation of the main facies types across the province, there is a general trend towards decreasing values of the component as one progresses northward.

Unlike the distribution pattern of other components, particularly quartz, bryozoan and molluscan, that of *Halimeda* appears to be influenced less by ancient strandline controls. The main factor affecting the facies development is the relative abundance of the *Halimeda* flora in the various areas. Living *Halimeda* has been found in almost every environment of the shelf down to depths of 40 fathoms. It favours the reef flat, reef lagoon and less silty inter-reef floor, where tidal currents and reduced wave action maintain energy conditions above a minimal level without reaching the extreme vigour of the surf zone.

The southern Marginal Shelf (the Swains Complex) provides a bathymetric and hydrodynamic situation that satisfies the requirements for prolific growth of *Halimeda*. The northern reefal shoal area of this complex is shallow, extensive and topographically irregular. It is also exposed to the enriched waters of the open ocean, waters which are funnelled under tidal pressures through the area and into the main complex. The flora provides an abundant supply of detritus because the segmented structure of *Halimeda* facilitates disintegration without being subjected to severe wave attack. On the other hand, the reefal shoals which consist largely of coral, lithothamnioid algae, and molluscs, are also below the level of severe wave action that is necessary for the destruction of these more compact organisms and so little detritus is supplied by them to the surrounding floor. Because of the prolific flora and the minor contribution from other organisms, the *Halimeda* facies reaches unusually high concentrations,

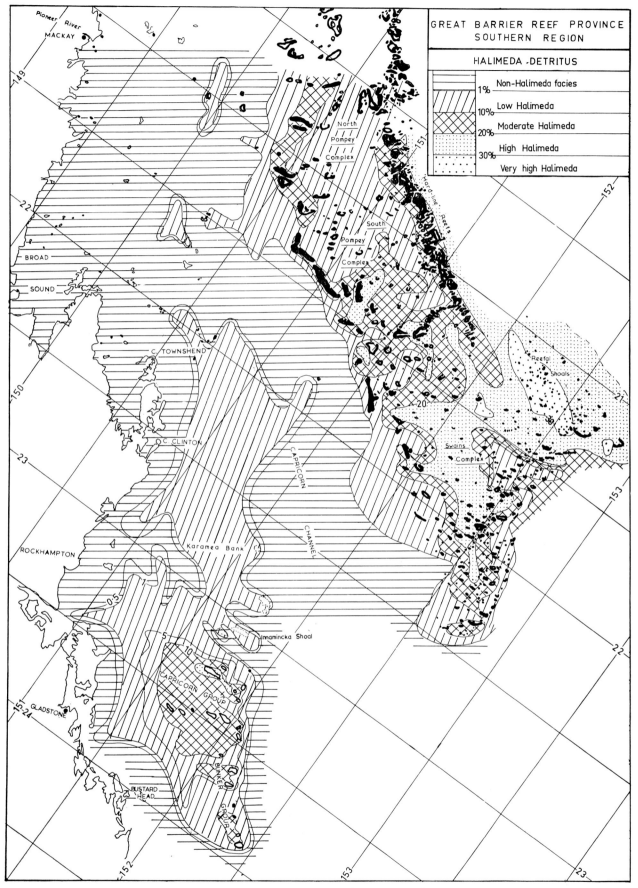

Fig. 153. Distribution pattern of *Halimeda* detritus.

frequently exceeding 65%. Such material is illustrated in Fig. 154. Similar hydrological conditions prevail within the main area of the Swains Complex, because the Shelf Edge reefs are sufficiently dispersed to permit ready penetration of oceanic water and the high tidal range favours efficient circulation. However, the reef surfaces are subjected to stronger wave attack and other components are swept into the area where they dilute the *Halimeda* concentration to a level below that found in the shoal area.

In the Southern Pompey Complex the moderate-*Halimeda* facies (10–20%) is dominant, although there are local concentrations of higher value. Hydrological conditions in the complex are less favourable than those further south because the Shelf Edge reefs effectively restrict penetration of oceanic water and circulation is generally poorer. Furthermore, the larger area of reef surface that is subjected to wave attack provides variable quantities of other components which contribute to the sediment. Behind the wall of Shelf Edge reefs, particularly near the narrow passages through this wall, extreme turbulence develops with changing tides and this, together with the fast currents through the passages, scours the immediate back-reef floor and removes most of the sediment.

In the Northern Pompey Complex, the low-*Halimeda* facies (1–10%) occupies the entire floor except for the narrow tongue of moderate values (10–20%) which occurs along the inner reef zone of the Marginal Shelf. As with the southern complex, the immediate back-reef zone of the Shelf Edge reefs is comparatively free of sediment because of extreme turbulence associated with tidal overfall. The decreasing content of *Halimeda* in the sediment as one progresses northward from the Swains Complex reflects the deteriorating hydrological situation caused by intensive Shelf Edge reef growth which leads to poor circulation. Furthermore, the decreasing width of the shelf permits greater intermixing of components from various sources. The reef zone of the Western Shelf (Capricorn–Bunker Complex) has *Halimeda* concentrations that are comparable with those of the Southern Pompey Complex. This moderate-*Halimeda* facies extends shorewards from the reefs for distances of 20 miles. North of the Capricorn–Bunker Complex, the reefal shoals provide little *Halimeda* detritus and the facies declines to the low-*Halimeda* level of 1–10%. Further north, these low values decrease even more because of the increasing quantity of bryozoan material that occurs on this part of the Inner Shelf.

Because of its mode of disintegration and because *Halimeda* flourishes most prolifically in zones below that

Fig. 154A, B. *Halimeda* sediment (Samples 3053, 3058), from the north-eastern floor of the Swains Complex (× 1.4).

of strong wave attack, the detritus is generally coarse-grained and its transportation is limited. The large segments are not readily lifted from the floor by tidal currents. Only in those areas where the flora is subjected to both wave and current action is there a degree of dispersal of the detritus. This accounts in part for the sharply defined facies limits of the component. Dilution by other components may obscure these limits, particularly near the reef masses and along older strandlines, but in general one of the main source areas of *Halimeda*, viz. the inter-reef floor, does not carry other component organisms (except foraminifera) in abundance. The absence of *Halimeda* detritus from the Southern Shelf Embayment is related to the unfavourable depth and substrate which preclude the existence of the organism, while distance from the reefal zones of the shelf prevents transportation from these sources. The same factors (except depth) account for its absence from the northern Inner Shelf.

*Coral component*

The coral component has a distribution pattern remarkably similar to that of *Halimeda*, and it is evident that similar factors have been responsible in both cases. Differences in the two patterns are due largely to the differences in source zones and in the manner of production of detritus. Whereas *Halimeda* disintegrates into its natural segments without the aid of wave energy and may accumulate on the inter-reef floor without transportation, coral on the other hand lives in the zone of highest energy and its detritus is produced through wave destruction. Its accumulation away from reefs requires transportation and unless currents of high competency are available the extent of transportation is very limited. In Fig. 155, the coral facies have been plotted on the basis of divisions at 1%, 5%, 15% and 30% levels.

The non-coral facies (less than 1%) occupies the Near Shore Zone, the Inner Shelf north of Broad Sound and the very southern part of the Shelf Embayment as well as a narrow, northern axial belt that projects southward into the embayment. In the central part of the Southern Pompey Complex and in the area between it and the Northern Pompey Complex very low values have also been recorded. The virtual absence of coralline material from the western areas is due to the poor development of fringing reefs around the continental islands and to the large volume of terrigenous sediment that is found there. In the Shelf Embayment, terrigenous muds have also succeeded in diluting the coral fraction to less than 1%, but at the same time, distance from reefs and the greater water depths have limited the amount of coralline detritus supplied to this area. In the two areas of the Pompey Complex, the coral fraction has been depressed by slight increase of *Halimeda*, molluscan and foraminiferal detritus. However, the main reasons for its near-absence are those which were considered in connection with the occurrence of the relict-quartzose facies in these two areas. The dense wall of Shelf Edge reefs has adversely affected hydrological conditions in the back-reef zone and restricted reef growth here. The supply of reef detritus is negligible and effective tidal action inhibits deposition of even small amounts of carbonate. The main sediment that is found is the terrigenous material that was deposited during the time of the 32-fathom sea level when the western shelf was exposed, and the debris from

inter-reef benthos that invaded the area with rising sea level.

The low-coral facies (1–5%) forms a narrow fringe around the main moderate and high coral facies that are largely restricted to the reefal zones.

The moderate-coral facies (5–15%) has an interesting and significant pattern of distribution. It is the dominant facies of the Inner Shelf south from latitude 21°30′ S (i.e., from Pine Peak Island to Lady Musgrave Reef), and of the greater part of the Eastern Marginal Shelf. On the Inner Shelf the moderate-coral facies forms an irregular band averaging 50 miles in width except for the northern segment which is less than 25 miles. Two constrictions occur: one opposite the Fitzroy-Waterpark sector and the other off Cape Townshend. The main developments of the facies are in the Capricorn–Bunker Complex and in the area east of Cape Clinton. Its occurrence in the reef complex is normal. However, the extensive development of the facies further north, virtually on the same trend lines as the main bryozoan and high-quartz facies, is probably controlled by the 32-fathom strandline and possibly by a deeper strandline. The reefal shoals from Innamincka to Karamea rise from the 32-fathom level and provide evidence of reefal growth subdued by hydrological conditions that become progressively less favourable further north. Because of their depth these shoals are not subjected at the present time to the strong wave attack necessary for the production of coralline detritus. It would seem that the wide distribution of this material could be effected only when wave action was capable of producing a substantial supply and of dispersing it. This situation could arise during phases of lower sea level, when in addition to fragmenting reef material, wave activity would foster reef growth. In view of the other evidence—both bathymetric and sedimentary—it appears reasonable to suggest that with transgression from the 32-fathom strandline, reef colonisation occurred along this mud-free zone as far north as suitable hydrological conditions persisted, and that these reefs provided detritus for the adjacent floor until further transgression and deteriorating environment led to their decline and extinction. Thus the moderate-coral facies north of the present reefal shoals is probably largely relict. The encroachment on the coral facies by quartzose sand in the Fitzroy–Waterpark area and by sand and mud in the vicinity of Cape Townshend reflects stronger and probably later terrigenous sedimentation in these areas.

On the Eastern Marginal Shelf, the moderate-coral facies occupies more than half of the shelf floor and extends westward for nearly 10 miles into the eastern

*213*

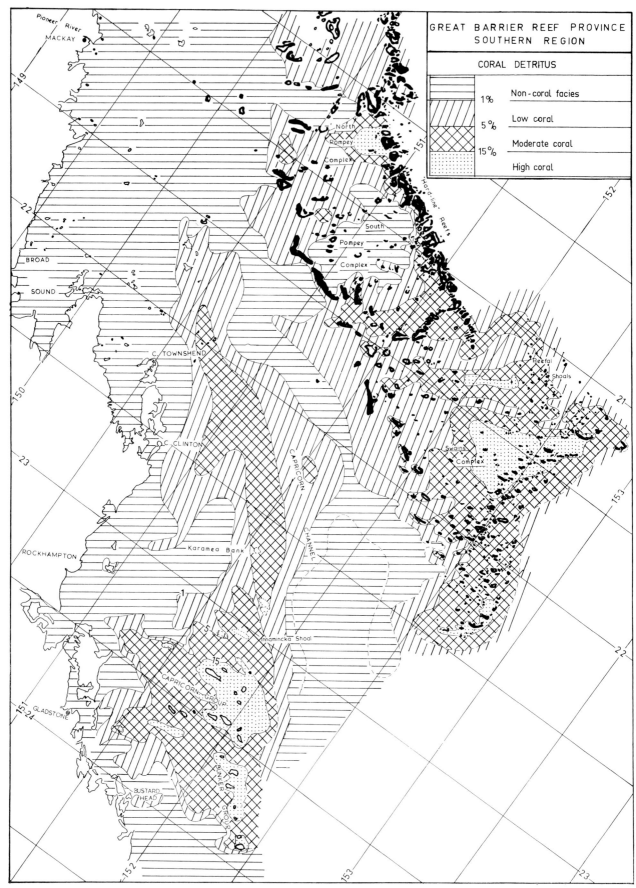

Fig. 155. Distribution pattern of coralline detritus.

side of the Shelf Embayment. Higher values are found in the facies of the Swains Complex than are found further north. This is largely a reflection of the greater abundance and more uniform distribution of reefs throughout the complex. In the Pompey Complex the Shelf Edge reefs have prevented a similar development and have also shielded the fewer leeward reefs from the severe wave attack to which the Swains Reefs are exposed.

The high-coral facies (greater than 15%) is found in the Capricorn–Bunker Complex and in the Swains Complex. Its occurrence in the Pompey Complex is virtually restricted to the Shelf Edge reefs. The concentration of coral detritus in these areas is clearly related to the abundance of reefs and the intensity of wave destruction. The short range of the facies from the parent reefs reflects the limited degree of dispersal that is possible in depths of 20–32 fathoms, depths that are found in the reef zones. This further supports the interpretation of a relict origin for the low coral facies of the Inner Shelf.

*Lithothamnioid component*

The lithothamnioid-facies pattern closely follows those of *Halimeda* and coral, but the concentrations of the lithothamnioid component are generally lower. In Fig. 156, where the facies has been plotted at intervals of 1%, 5%, and 10%, the lithothamnioid values are approximately one interval lower than those for *Halimeda* and coral in the corresponding areas. They exceed 15% only on the reef surfaces near the algal rims. Inter-reef areas rarely have values greater than 10% and in the non-reefal zones the values are less than 5%. Because lithothamnioid algae favour environments similar to those favoured by coral, viz. the shallow reef margin, it is not surprising that the distribution patterns of their detrital components show a close correspondence. Coral has a wider range of growth—reef slope as well as reef surface— and this accounts in part for the greater spread of its detritus. At the same time lithothamnioid algae, because of their tightly encrusting habit and compact structure, are more resistant to wave attack and provide a smaller supply of detritus to the surrounding environment. This accounts for its more restricted dispersal as well as its lower concentrations. From the distribution pattern in the reef zones, it is obvious that the component has been derived mainly from the algae of the reef surfaces. The possibility of fragmenting the strong, skeletal structure of such algae below the surf zone is quite small, and its occurrence beyond the main reefal zones provides further evidence of pre-existing reefs.

The non-lithothamnioid facies (less than 1%) covers approximately half of the Southern Region, being most extensive in the Southern Shelf Embayment and on the northern Inner Shelf. Large areas also occur in the central parts of the Pompey and Swains Complexes. The barren areas of the Pompey Complex co-incide with those in which quartzose sediments have been found. In the Swains Complex the areas of virtually no lithothamnioid material have a considerable concentration of *Halimeda*.

The low-lithothamnioid facies (1–5%) extends as a narrow belt along the Inner Shelf margin, southward from latitude 21°30'S, and it widens to more than 32 miles as it approaches the Karamea–Innamincka reefal shoals. In the Capricorn–Bunker Complex it has an average width of 45 miles, the greater part of the facies being in the back-reef zone. Off Waterpark, the Fitzroy and Gladstone Harbour entrance, the non-lithothamnioid sediment (mainly quartzose sand) encroaches on to the low-lithothamnioid facies, and between North West Reef and Douglas Shoal this facies extends as a narrow tongue to the Shelf Edge. The long, narrow band of low-lithothamnioid sediment north of the Capricorn–Bunker Complex occurs well beyond the range of existing reefs and, like the other components of this zone, probably represents a relict facies formed from reefs that developed on the old 32-fathom strandline and subsequently degenerated with further transgression of the sea. On the Eastern Marginal Shelf the low-lithothamnioid facies covers more than 70% of the shelf floor.

The moderate-lithothamnioid facies (5–10%) forms narrow fringes, less than 3 miles in width, around the reef masses.

The high-lithothamnioid facies (greater than 10%) is restricted to the reef surfaces and very narrow off-reef fringes. Only on the reef surfaces does it reach values in excess of 15%, but on parts of the reef rim the values may be as high as 40%.

*Foraminiferal component*

The foraminiferal-facies pattern departs significantly from those of other components. The strong trends parallel with the coastal direction found in the other components still persist, but in the southern part of the region, marked cross-trends have developed. This new pattern is illustrated in Fig. 157, where the facies intervals have been drawn at 5%, 10%, 20% and 30%.

The non-foraminiferal facies (less than 5%) exists in the Near Shore Zone, the Inner Shelf north of Broad Sound and in a very narrow band along the north-

215

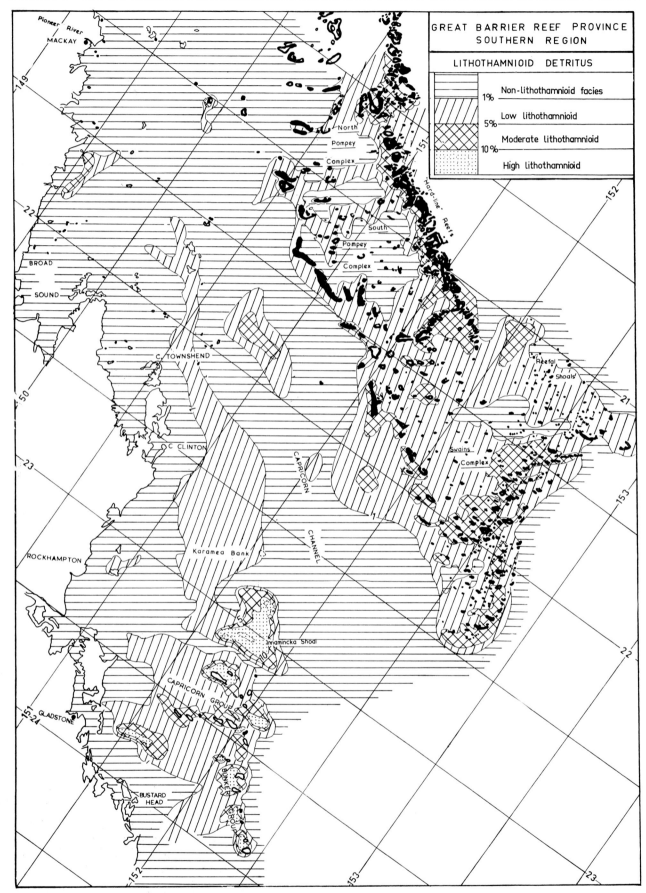

Fig. 156. Distribution pattern of lithothamnioid detritus.

eastern margin of the Shelf Embayment. The few species recorded from these areas are mainly pelagic.

The low-foraminiferal facies (5–10%) forms a narrow, marginal zone to the previous facies and consists largely of the abraded and fragmented tests of inter-reef and reef-surface forms: *Alveolinella*, *Marginopora*, *Elphidium*, and *Operculina*. Very irregular developments of the facies occur on the Marginal Shelf. A large part of the reefal shoals on the northern margin of the Swains Complex and the back-reef zone of the Shelf Edge reefs in the Pompey Complex, have low-foraminiferal values. In the Swains Complex this is due to dilution by the abundant *Halimeda* detritus and in the Pompey Complex tidal scour and lack of sedimentation are responsible.

The moderate-foraminiferal facies (10–20%) is an extremely narrow belt on the Inner Shelf as far north as latitude 21°40′S, where it widens abruptly and then reverts south-eastward into the Southern Shelf Embayment. Near latitude 22°15′S, this wider band curves east-north-eastward and extends through the Swains Complex to the northern reefal shoals near the Shelf Edge. A second, irregular development of the facies extends northwestward along the Marginal Shelf floor, behind the Shelf Edge reefs, and in the northern part of the Southern Region it expands westward over the Inner Shelf. One arm of the Marginal Shelf facies fringes the western side of the reef zone and encroaches the Shelf Embayment. The significant features of this distribution pattern are the very small width of the Inner Shelf facies, the strong cross-trend that develops from the Shelf Embayment to the Shelf Edge of the Northern Swains, and the unusual expansion of the northern facies from the Marginal Shelf to the Inner Shelf.

The small width of the facies on the Inner Shelf reflects the abruptness of transition from the non-foraminiferal to the predominantly foraminiferal sediments of the shelf, a transition that occurs between 18 and 30 fathoms and corresponds approximately with the highly quartzose facies (20–60% quartz, less than 10% mud). The association of the two types of sediment—moderate foraminiferal and high, mud-free quartz—may reflect a substrate control on the distribution of living benthic foraminifera, the depth range being sufficient to prevent extensive dispersal of their dead tests by wave action. The transitional facies also coincides approximately with the belt of *Halimeda*, coral and molluscan material that has been interpreted as relict in character but this does not imply a similar origin for the foraminifera. The large area of moderate-foraminiferal sediment that extends further east is not consistent with such an origin for foraminiferal detritus in the Inner Shelf band. It seems that the sharp transition has been caused by the change in the substrate of the benthos, a change that has resulted from the survival of other relict sediments.

The strong cross-trend from the Shelf Embayment through the Swains Complex to the Shelf Edge appears to be related to tidal-current activity. In the earlier examination of the *Halimeda* and bryozoan detrital patterns, the strong tidal flow through the northern reefal shoals of the Swains Complex was considered as one of the controlling factors in their distribution. The cross-trend of the moderate foraminiferal facies, as well as those of the high-foraminiferal and very-high-foraminiferal facies are aligned with the general direction of tidal-current movement. In the more exposed Shelf Embayment, current activity is augmented by the westward drift induced by the prevailing South-East Trade wind. The bulk of the foraminiferal detritus is derived from the rich inter-reef faunas of the Swains Complex and carried across the embayment by tidal current and wind drift. In the deeper, southern part of the embayment, foraminiferal values decline and the cross-trend becomes more obscure. The moderate-foraminiferal facies of the Pompey Complex is subjected to strong, localised current action and in the immediate back-reef zone its values have been reduced considerably. However, the tidal flow has been insufficient to carry significant quantities beyond the Marginal Shelf. The northern expansion of the facies across the Inner Shelf appears to be related to the occurrence of numerous fringing reefs around the many small continental islands.

The high foraminiferal facies (20–30%) is most extensive in the southern half of the Southern Region where least protection is afforded by reefs. It is absent from the northern Inner Shelf. Two narrow belts enclose the Capricorn–Bunker Complex and converge north of the Karamea reefal shoal where they are joined to the main development that extends eastward across the Southern Shelf Embayment through and around the Swains Complex. A large area is covered by the facies near the junction of the Swains and Pompey Complexes, and it is also developed extensively further north where it is the dominant foraminiferal facies of the western part of the Marginal Shelf. The higher concentrations of the Swains Complex border the zones of strong current activity and probably provide the main supply of material to the belts crossing the Shelf Embayment. The more northern occurrence of the facies is in the vicinity of the inner reefs of the Marginal Shelf: Kindemar to Herald's Prong. It forms

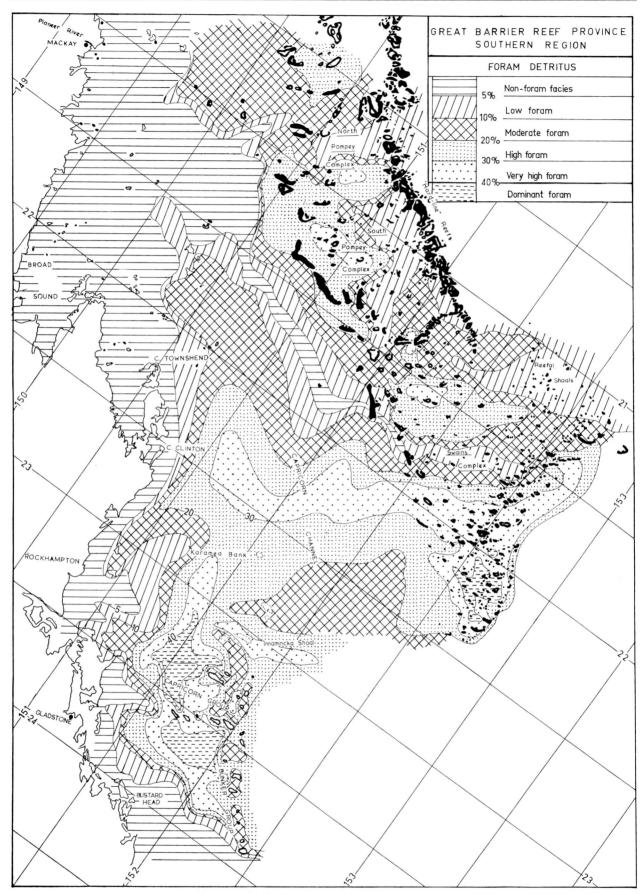

Fig. 157. Distribution pattern of foraminiferal detritus.

a narrow fringe on the western side of these reefs and expands considerably in the eastern back-reef area, where the open inter-reef environment favours foraminiferal growth and where detritus from the larger reef surfaces is also deposited.

The very-high-foraminiferal facies (greater than 30%) is found mainly in the back-reef areas of the Capricorn–Bunker Complex and the Swains Complex, and in the wide band crossing the Southern Shelf Embayment. Small occurrences are found in the axial part of the Pompey Complex. The higher concentrations in the back-reef areas are due to the favourable environment in which the inter-reef benthos can thrive. Additional contributions from the adjacent reefs as well as the influx of pelagic forms also help to increase the concentrations. In the Southern Shelf Embayment the very high values are due to both pelagic and benthonic material, some of which has been carried in from the reef zones. The smaller occurrence of the facies in the Pompey Complex is a reflection of the less suitable conditions caused by the strong wall of Shelf Edge reefs which inhibit circulation in the western and axial part of the complex.

*Distribution of aragonite, high-magnesium calcite and low-magnesium calcite*

The percentages of aragonite and calcite in the carbonate fraction of the sediments have been determined and their distribution patterns are presented in Fig. 158–160. The patterns largely reflect the distribution of the dominant skeletal components as well as the contribution made by material derived from old reef surfaces. In most cases this material has been altered from its original composition and tends to increase the content of low-magnesium calcite in the sediment. The main source of aragonite is from coral, *Halimeda*, and mollusc. Lithothamnioid algae and benthonic foraminifera provide high-magnesium calcite while bryozoans, pelagic foraminifera and lithified reef surface material are responsible for the low-magnesium calcite.

In Fig. 158, the highest concentration of aragonite is seen to occur in the Swains Complex where it corresponds closely with the very-high-*Halimeda* facies extending south-westward from the reefal shoals. In this instance the direct relationship between organism and mineralogical composition of the sediment is strikingly obvious. The high-coral facies also overlaps the same area and augments the aragonite fraction. In the Capricorn–Bunker Complex the same relationship is found although all three have a more restricted areal distri-

bution. The weak-aragonite facies (30–40%) is found on the Inner Shelf and Southern Shelf Embayment and in small, isolated areas of the Pompey Complex. On the Inner Shelf, its occurrence corresponds broadly with the main bryozoan band that has been interpreted as a relict facies. The low values of coral, *Halimeda*, and mollusc in this zone have also helped to depress the aragonite fraction. In the southern part of the Shelf Embayment the small values of aragonite are probably related to the existence of both pelagic foraminiferal detritus and bryozoa. In the Swains and Pompey Complexes, bryozoans are mainly responsible for the small values.

The distribution of high-magnesium calcite is generally complementary to that of aragonite. With the exception of the Capricorn–Bunker Complex where high-magnesium calcite has concentrations greater and more extensive than those of aragonite, the calcite fraction is generally the smaller. On the Inner Shelf a marked trend is seen to co-incide with the 32-fathom zone, a trend that is consistent with those recognised in the bryozoan, coral, mollusc and *Halimeda* distributions. The weaker values to the west are related to the increasing dominance of aragonitic molluscan components in the benthos and to the supply of land derived low-magnesium calcite. In the Southern Shelf Embayment, to the east of the 32-fathom zone, weaker values of high-magnesium calcite correspond with the increase in bryozoan detritus and also with increasing pelagic foraminiferal content. On the Marginal Shelf, the values are similar to those of the Capricorn–Bunker Complex (40–60%), but in the area of strong *Halimeda* concentration in the northern part of the Swains Complex they fall below 20%. Strongest values of high-magnesium calcite are found on the reef surfaces and in their immediate surroundings.

Low-magnesium calcite has an interesting distribution pattern in as much as its values increase with distance from reefs and proximity of the land—a relationship that is essentially the reverse of that for the other two carbonates. In the Near Shore Zone and shallow part of the Inner Shelf, its values exceed 40%. From here to the Shelf Edge there is a progressive decline in values, with an interruption in the southern part of the Shelf Embayment where stronger concentrations of low-magnesium calcite re-appear. The Capricorn–Bunker Complex and the northern 32-fathom zone both have depressed values. Within the Pompey Complex there are small areas where increased values occur. The distribution of low-magnesium calcite is related to three factors, viz. the supply of carbonate from the coastal area, the supply from old reef surfaces and shell

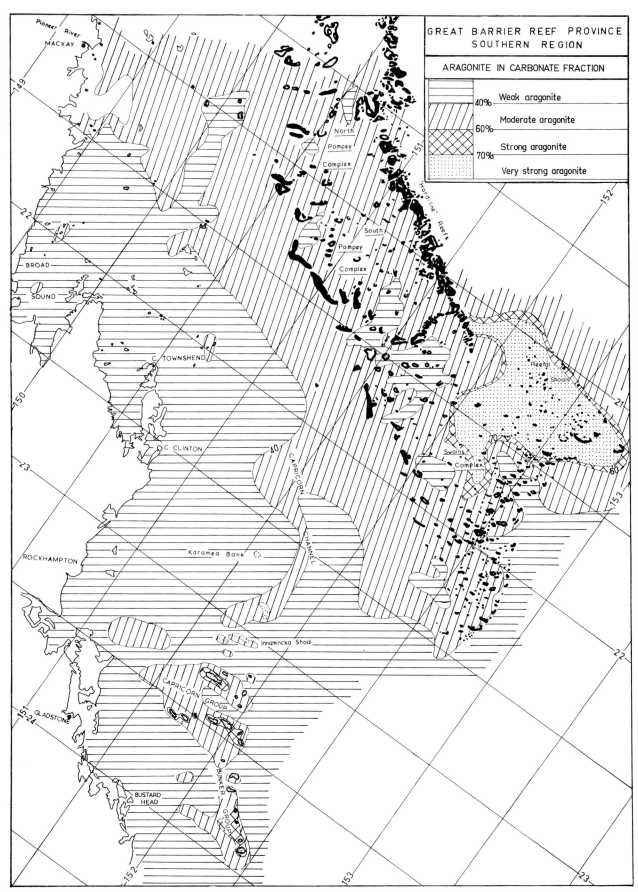

Fig. 158. Distribution pattern of aragonite in the carbonate fraction.

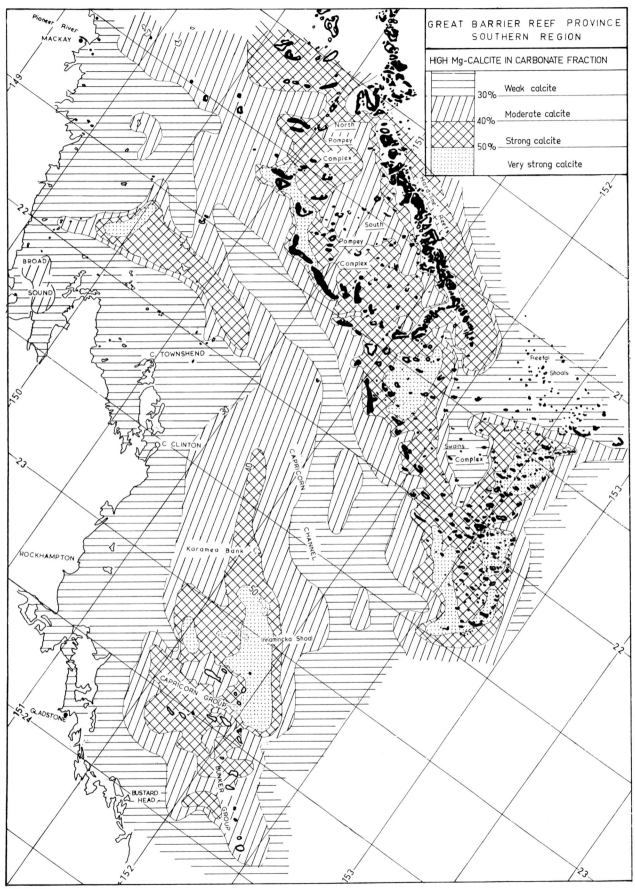

Fig. 159. Distribution pattern of high-magnesium calcite in the carbonate fraction.

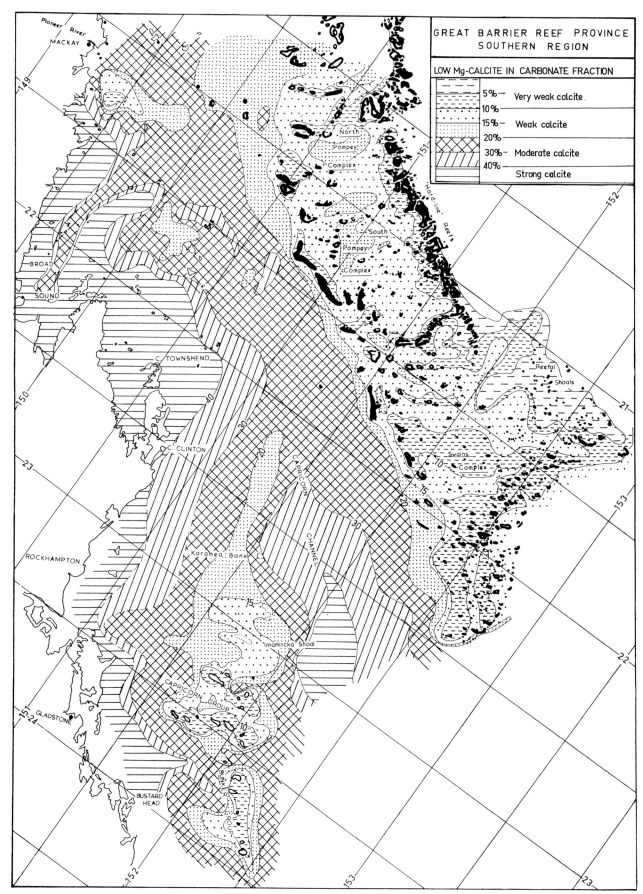

Fig. 160. Distribution pattern of low-magnesium calcite in the carbonate fraction.

gravels that have been sub-aerially weathered, and the contribution of skeletal detritus from organisms such as pelagic foraminifera and bryozoans. Low-magnesium calcite may be a useful indicator of the relative contributions of detritus from dead reef and living reef, since the ratio of low-magnesium calcite to the lithothamnioid–foraminiferal content is greater for material derived from old reef surfaces where sub-aerial weathering results in the conversion of the originally high-magnesium calcite of the organisms to the low-magnesium form.

### VARIATION IN COMPOSITION AND TEXTURE

The wide range of variation in the composition of sediments from the Southern Region has been demonstrated in the distribution patterns of the main components. In addition to this, there is considerable diversity in their textural character, a diversity that results from the inter-action of several factors, most important of which are the type and abundance of the various source materials, the effectiveness of hydrodynamic forces and the distribution of relict facies.

The variation in sedimentary character is best illustrated by samples and their granulometric analyses, from traverses extending from the coast line to the Shelf Edge. Four such traverses have been selected in the Southern Region. The northern one (Fig. 161) extends from Mackay across the shelf into the northern Pompey Complex, the second (Fig. 162) from Broad Sound to the Shelf Edge reefs, the third (Fig. 163) from Port Clinton across the northern end of the Shelf Embayment and the Swains Complex to the Shelf Edge, and the fourth (Fig. 164) from Cape Capricorn into the Southern Swains Complex.

Photographs of the sediment from several sample locations on each of the above-mentioned lines are presented in the four figures (Fig. 161–164), together with histograms illustrating the granulometric character of each one. From these, the extreme diversity in sedimentary type is obvious. Furthermore, it is clear that all except the sample 3106 on Fig. 163 which is from a reef surface, are bimodal or polymodal in grain-size distribution. This polymodality is a reflection of the particular grades favoured by skeletal material from specific organisms, of the inter-mixing of relict sediments with material of more recent origin and of the normal infiltration of muds into coarser sediment. Detailed assessment of the granulometric character of the sediments is beyond the scope of the present work, but it is important to recognise the dominant control

exerted by organisms and to realise the difficulties which this raises in any attempt to interpret energy conditions on the basis of the grain-size distribution.

Where foraminiferal material constitutes the main sediment fraction, the mode is determined by the size of the tests, and in most species the size variation is within very narrow limits. Where two or more living genera are present, e.g., *Marginopora* (disc-shaped), *Alveolinella* (cylindrical) and *Elphidium* (sub-spherical) several strong modes are common in the sediment. As one moves across an area, environmental conditions may change to the advantage of one genus and to the disadvantage of another, and this is reflected in a corresponding adjustment in the several modal values. In another situation, we find relict inter-tidal carbonate accumulations in which molluscs are dominant (e.g., Fig. 164, sample 20) giving a wide size range, while the adjacent quartzose facies has a more restricted size range (e.g., Fig. 164, sample 18) and nearby transitional terrigenous–carbonate (Fig. 164, sample 221) is similarly restricted. In the case of the quartzose material, the better sorting is a reflection of energy conditions of a previous age; in the case of the transitional terrigenous–carbonate sediment it is doubtful whether the co-existence of similarly sized quartz and skeletal material has the same significance.

The polymodality of sample 3011 (Fig. 163), from an 18-fathom floor in the Swains Complex, has resulted from three main organic groups: *Halimeda*, *Marginopora*, and *Operculina*. Each favours a different and relatively constant size range. Contributing to the other grades of this sediment is detritus derived from molluscs, coral, lithothamnioid algae, bryozoans and other foraminiferal genera. In this instance, *Halimeda* and the foraminifera represent the "in situ" flora and fauna which have been subjected to minimum attack by wave and current. On the other hand, detritus from coral and lithothamnioid algae has been derived from adjacent reefs under strong wave attack and it has been transported into the area of deposition. Thus, the major part of the sediment has a uniform grain size inherited from the living organism, while the minor fraction has a wider size range which, in theory, should reflect something of the energy conditions of both its source and depositional areas.

In this brief treatment of the sediments, their textural diversity and the controlling influence of skeletal composition on texture have been emphasised in order to demonstrate the complexity of the sedimentary problem and the difficulties involved in regional interpretation. More detailed assessment is being pursued currently by a number of workers whose results should contribute significantly towards the better understanding of the sedimentary cover in the Great Barrier Reef Province.

In a marine province such as that of the Great Barrier Reef it is not unreasonable for one to assume that a large quantity of sediment is being deposited on the sea floor, sediment that is being derived from the innumerable reefs that are under constant and severe wave attack, and from the many coastal rivers that discharge their loads along the thousand miles of coastline. This assumption, however, has not been substantiated. On the contrary, the evidence that is currently emerging leads one to the view that the rate of sedimentation on the Queensland Continental Shelf has been extremely slow since the lowest stand of sea level after the Tertiary, and certainly since the time of the 32-fathom sea level. At the present time the evidence is not conclusive, and until geophysical studies of the unconsolidated surface layer have been completed the true thickness of the sediment cover will remain in doubt.

However, three types of information already lend support to the view that negligible sedimentation is occurring on the shelf today.

The first type relates to the large areas of the Marginal Shelf reef zones which have hard, sediment-free floors. These areas are located behind the densely populated Shelf Edge reefs of the Southern and Northern Regions. The inability to recover sediment, using a variety of techniques which have been successfully applied throughout the rest of the province, was the first indication of the lack of sediment. This was supported by the change in the character of the echogram in these areas. Absence of sediment from the back-reef area is not, in itself, evidence of a low rate of deposition throughout the entire province, since extreme tidal scour occurs behind the Shelf Edge reefs and little sediment would survive. However, when the bathymetric level of the sediment-free area is compared with that of the adjacent floor where sediment is readily recovered, it is found that there is no measurable difference between the two. In the Marginal Shelf, the floor maintains a comparatively constant depth of 32 fathoms. Where deeper channels and depressions have incised the floor, they too are frequently free of sediment. It is reasonable then to infer that where sediment has been found on the Marginal Shelf, it is resting on the same hard 32-fathom surface that occurs in the scoured back-reef area, and since there is no recognis-

able bathymetric difference, the sediment thickness must be minimal.

The second type of information is derived from bathymetric and sedimentary analysis and concerns ancient strandlines and strandline deposits. The persistence of bathymetric features at constant depth throughout the province is regarded as evidence of their strandline origin, and the character of the sediments in the vicinity of these features supports this interpretation. If the rate of sedimentation on the shelf were substantial, then the topographic features would have been obscured by the sedimentary cover and furthermore the relict facies that are associated with them would also have disappeared. Because both are clearly recognisable it would seem that negligible deposition has occurred since their formation.

The third source of information is from echogram patterns. By using a low-frequency sounder, it is possible to obtain deeper penetration of the bottom sediment and to produce a reflection from the hard surface underlying the unconsolidated sediment. This has been achieved on a traverse (Fig. 165) along the central part of the Inner Shelf from Cairns to the Whitsunday Group. Except for the Near Shore muds at the entrance to Cairns Harbour where the thickness is of the order of 40 ft., the greater part of this traverse reveals a sediment cover of less than 15 ft. The main deposition has occurred in old channels, presumably ancient stream beds, and these are readily recognised on the echogram.

If the inference of negligible deposition is correct, then the problem of disposing of reef detritus must be considered. As one witnesses the tremendous destructive power of waves on the reef margin and surface, the image of large volumes of detritus being swept across the province comes readily to mind. However, when the surface area of all the reefs in the province is estimated and compared with the total area of the shelf floor it is found that the reefs form less than 2% of the shelf area. Furthermore, if total destruction of the top 15 ft. of the reefs occurred, and the detritus were spread over the entire shelf, less than 4 inches of sediment would form. At the same time, the supply of terrigenous sediment would continue, but this too is small. The approximate annual discharge of the eastern streams is less than 20,000 square mile-feet, which spread across the shelf amounts to less than 3 inches of water per annum, and in terms of the sediment which could be moved by this volume of water, the amount would be infinitesimally small. While it is true that the rate of reef destruction is offset by new growth, it is obvious that the total contribution of reef detritus and

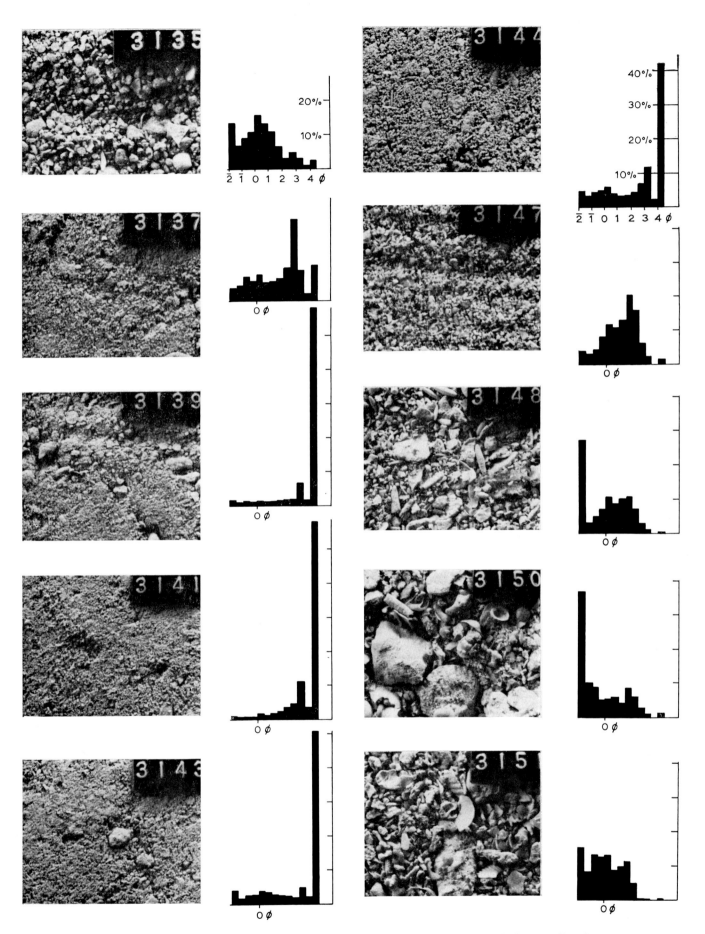

Fig. 161. Sedimentary samples and their histograms on traverse line from Mackay into the Pompey Complex.

225

Fig. 162. Sedimentary samples and their histograms on traverse line from Broad Sound to the Shelf-Edge reefs.

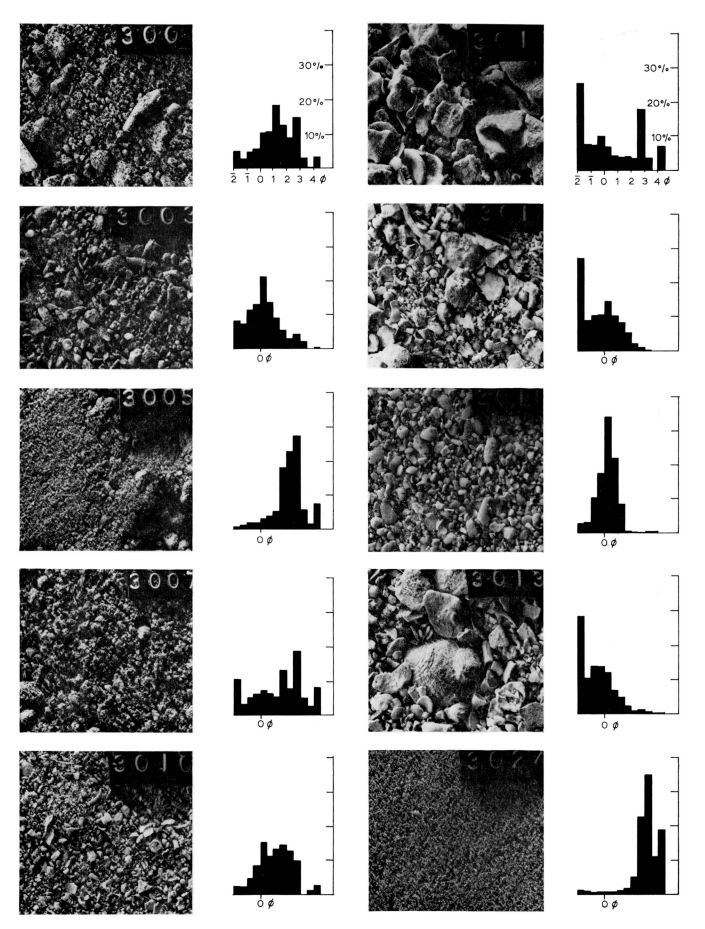

Fig. 163. Sedimentary samples and their histograms on traverse line from Port Clinton into the Swains Complex.

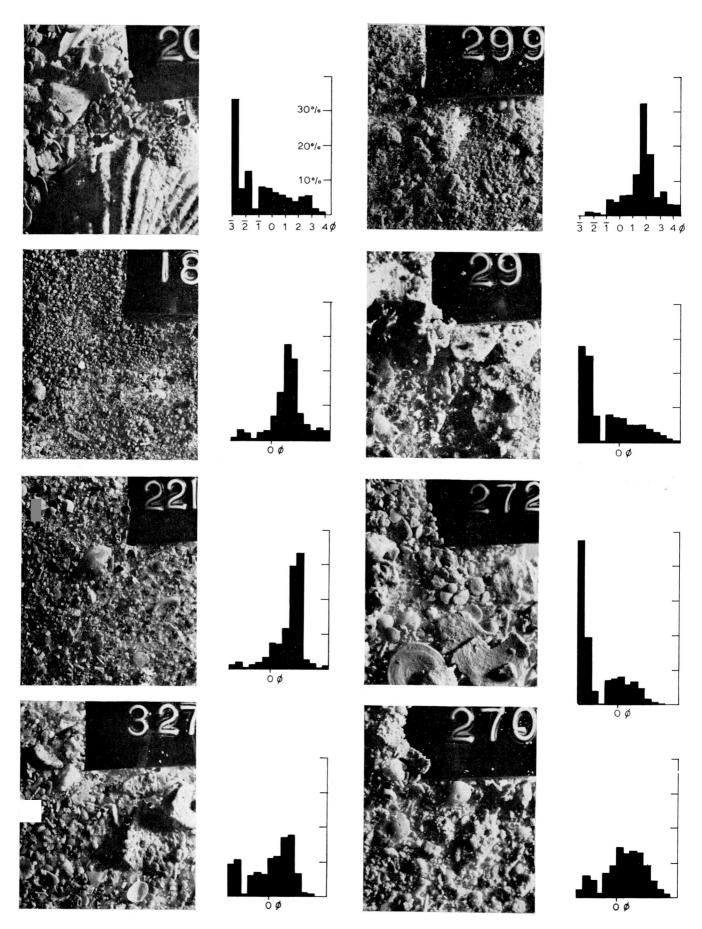

Fig. 164. Sedimentary samples and their histograms on traverse line from Cape Capricorn into the southern Swains Complex.

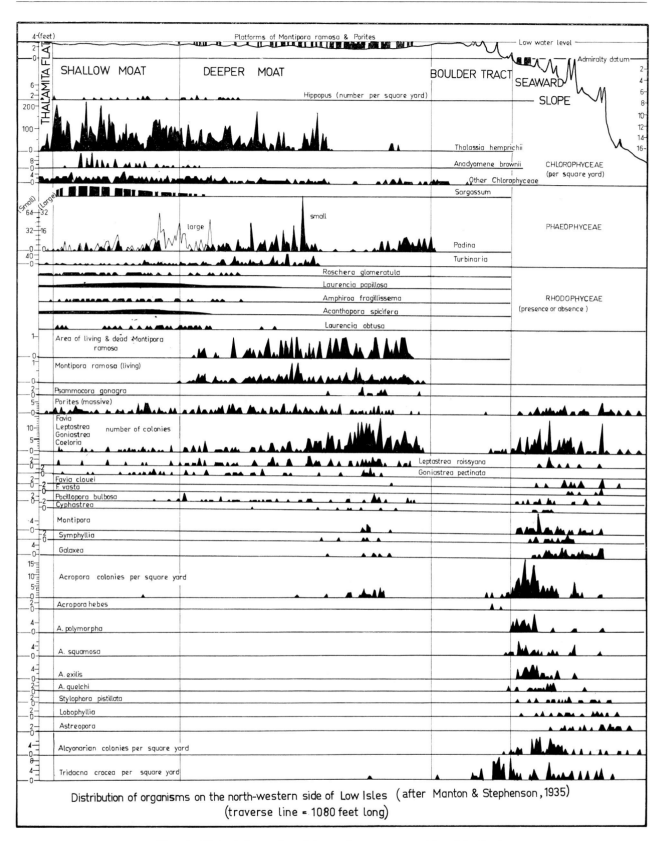

Fig. 165. Biological zonation of the north-western part of Low Isles Reef.

terrigenous material to the shelf at the present time is not sufficient to produce a substantial thickness of sediment. Greater exposure of reefs and higher stream energies with consequent increase of load would be necessary to produce appreciable deposition. For this situation to develop a regression of the order of 20–30 ft. would have to occur.

The restricted distribution of skeletal material from the reef surface is quite striking. A particularly significant indication of this is provided by the foraminiferal genera *Baculogypsina* and *Calcarina*. They constitute up to 95% of some of the sands on the algal rim and reef flat, but in no area of the off-reef floor have their values exceeded 5%, and beyond distances of 1 mile from the reef the forms are rarely found. If reef-surface detritus were transported in quantity, then one would expect to find these common genera more strongly represented in the sediment. The same situation exists with respect to the lithothamnioid algae. While a proportion of detritus is carried over the reef edge, a greater amount is swept across the reef flat into the lagoon and the shallow back-reef zone where extensive aprons develop. Maximum production of reef detritus occurs on reef surfaces that are exposed to subaerial weathering. This is clearly recognisable on the high reefs of the Inner Shelf in the Northern Region. Their sedimentary cover is more extensive than that of other types of reef and their high cays and shingle banks are being actively eroded. By contrast, the reefs of the Marginal Shelf carry less sediment and their surfaces are rarely exposed. Since most intensive erosion occurs in the surf zone where wave attack is effective to depths of only a few feet, the actual production of detritus on the deeper Marginal Shelf reefs is considerably less. This poor supply together with the limited terrigenous supply from the distant land source accounts for the sparse sedimentary cover of the Marginal Shelf zone.

### PROCESSES OF SEDIMENTATION

In view of the previous considerations, it would seem that the processes of sedimentation in the province are not very effective in terms of the amount of material that is being deposited at the present time. This is due largely to the recent eustatic changes and the comparatively mature character of the adjacent land mass. Both have resulted in declining supplies of reefal and terrigenous detritus. Sediment of the shelf is derived from four main sources.

The land areas provide mud which is brought into the province by the eastern rivers. Because of the maturity of the terrain and the climatic character, weathering processes lead to the formation of muds which are deposited mainly in the Near Shore Zone. The generally low competency of the streams restricts the supply of coarser, terrigenous sediment.

A second important source of shelf sediment is in the coastal dune systems, particularly in the Southern Region. Their origin has been considered in an earlier chapter, where it was shown that they formed far larger systems in the pre-Recent. Undercutting by waves, as well as wind and stream erosion, are responsible for the movement of this aeolian sand into the Near Shore Zone and Inner Shelf where it forms a major component of the sediment. However, the total volume of these dunes is insignificant in terms of shelf dimensions, and their total contribution to shelf sediment is quite small.

Related to the dunes is the third source of sediment: the submerged, pre-Recent dunes and bars. Most of these are below the present level of effective wave action, but during the previous stages of transgression they could have contributed on the same scale as the present dunes.

The fourth source of shelf sediment is found in the faunas: inter-tidal, inter-reef and reef. Their contribution depends on the size and rate of reproduction of the various assemblages and on the extent to which they are exposed to wave action. The inter-reef faunas are subjected to few external forces and they produce a sediment that is essentially unsorted, unabraded, and extensive in its occurrences. Inter-tidal faunas provide skeletal debris as well as unbroken tests, and in most cases this material is reworked and frequently transported or concentrated. It is more restricted in its areal extent than inter-reef sediment. Reefal faunas provide the bulk of detritus that spreads leeward into the lagoon or back-reef area. Skeletons of non-sessile organisms survive with less abrasion and fragmentation than do those of coral and encrusting algae. The extent of transportation of reefal detritus is limited by the considerable depths from which the reefs rise, so that within short distances most of the material falls into zones of negligible energy.

The main forces acting on the material are hydrodynamic and biological. Biological forces are active in the production of detritus: e.g., carnivourous species destroy other species, some fragment the skeletal structure (e.g., crabs, echinoids); boring algae and fungi weaken skeletal structure and render it less resistant to physical forces; boring molluscs perform the same role. Of the hydrodynamic forces, wave action disintegrates reefal and coastal formations and furthermore, in suitable

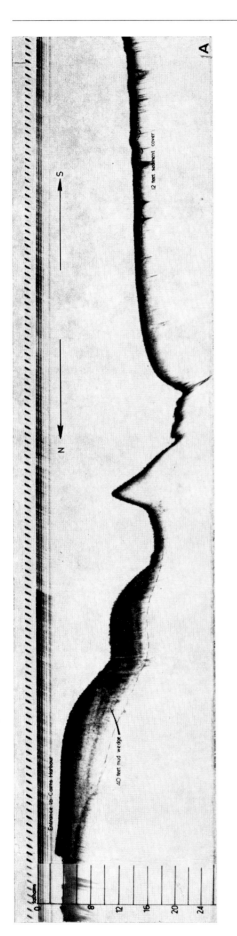

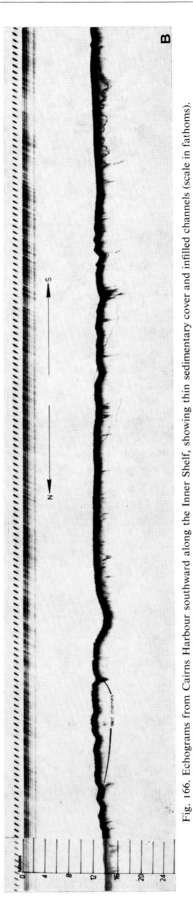

Fig. 166. Echograms from Cairns Harbour southward along the Inner Shelf, showing thin sedimentary cover and infilled channels (scale in fathoms).

depths, it lifts material into suspension thereby facilitating transport by currents. Tidal currents are important in that they carry sediment, but because of their semidiurnal reversals of flow, the net transport of material may be quite small. They are also important in scouring the sea floor, particularly in reefal and constricted coastal areas.

The four main sources of sediment and the mechanisms for its production and transportation, are obviously inadequate for large scale sedimentation and this inadequacy derives from the recent geological and eustatic history of the province.

When the sea was at its lowest level, after the Tertiary, the land mass was reduced by active erosion, streambeds were deeply incised and considerable quantities of sediment were carried towards the Shelf Edge. As the sea transgressed, base level was raised, erosion became less effective and much of the stream load was deposited in the previously deepened valleys. With transgression, existing reefs grew surfaceward and were not eroded until they reached the surf zone. Thus the transgressive phase encouraged reef growth but reduced the scale of deposition.

Temporary regression could reverse this trend by lowering base level, increasing erosion and stream discharge from the land and exposing greater areas of reef to sub-aerial and surf weathering. The most recent change in sea level has been a minor regression, but with the exception of some of the Inner Shelf and Near Shore reefs, equilibrium appears to have been re-established. The magnitude of this regression has not been sufficient to reverse the effects of the main transgressive phase. The amount of sediment produced before the present state of near-equilibrium was reached has been negligible, and the facies pattern of the shelf is essentially a transgressive one, viz. old strandline and near-shore deposits, separated and encroached upon by more slowly accumulating, finer sediments of mainly terrigenous origin. Carbonate facies have been superimposed on these in areas where reef density is sufficient to provide a veneer of off-reef detritus and protection for the inter-reef faunas. The comparatively abrupt transitions between the carbonate, muddy terrigenous and sandy terrigenous facies is further evidence of the low rate of movement of sediment and of the generally low rate of deposition. In spite of the vigorous wave action and the high velocities of tidal currents in the province, the average depth of the present shelf is sufficient to prevent their effective movement of sediment. The sedimentary pattern that exists on the shelf is essentially one that has developed during the main transgressive phase of the sea, when the zone of effective hydrodynamic action migrated across the shelf as the strandline moved westward. Modification to this advancing system has been effected by reef growth and mud deposition, but in the former case dispersal of reef detritus has been limited and in the latter case the rate of mud deposition has been slow. The pattern that we find today will persist until major regression occurs and the processes of sedimentation are intensified.

# *Chapter 9* | Conclusion

The initial framework on which the Great Barrier Reef Province has developed, formed as a result of tectonic adjustments, some of which were initiated as early as Precambrian time and are still in various stages of activity. This framework can be recognised today in the meridional-trending basins and highs of the Tasman Geosynclinal Belt. The highs have provided the foundations on which the main reef zones have been established, whereas the basins have provided the source of sediments that were later deposited on the shelf. Latitudinal trends in the framework are manifested as low, broad crustal upwarps that have modified the drainage systems, the depositional areas and the distribution of reefs. Where the evolving framework favoured the concentration of sand, particularly along the shoreline near older basins, new potential zones of reef colonisation were established.

From the time that reef organisms invaded areas of suitable substrate and suitable bathymetry, their survival and expansion depended on the hydrological and bathymetric character of the shelf. This was controlled largely by the water masses and circulatory system of the South-West Pacific. The unique bathymetric situation as well as the unusually active hydrodynamic system, related to high tidal range, favoured intensive reef growth on the Marginal Shelf of the Northern and Southern Regions. Warm surface waters swept into the province under the influence of the Trade Wind Drift and Eastern Australian Current, while the deeper cooler waters of the Coral Sea and the Queensland Trench provided the carbonate enrichment in those areas where steep slope gradients permitted their rapid entry into the province. As the reefs developed, their influence on water circulation increased and ultimately the density of the Shelf Edge system determined the manner and degree of reef growth on the inner areas of the shelf.

Eustatic fluctuation was the third factor fundamental to the evolution of the province. With successive rises of sea level, new strandline features were developed, older features were submerged and new invasions of reef organisms resulted in the colonisation of these older features. Some reef areas were adversely affected by the changing sea level and reefs degenerated or even disappeared. With regression of the sea, wide areas of reefs and earlier Near Shore Zones were exposed to severe sub-aerial erosion that resulted in the planation of reefs and the removal of sediment from the coastal zone. During such phases intensive sedimentation, both carbonate and terrigenous, occurred on the shelf and strong strandline features were formed: dune systems, river bars, beaches, off-shore bars. With renewed transgression, many of these features were left below the level of effective wave action and some provided sites for reef colonisation. The planed surfaces of the old reef zones were also re-colonised and in most cases reef growth continued on the earlier pattern. In other, fewer cases, the new hydrological situation was less favourable and reefal shoals survived in place of true reefs. However, transgression was generally accompanied by an expansion of the reef population. Where new areas were submerged and suitable substrate existed, reefs developed provided the necessary supply of undepleted oceanic water was available and the hydrodynamic forces—waves and currents—were adequate to maintain aeration and removal of organic waste. In the province, the limiting distance of reefs from open oceanic water is approximately 30 miles. Proximity of land and of stream discharge has little direct effect on reef distribution.

The most recent eustatic change has been a fall of approximately 10 ft. This resulted in the exposure of the inner Near Shore Zone and reef surfaces. Dessication caused the extinction of surface organisms and a degree of lithification ensued. Severe sub-aerial weathering as well as wave destruction removed most of the lithified material from all but the Inner Shelf reefs of the Northern Region, and re-population of the eroded surfaces has since occurred. In the Northern Region erosion of the surface material is proceeding more slowly and less efficiently because of the lower energy levels in this somewhat protected zone. The regression has been minor in scale and no clear reflection of this phase has been recognised in the sedimentary pattern of the shelf.

The eustatic history of the area has been predominantly

transgressive and consequently the degree of sedimentation has been relatively small. The main sedimentary pattern has been controlled by the ancient stream systems that crossed the shelf, carrying substantial quantities of material derived from the granites, metamorphic rocks and Mesozoic sandstones of the Tasman Geosynclinal Belt. When sea level was at its lowest and erosive processes were most active, this material was deposited on the outer part of the shelf where it was re-worked and redistributed during subsequent eustatic phases. Much of it was concentrated in large coastal dune systems, that later provided sediment to the Near Shore Zone. As sea level rose, the deeper basins formed through crustal subsidence and cross-flexure became the site of mud deposition. Reefs provided fringing deposits of carbonate that were

distributed over wider areas only during phases of regression. The strong tidal currents, typical of the province, probably played an important role in sediment distribution during such phases, but at the present time their main influence is on reef growth.

Today, the Great Barrier Reef Province appears to be in a state of equilibrium. The limit of reef expansion has been reached and reef growth would seem to be restricted to those parts where wave destruction tends to upset the normal balance. Sedimentation also appears to have reached a stage of low activity. Until eustatic or tectonic factors intervene, this state of equilibrium should persist with no major changes in the distribution pattern of reefs or the facies pattern of the sediments.

# References

ADAMS, R. D., 1962. Thickness of the earth's crust beneath the Campbell Plateau, *New Zealand J. Geol. Geophys.*, 5: 74–85.

AGASSIZ, A., 1903. On the formation of barrier reefs and the different types of atolls. *Proc. Roy. Soc. (London)*, 71: 412–414.

BRYAN, W. H., 1928. The Queensland continental shelf. *Rept. Great Barrier Reef Comm.*, 2: 45–50.

BRYAN, W. H., 1930. The physiography of Queensland. In: *Handbook of Queensland*, Australian Assoc. Advan. Sci., Brisbane, pp. 17–22.

CLOUD, P. E., 1962. Environment of calcium-carbonate deposition west of Andros Island. *U.S., Geol. Surv., Profess. Papers*, 350: 1–138.

COLLINS, A. C., 1958. Foraminifera. *Sci. Rept. Great Barrier Reef Expedition*, 6 (6): 335–437.

CONAGHAN, P. J., 1964. Sediments and sedimentary processes in Gladstone Harbour, Queensland. *Univ. Queensland Papers, Dept. Geol.*, 6 (1): 1–52.

CRIBB, A. G., 1966. The algae of Heron Island, Great Barrier Reef, Australia. *Great Barrier Reef Comm., Univ. Queensland*, 1 (1): 1–23.

DANA, J. D., 1872. *Corals and Coral Islands*. Dodd, Mead and Co., New York, N.Y., 440 pp.

DARWIN, C., 1842. *The Structure and Distribution of Coral Reefs*. Smith, Elder and Co., London, 214 pp. (Reprinted in 1962 by Univ. Calif. Press, Berkeley–Los Angeles, Calif.)

DICK, R. S., 1958. Variability of rainfall in Queensland. *J. Trop. Geograph.*, 11: 32–42.

DIETRICH, G., 1963. *General Oceanography*. Wiley, New York, N.Y. - London, 588 pp.

DOOLEY, J. C., 1959. Preliminary report on underwater gravity survey, Hervey Bay, Queensland. *Records Bur. Mineral Resources Australia, 1959*, 68: 1–4.

DOOLEY, J. C., 1965. Gravity surveys of the Great Barrier Reef and adjacent coast, North Queensland, 1954–60. *Rept. Bur. Mineral Resources Australia*, 73: 1–26.

DOOLEY, J. C. and GOODSPEED, M. J., 1959. Preliminary report on underwater gravity survey, Great Barrier Reef area—Rockhampton to Gladstone. *Records Bur. Mineral Resources Australia, 1959*, 69: 1–5.

ELLIS, P. L., 1966. The Maryborough Basin. *J. Australian Petrol. Exploration Assoc.*, 1966: 30–36.

ENDEAN, R., KENNY, R. and STEPHENSON, W., 1956. The ecology and distribution of intertidal organisms on the rocky shores of the Queensland mainland. *Australian J. Marine Freshwater Res.*, 7 (1): 88–146.

FAIRBRIDGE, R. W., 1950. Recent and Pleistocene coral reefs of Australia. *J. Geol.*, 58 (4): 330–401.

FERRANTE IMPERATO, 1599. Quoted in: YONGE, C. M. 1930. *A Year on the Great Barrier Reef*. Putnam, London–New York, N.Y., 245 pp.

GARDINER, J. S., 1898. The coral reefs of Funafuti, Rotuma and Fiji, together with some notes on the structure and formation of coral reefs in general. *Proc. Cambridge Phil. Soc.*, 9: 417–503.

GARDINER, J. S., 1931. *Coral Reefs and Atolls*. MacMillan, London–New York, N.Y., 181 pp.

GLAESSNER, M. F., 1950. Geotectonic position of New Guinea. *Bull. Am. Assoc. Petrol. Geologists*, 34 (5): 856–881.

GOODSPEED, M. J. and WILLIAMS, L. W., 1959. Preliminary report on underwater gravity survey, Great Barrier Reef area, Thursday Island to Rockhampton. *Records Bur. Mineral Resources Australia, 1959*, 70: 1–6.

GUPPY, H. B., 1888. A criticism of the theory of subsidence as affecting coral reefs. *Scott. Geograph. Mag.*, 4: 121–137.

GUPPY, H. B., 1890. The origin of coral reefs. *Victorian Inst. J., (Phil. Soc. Great Britain)*, 23: 51–68.

HARTMANN, R. R., 1962. *A Preliminary Interpretation of Airborne Magnetometer Profiles over Barrier Reef, Queensland, Australia*. Rept. for Australian Oil Gas Corp. Ltd. (unpublished).

HEDLEY, C., 1925. The natural destruction of a coral reef. *Rept. Great Barrier Reef Comm.*, 1: 35–40.

HILL, D., 1951. Geology. In: *Handbook of Queensland*. Australian Assoc. Advan. Sci, Brisbane, pp. 13–24.

HILL, D. and DENMEAD, A. K. (Editors), 1960. Geology of Queensland. *J. Geol. Soc. Australia*, 7: 1–474.

HOUTZ, R. E. and PHILLIPS, K. A., 1963. Interim report on the economic geology of Fiji. *Geol. Surv. Dept. Suva, Econ. Rept.*, 1: 1–36.

ILLING, L. V., 1954. Bahaman calcareous sands. *Bull. Amer. Assoc. Petrol. Geologists*, 38: 1–94.

INMAN, D. L., 1963. Sediments: physical properties and mechanics of sedimentation. In: F. P. SHEPARD (Editor), *Submarine Geology*, 2 ed. Harper and Row, New York, N.Y., pp. 101–151.

ISIDORE, Bishop of Seville (6th century): Quoted in: PAULY, *Encyclopedia der Klassischen Altertumswissenschaft*, 9 (2): 2069.

JARDINE, F., 1925. The development and significance of benches in the littoral of eastern Australia. *Rept. Great Barrier Reef Comm.*, 1: 111–130.

JARDINE, F., 1928. The Broad Sound drainage in relation to the Fitzroy River. *Rept. Great Barrier Reef Comm.*, 2: 88–92.

JENNY, W. P., 1962. *Aerial Magnetic Report, Authority to Prospect 88P, Queensland, Australia*. Rept. Gulf Interstate Overseas Ltd (unpublished).

JUKES, J. B., 1847. *Narrative of the Surveying Voyage of H.M.S. Fly*. Boone, London, 1: 424 pp.; 2: 362 pp.

KUENEN, Ph. H., 1933. Geology of Coral Reefs. In: *The Snellius Expedition*, 5 (2): 125 pp.

MANTON, S. M. and STEPHENSON, T. A., 1935. Ecological surveys of coral reefs. *Sci. Rept. Great Barrier Reef. Expedition*, 3: 273–312.

MARSHALL, S. M. and STEPHENSON, T. A., 1933. Sedimentation on Low Isles Reef and its relation to coral growth. *Sci. Rept. Great Barrier Reef Expedition*, 3 (8): 219–245.

MAXWELL, W. G. H., JELL, J. S. and MCKELLAR, R. G., 1964. Differentiation of carbonate sediments in the Heron Island Reef. *J. Sediment. Petrol.*, 34 (2): 294–308.

MENARD, H. W., 1964. *Marine Geology of the Pacific*. McGraw-Hill, New York, N.Y., 271 pp.

MURRAY, J., 1880. On the structure and origin of coral reefs and islands. *Proc. Roy. Soc. Edinburgh*, 10: 505–518.

OFF, T., 1963. Rhythmic linear sand bodies caused by tidal currents. *Bull. Amer. Assoc. Petrol. Geologists*, 47 (2): 324–341.

ONIONS, C. T., 1966. *Oxford Dictionary of English Etymology*. Clarendon Press, Oxford, 1040 pp.

PEYSSONNEL, 1753. Quoted in: C. M. YONGE, 1930. *A Year on the Great Barrier Reef*. Putman, London–New York, N Y., 245 pp.

PYRARD DE LAVAL, F., 1605. Quoted in: C. DARWIN, 1842. *The Structure and Distribution of Coral Reefs*. Smith, Elder, London, 214 pp. (Reprinted in 1962 by Univ. Calif. Press, Berkeley–Los Angeles, Calif.)

ROCHFORD, D. J., 1959. Scientific reports of a cruise on H.M.A. Ships Queenborough and Quickmatch. a. Hydrology. *Australian C.S.I.R.O., Div. Fisheries Oceanog. Tech. Paper*, 24: 1–24.

ROUTHIER, P., 1953. Étude géologique du versant occidental de la Nouvelle Caledonie entre le Col de Broghen et la Pointe d'Arama. *Mem. Soc. Geol. France*, 67: 1–266.

SAVILLE-KENT, W., 1893. *The Great Barrier Reef of Australia*. Allen, London, 387 pp.

SEXTUS EMPIRICUS (6th century). Quoted in: PAULY. *Encyclopaedia der Klassischen Altertumswissenschaft*, 2 (2a, 2).

SPENDER, M. A., 1930. Island reefs of the Queensland coast. *Geograph. J.*, 76: 194–214, 273–397.

STANLEY, G. A. V., 1928. The physiography of the Bowen district and of the northern isles of the Cumberland Group. *Rept. Great Barrier Reef Comm.*, 2 (1): 1–51.

STEERS, J. A., 1929. The Queensland coast and the Great Barrier Reef. *Geograph. J.*, 74: 232–257, 341–370.

STEERS, J. A., 1938. Detailed notes on the islands surveyed and examined by the geographical expedition to the Great Barrier Reef in 1936. *Rept. Great Barrier Reef Comm.*, 4 (3): 51–96.

STEPHENSON, W. and WELLS, J. W., 1956. The corals of Low Isles, Queensland. August 1954. *Zool. Papers, Univ. Queensland*, 1 (4): 1–59.

STEPHENSON, T. A., STEPHENSON, A., TANDY, G. and SPENDER, M., 1931. The structure and ecology of Low Isles and other reefs. *Sci. Rept. Great Barrier Reef Expedition*, 3 (2): 17–112.

SUSSMILCH, C. A., 1938. The geomorphology of eastern Queensland. *Rept. Great Barrier Reef Comm.*, 4 (3): 105–134.

SVERDRUP, H. U., JOHNSON, M. W. and FLEMING, R. H., 1942. *The Oceans, Their Physics, Chemistry and General Biology*. Prentice-Hall, New York, N.Y., 1060 pp.

THOMAS, B. M., 1966. *The Marine Geology of the Whitsunday Passage Area, Queensland*. Honours Thesis, Univ. Queensland, 89 pp. (unpublished)

VAUGHAN, T. W., 1919. Corals and the formation of coral reefs. *Smithsonian Inst. Ann. Rept. for 1917*, pp. 189–276.

VON ARX, W. S., 1962. *An Introduction to Physical Oceanography*. Addison-Wesley, Reading–London. 422 pp.

WELLS, J. W., 1955. A survey of the distribution of reef coral genera in the Great Barrier Reef region. *Rept. Great Barrier Reef Comm.*, 6 (2): 1–9.

WHITEHOUSE, F. W., 1963. The sandhills of Queensland—coastal and desert. *Queensland Naturalist*, 17 (1/2): 1–10.

WHITEHOUSE, F. W., 1964. Sediments forming. *Queensland Naturalist*, 17 (3/4): 51–58.

WOOD-JONES, F., 1910. *Coral and Atolls*. Lovell-Reeve, London, 392 pp.

WYRTKI, K., 1960. The surface circulation in the Coral and Tasman Seas. *Australia, Commonwealth Sci. Ind. Res. Organ. Div. Fish. Oceanog., Tech. Papers*, 8: 1–44.

YONGE, C. M., 1930. *A year on the Great Barrier Reef*. Putnam, London–New York, N.Y., 245 pp.

YONGE, C. M., 1940. The biology of reef-building corals. *Sci. Rept. Great Barrier Reef Expedition*, 1 (13): 353–391.

# Index

*B. compacta*, 175
*B. hantkeniana*, 175
*B. quadrilatera*, 175
*B. rhomboidalis*, 175
*B. subtenuis*, 175
*B. tortusa*, 175
*B. zanzibarica*, 175
*Bolivinella elegans*, 175
Booby Island, 72
*Boodlea composita*, 180
Borderland, 8, 73
Bore, tidal, 80
*Botellina tasmanica*, 173
*Botulopa silicula*, 169
*Botrythis magnicoecus*, 171
Boulder tract, 106, 114, 115, 124, 142–145, 162, 167, 169, 170
    zone, 105, 106
Boult Reef, 125
Bounty Rise, 3, 5
    Trough, 3, 5
Bowen, 35, 62, 73, 89, 146, 191, 192
    basin, 21, 24, 29
Boyne River, 51
Brachyura, 170
Brain coral, 2, 115, 154, 158, 159, 163, 171
Branching coral, 2, 154, 171
Brisbane, 15, 73
Brittle stars, 179
Broad Sound, 41, 43, 47, 52, 57–62, 67, 73, 75, 78–81, 84, 197, 198, 202, 204, 206, 207, 210, 213, 215, 223, 226
Broken Hill, 19
*Bronnimannia haliotis*, 175
Brown algae, 115, 179
BRYAN, W. H., 24, 26, 51, 235
Bryozoan, 171, 183, 199, 219, 223
    accumulation, 151, 206, 207
    community, 204
    component, 206, 207, 210
    detritus, 204, 206–208
    facies, 204, 206–208, 213
    fauna, 204, 206–208
    material, 201, 206, 207, 212
    sediment, 207
    skeletal material, 207
Bryozoan facies, 204–208
    high, 207
    low, 206
    moderate, 207
    non-bryozoan, 206
Buckland Tableland, 25
*Bulimina barbata*, 175
    *B. marginata*, 175
    *B. oblonga*, 175
    *B. rostrata*, 175
*Buliminella latissima*, 175
    *B. milletti*, 175
    *B. cf. parallela*, 175
    *B. spicata*, 175
Buliminidae, 175
*Buliminoides williamsonianus*, 175
Bunker Group, 43, 47, 51, 84, 106, 120, 124, 151, 190, 192, 198, 202, 204, 207, 210, 212, 213, 215, 217, 219
    High, 26, 29
    Reefs, 43, 47, 51, 84, 86, 106, 151, 206
Burdekin River, 25, 26, 52, 60, 61, 189, 190, 191, 197, 200, 202
Bureau of Mineral Resources, 26
Burnett River, 25, 26, 51, 57, 60, 197
Burrum River, 51
Bustard Head, 189, 197, 198, 202

Button shell, 162
Buttress, 99
Byron, Cape, 12

*Cadus rufus*, 162, 163
Cainozoic, 19, 23, 24, 25
Cairns, 25, 35, 72, 90, 190, 200, 224, 231
    Reef, 164, 165
*Calappa hepatica*, 170
*Calcarina*, 112, 172, 230
    *C. calcar*, 176
    *C. venusta*, 176
Calcarinidae, 176
Calcareous algae, 115, 153, 159, 160, 179
Calcite, 219
    high-magnesium, 219, 221, 223
    low-magnesium, 219, 222, 223
*Callianassa australiensis*, 170
Calliope River, 51
*Calothrix crustacea*, 180
    *C. pilosa*, 180
Campbell Plateau, 3, 5, 20
*Canarium canarium*, 163
*Cancris auriculus*, 175
Cape Byron, 12
    Capricorn, 223, 228
    Clinton, 47, 57, 59, 62, 199, 213
    Flattery, 26, 30, 198
    Melville, 31
    Townshend, 29, 31, 43, 197, 200, 213
    Tribulation, 98
    York, 8, 12, 24, 52, 71, 73, 90
    York Complex, 21
    York Peninsula, 25, 29, 150
*Caphyra laevis*, 171
Capricorn Basin, 26, 29, 60, 61
    Channel, 8, 26, 29, 86
    Group, 43, 47, 51, 86, 91, 104, 106, 107, 120, 124, 151, 190, 192, 198, 202, 204, 207, 210, 212, 213, 215, 217, 219
    Reefs, 43, 47, 84, 86, 91, 104, 106, 107, 151, 192, 204, 206, 210
Carbon dioxide, 135, 154
Carbonate, 184–186
    debris, 2, 4, 189, 192, 197
    facies, 4, 183–186, 189–192
    mud, 145, 190, 202
    sediment, 189, 204
    sedimentation, 24, 204, 233
    solubility, 135
Carbonate facies, 3, 184–186, 189–192, 197, 202
    high, 189–192
    impure, 189–192, 197
    transitional, 189–192
Carboniferous, 26
Cardiidae, 169
*Cardita incrassata*, 166, 179
*Caretta caretta*, 177
Caribbean, 1
Carnarvons, 25
Carpentaria, Gulf of, 73, 88
*Carpenteria monticularis*, 176
*Carterina spiculotesta*, 173
Cassidae, 162
*Cassis cornuta*, 162, 163, 179
*Cassidulina elongata*, 175
    *C. laevigata*, 175
Cassidulinidae, 175
*Casuarina*, 119, 121

*L. nordgardii*, 180
*L. semiplena*, 180
*L. rivularianum*, 180

McIvor River, 52
Mackay, 8, 59, 60, 72, 73, 75, 146, 190, 197–200, 202, 204, 206, 207, 223, 225
McKellar, R. G., 236
*Macrophiothrix longipeda*, 166, 170
Madagascar, 67
Main Divide, 24, 25
Malay Reef, 8
*Malleus malleus*, 168, 179
*Mancinella mancinella*, 163
Mangrove, 58, 59, 63, 106, 119, 120, 124, 143, 145, 177, 198, 200
    park, 142, 179
    swamp, 43, 95, 98, 122, 124, 142, 162
Manton, S. M., 179, 235
*Marchia clavus*, 167
Margin. lagoonal, 96, 101, 103, 104, 117, 125, 142, 158, 170
    reef, 110, 124, 126, 133, 171, 200, 215, 224
    shelf, 43, 84, 99, 107, 135
Marginal Shelf, 43, 47, 59, 92–97, 100, 106, 126, 127, 136–139, 141, 143–148, 151, 179, 183, 189, 192, 197–202, 204, 206–208, 210, 212, 213, 217, 219, 224, 230, 233
    Eastern, 43, 47, 92, 93, 207, 213, 215
    inner, 114, 136, 138, 142
    Western, 43, 47, 51, 91, 119, 202
*Marginopora*, 78, 112, 172, 174, 179, 183, 217, 223
    *M. vertebralis*, 174
*Marginulina glabra*, 174
Marine Basin, 19
Marion Reef, 8
Maritime air, 88
Marrett River, 52, 63
Marshall, S. M., 235
*Marsipella cylindrica*, 173
Mary River, 51, 52, 57, 60, 197
Maryborough Basin, 24, 26, 29, 197, 198
*Massilina*, 173, 179
    *M. corrugata*, 173
    *M. minuta*, 173
    *M. secans tropicalis*, 173
    *M. subrogosa*, 173
Massive coral, 179
Masthead Reef, 113, 120
*Mastigocoelus testarum*, 180, 181
Maxwell, W. G. H., 115, 236
Meandrine coral, 156, 158, 159
*Melanerita melanotragus*, 162
Melanesia, 19, 20
*Melaraphe*, 162, 179
*Melina nucleus*, 168
*Melitodes*, 160
*Meloamphora*, 179
Melville, Cape, 31
*Membranipora membranacea*, 171
Menard, H. W., 19, 20, 236
*Menathais pica*, 162, 167
    *M. mancinella*, 167
    *M. kieneri*, 167
*Merulina*, 159
Mesh reef, 96, 101, 125–127, 133
Mesozoic, 19-21, 23–27, 29, 31, 63, 64, 85, 197, 200, 234
*Messerschmidia argentea*, 122
Metamorphic, 20, 21, 23, 25, 26, 27, 29, 150, 200, 234
*Metasepia*, 169

Microatoll, 115, 157–159
*Microcoleus tenerrimus*, 180
*Microdictyon obscurum*, 180
Microphytic algae, 159
Miliolidae, 173, 174
Miliolidea, 173
*Millepora*, 157, 160
    *M. tenera*, 156
*Mimachlamys gloriosus*, 179
*Mimosina affinis*, 175
    *M. echinata*, 175
    *M. rimosa*, 175
Mineral component, 201
Mineral Resources, Bureau, 26
Mineralogical composition, 183, 219
Mineralogy, 1
Minerva Reef, 17
*Miniacina miniacea*, 176
Miocene, 20
*Mississippina pacifica*, 175
Mitre shells, giant, 167
Mitridae, 167
*Mitra mitra*, 164, 167
    *M. pontificalis*, 167
Mixed tide, 69
Moat, 142, 160
*Modiolus auriculatus*, 165, 169
Mollusc, 153, 161, 162, 167, 183, 192, 199, 210, 217, 219, 223, 230
Molluscan facies, 208–210
    high, 208, 210
    low, 208
    moderate, 208
    non-, 208
*Monalysidium politum*, 174
*Monostroma*, 180
Monsoon, 8, 16, 88–90, 147
*Montipora*, 154, 155, 159
    *M. ramosa*, 179
Montmorillonite, 183
Moon shell, 162
*Mopsella*, 161
Moresby Bank, 52
Morobe Arc, 20
Morphology, reef, 91, 98
Morphological zonation, 98, 101, 107
Mossman River, 52
Mt. Isa, 19, 29
Mountains, coastal, 138, 150
    Finisterre, 20
    Owen Stanley, 20
Mowbray River, 43, 98, 146
Mud, 78, 79, 81, 137, 142, 145, 183, 190, 193–195, 197, 200, 230
    carbonate, 145, 190, 202
    terrigenous, 151, 190, 199, 213
Mud deposition, 52, 81, 198, 201, 234
    facies, 145, 202
        pure, 197, 200
        sandy, 197, 200
    flat, 200
Mud–sand ratio, 198
Mulgrave River, 52
Murdoch Point, 64
Murex shell, 167
    giant, 167
    rudder, 167
    spiny woodcock, 167
Muricidae, 167
Murray, J., 95, 236
Murray Basin, 21